IMAGES
of America

HISTORIC DOWNTOWN PLANO

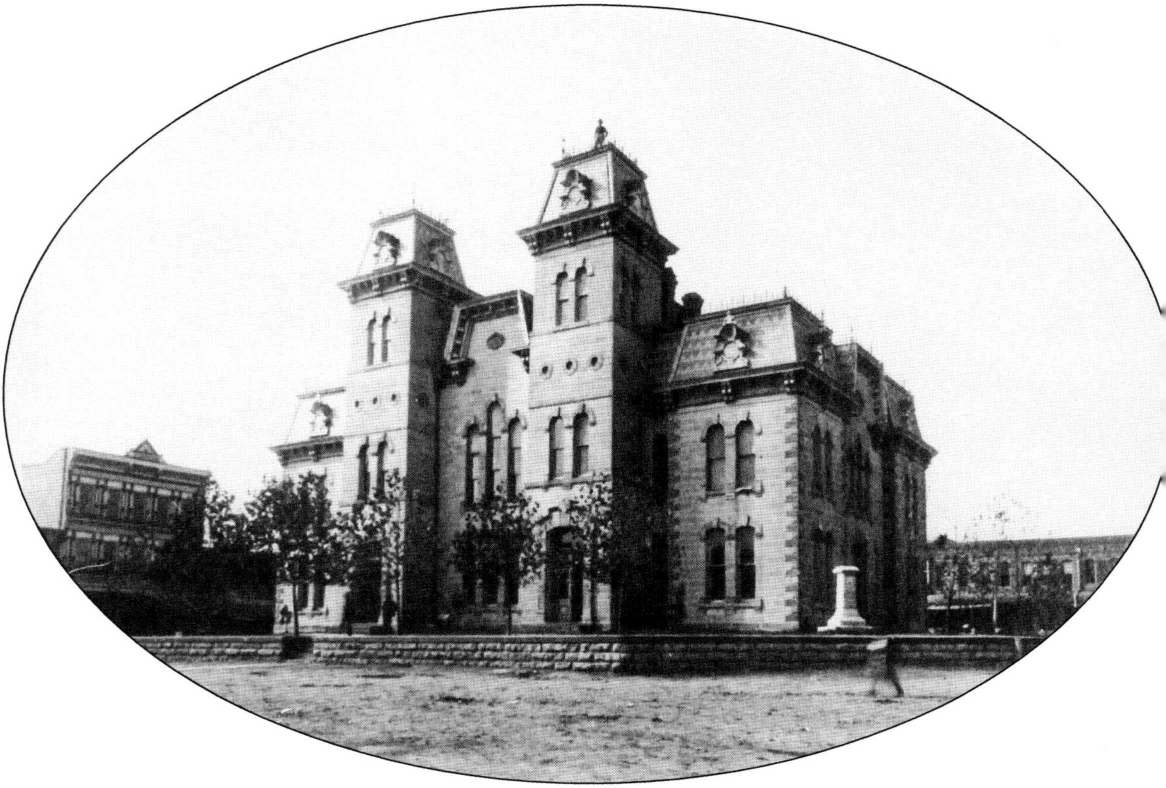

Plano is located in Collin County in north central Texas. The earliest county courthouse was in McKinney on the Town Square and dates back to 1874. In 1927, extensive exterior and interior renovations were completed resulting in a Classical Revival edifice commonly known as the "Temple of Justice." The author was married in the Collin County Courthouse in 1973 and now serves on the Collin County Historical Commission, which uses the building for meetings. The district courtroom of the 1927 courthouse is now the McKinney Performing Arts Center. The judge's dais was replaced by a stage. (Photograph courtesy of Rodney Haggard.)

On the Cover: During the early years, Dr. Henry Dye, who is credited with naming Plano, owned land on the south side of Mechanic Street (now Fifteenth Street) where this store was located. After the devastating fire of 1895, this building at 1008 Fifteenth Street was rebuilt of brick. It has since housed a grocery, saloon, café, and was the site of Love Photography for more than 30 years. (Photograph courtesy of Rick Fambro.)

IMAGES
of America

Historic Downtown Plano

Janice Craze Cline

ARCADIA
PUBLISHING

ISBN 978-0-7385-7902-3

Published by Arcadia Publishing
Charleston, South Carolina

Printed in the United States of America

Library of Congress Control Number: 2010923104

For all general information, please contact Arcadia Publishing:
Telephone 843-853-2070
Fax 843-853-0044
E-mail sales@arcadiapublishing.com
For customer service and orders:
Toll-Free 1-888-313-2665

Visit us on the Internet at www.arcadiapublishing.com

This book is dedicated to my grandchildren, Skylar and Spencer Belloni, as inspiration to revisit the history of their birthplace in these vintage images. They are precious pioneers in the new millennium.

Contents

ACKNOWLEDGMENTS

My four years on the Plano Heritage Commission taught me a lot about downtown and the surrounding neighborhoods. *Plano, Texas: The Early Years*, published in 1985 by the Friends of the Plano Public Library, inspired this project and is the "bible" on early Plano, thanks to the remarkable work of the book committee: Mozelle Jones Campbell, Maribelle McLaurine Davis, Betty Harrington Stranz, Francis Bates Wells, and Shirley Carter Schell. Their work paved the way for the rest of us who are interested in the history of Plano.

The Francis Wells Collection in the Texana Collection of the Genealogy, Local History, Texana, and Archives Division (GLHTA) of the Plano Public Library System holds volumes of images used in *Plano, Texas: The Early Years*. Unless otherwise noted, most of the early images in the first few chapters are from the Francis Wells Collection and are reprinted here with permission from the library. David Hardin, Cheryl Smith, and Tom Turner in the GLHTA at W.O. Haggard Library were helpful in determining resources and doing the heavy lifting of scanning images. Other images from the early period are found in the Corral Barn at Fairview Farms and are reprinted courtesy of Rodney Haggard. Rodney also provided written histories of the fire department and Skaggs Grocery.

The Texas State Historical Association and the *Southwestern Historical Quarterly* were also great resources, with much of the Collin County, Peters colony, and early pioneer research submitted by J. Lee and Lilian J. Stambaugh, E. Wade, Victoria S. Murphy, Seymour V. Connor, Wayne Gard, J. Evetts Haley, and others.

The developmental history of Plano was found in the city's early preservation plans, heritage commission and parks and recreation files, maps, the municipal library, and other studies and reports paid for by the City of Plano. Recent images are courtesy of the City of Plano and the author's collection.

Following Arcadia's Images of America series on *Plano: An Historic Walking Tour* by Nancy McCulloch in 2000 and, most recently, its Images of Rail series on *Plano and the Interurban Railway* by the Plano Conservancy for Historic Preservation, Inc. in 2009, it was challenging to find unpublished vintage images of Plano. Homes pictured in *Plano: An Historic Walking Tour* have been intentionally omitted here due to my focus on the government and business district of old Plano.

The Cox School Museum provided much of the rich educational and developmental history of Plano. I appreciate the contributions of many who have made "indelible etchings" on Plano, especially the founding families and their descendants, school board members, and superintendents, mayors, councilmen, and teachers through the years.

My heartfelt gratitude goes to Peggy Mitchell and Dorothy Mitchell Johnston, native Planoites, who opened their collections and lent their support, providing heretofore-unpublished images reflecting life during the 1940s and 1950s. Peggy referred to downtown as "uptown" at one of our lunches, and I have interspersed that reference in the last chapter because the subject is truly "uptown" now.

I appreciate the patient guidance and encouragement of Kristie Kelly with Arcadia and the inspiration and contributions to this labor of love by Melissa O'Neal, Cynthia Hudson Reed, Brenda Kellow, Joy Gough, Doug Cargo, Jim Hiegel, Judy Moore, Randy Brodhead, Rick Fambro, Mary Katherine Carpenter, Jim Fox, Jon Hubach, Frank Turner, and Steve Sims.

Most importantly, I appreciate the love and patient support of my husband, Steve, and the encouragement and inspiration of our children, Kris, Tammy, and Adam, each of whom has accomplished their own milestones. Thanks always to my sister Annette—my first teacher and final editor.

Introduction

The first settlers arrived in the Plano area in the early 1840s. These Peters colonists came from Kentucky and Tennessee to settle in north central Texas after Sam Houston, then governor of Tennessee, touted its rich soil for farming.

The original name for Plano was probably Forman, after William Forman, a Kentuckian who opened a store and post office in 1851. The village was known for a brief period as Fillmore, in honor of Pres. Millard Fillmore. The origin of the name Plano is unclear, but Dr. Henry Dye is credited with naming it for the "plain" on which it was located.

These early settlers found a vast prairie with Spring, Rowlett, and White Rocks Creeks providing necessary water for sustenance. They toiled through drought, storms, and Indian raids to carve out a life on the Blackland Prairie. The last Indian raid is depicted in a marker at Collin College on Spring Creek as the Muncey Massacre of 1844.

Raising livestock and farming provided a life for the early settlers. The flat Blackland Prairie was ideal for growing cotton, the primary crop of this region. Several cotton ginning and milling operations were located in Plano, though none of them remain today. As the Shawnee trail developed along present-day Preston Road through Plano and across the Red River to Oklahoma and on to Missouri, cattle herds were taken up the trail to market.

The Houston & Texas Central Railroad (H&TC) opened Plano to the world in 1872, followed shortly thereafter by the St. Louis, Arkansas & Texas Railway—known as the Cotton Belt—and the community experienced new growth with a population of 500. Introduction of the railroad also had a great impact on local agriculture and regional prosperity. Plano was the first rail stop entering Collin County from Dallas to the south. Lumber was brought in from Jefferson, Texas, and homes and buildings sprung up around the railroad.

Fires repeatedly destroyed the business district in the 1880s and 1890s, but the resilient founding fathers began to build modern brick buildings and the town flourished. Almost anything could be bought or traded in Plano. Economic dependence on agriculture continued through the 1960s.

The Great Depression of the 1930s, oddly enough, led to Plano's second growth spurt. The Plano school system had a good reputation, a new building, and, most importantly, it paid teachers in cash, not vouchers. By attracting good teachers, it also attracted students from the outlying rural population. In 1935, with funding from the federal government's Works Progress Administration, a gymnasium was built adjacent to the school building. The gymnasium had an immediate impact on the growth of sports in Plano and in social life of Plano's residents.

Throughout much of the 20th century, Plano relied on surrounding farms and ranches for its livelihood. The Depression years of the 1930s were hard-felt, but soil conservation, faith in the land, and survival techniques showed the strength of the pioneer farmers. The 1940s were marked with the conservation of goods and young men enlisting in the war efforts.

After World War II, with soldiers returning home and the emergence of the baby boomer years, families began to move out of the big city of Dallas for more affordable homes and good schools. The postwar homes built in the Haggard Addition, Southwood Estates Addition, and Belle View Additions are prime examples of the desirable neighborhoods Plano offered. Most of the land east of K Avenue was farmland, and remained that way until the late 1960s.

In the 1960s and 1970s, multifamily housing was developed in the old neighborhoods, along with modern shopping centers around the downtown core. Several churches and businesses were also scattered near downtown. Mendenhall Elementary School was the first freestanding elementary school built in Plano, on Eighteenth Street north of K Avenue in the 1960s. Williams High School, in the Old Towne neighborhood, was designed to be the high school for Plano. Today, the old neighborhoods are composed of a diverse mixture of individuals representing many ethnic heritages. Mature shade trees line streets in Old Towne and the Haggard Park Heritage District, giving a feeling of nostalgia and a sense of stability, which residents want to preserve.

With the construction of Highway 75 (North Central Expressway) in the 1960s and the US population beginning its historic shift to the Sunbelt in the 1970s, Plano welcomed newcomers with open arms and became one of the fastest growing cities in Texas and America. Plano North Shopping Center opened at K Avenue and Eighteenth Street in 1968, bringing the first real competition to downtown.

Concerned about the future of downtown and the historic homes standing in the path of progress, the city adopted the Historic Landmark Preservation ordinance in 1979. In 1981, with a population of 76,400, Plano celebrated the opening of Collin Creek Mall to keep up with growth west of the Central Expressway. Downtown's mom-and-pop stores suffered for the following 10 years.

Corporate headquarters for JC Penney, Frito-Lay, and Electronic Data Systems (EDS) relocated west of downtown as Plano incentivized big businesses to locate to its central location, good climate, and friendly neighbors. As a result, new retail centers sprung up in the new epicenter of Plano. An upscale urban town center, the Shops at Legacy, as well as the Shops at Willowbend Mall, were developed along the Dallas North Tollway to answer the booming demand for retail in the early 2000s. While the historic Haggard Farm still encompasses many acres along the Tollway, many new residents are unaware of Plano's historical downtown just 10 or so miles east.

Downtown Plano's architectural assets are still in place, contributing to an old Texas town character, which cannot be replicated. Much of the historic retail core of Plano was developed after fires plagued downtown in the 1890s. Design guidelines were set in place in 1993 to maintain the century-old architectural and historical character of downtown while encouraging economic growth. Redevelopment began with the Interurban Railway building in downtown Plano.

In 2003, after 130 years, downtown Plano was recognized as a historic district. Former first lady Laura Bush recognized preservation efforts by awarding Plano the "Preserve America" designation in 2006 to promote education and a greater appreciation of historic treasures.

Much progress has been made downtown to revitalize and redevelop the historic district in the past five years. Residents and visitors are greeted with a historically significant commercial and residential town center and an attractive place to live and conduct business. Continued restoration has the potential to uncover more treasures and explore Plano's past, while incorporating new technology and development.

It is my earnest goal in this book to educate residents and visitors about the history of this once sleepy farming community that has risen to a nationally acclaimed All-America city of 270,000 residents. Downtown Plano has a rich history, and this book is a tribute to the courage and resilience of its forefathers.

One

Peters Colonists, Legendary Men, and Mules

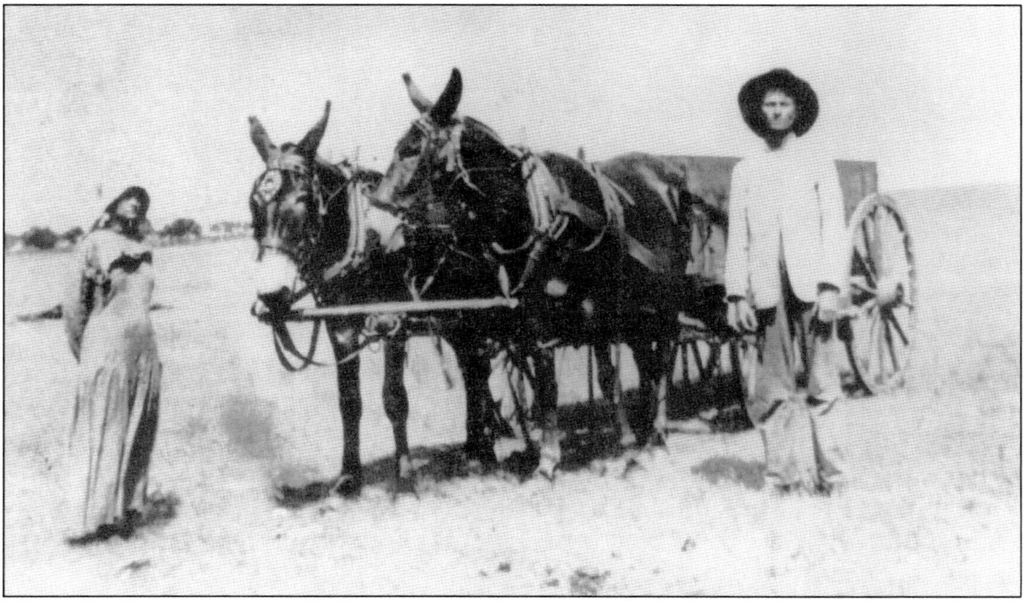

In 1841, the Congress of the Republic of Texas granted land to agents for the establishment of colonies. Sam Houston, the first president of the republic, touted the vast fertile prairie of North Texas to entice settlers. Pioneers moved west for the promise of free land, using an existing American Indian path reaching from the Red River to Austin. Originally known as the Shawnee Trail, the road was later named for William G. Preston, a captain in the Texas Revolution. Here, early settlers Lawrence and Josie Bush Faulkner make their way across the prairie.

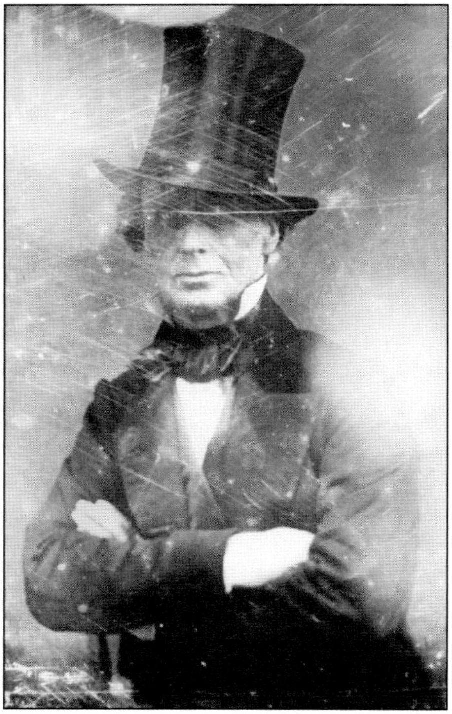

The Peters colony, headquartered in Louisville, Kentucky, recruited settlers to migrate into north central Texas with the offer of 640 acres for heads of families and 320 acres for a single person. Henry Oliver Hedgcoxe was one of the early agents of the Peters colony, the largest of all the land reserves. Texas became a state in 1845 and Collin County was carved out of Fannin County in 1846. Subsequently, in 1852, controversy over boundaries and land titles led to an incident known as the Hedgcoxe War, though "nary" a shot was fired, according to an early newspaper article.

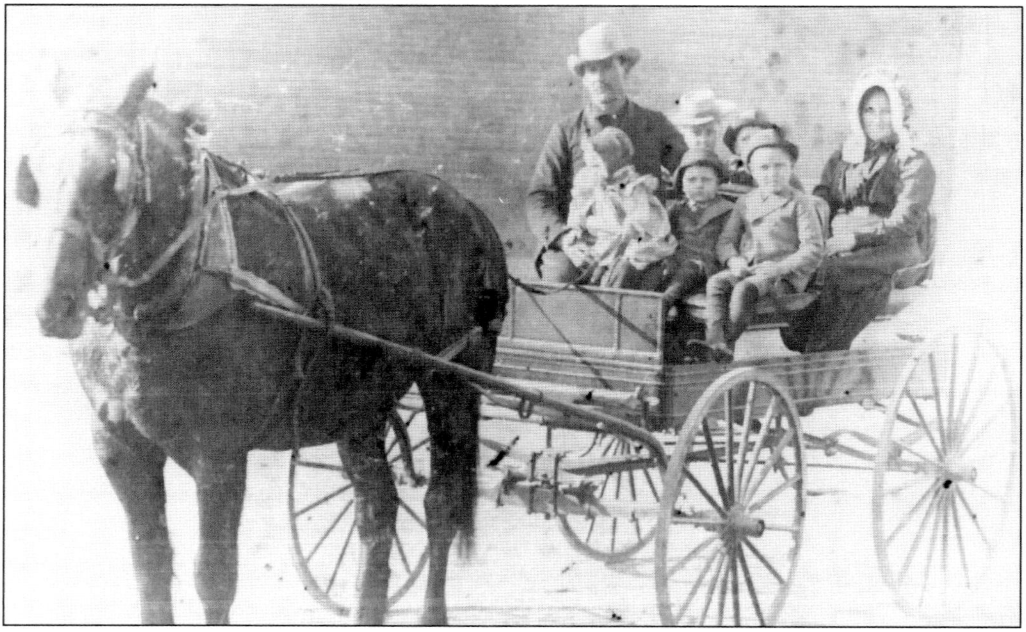

Early pioneers settled along the creeks to be close to water and timber for daily living needs and shelter. In 1842, Jeremiah Muncey settled his family in the Plano area. In 1844, some men came upon Muncey's hut and found the savagely slain bodies of the Munceys, the earliest known family in the Plano area. That was the last American Indian raid in Collin County and is commemorated with a marker entitled "The Muncey Massacre." Settlers like the Bishop family, shown here in the early 1900s, kept coming to Texas, ever vigilant and determined to carve out a new life on the fertile Blackland Prairie. (Courtesy of Rodney Haggard.)

Peters colonist Oliver Loving came to the Plano area along with Sanford Beck, Alfred and Silas Harrington, and James Salmons, to claim land in 1845. Loving bought a general store on the main crossroads in Plano in 1856. Sometime after the Civil War, he and Charles Goodnight, a former Texas Ranger and Indian scout, ran cattle on a trail that became known as the Goodnight-Loving Trail. Here, two unidentified men stand near the main crossroads.

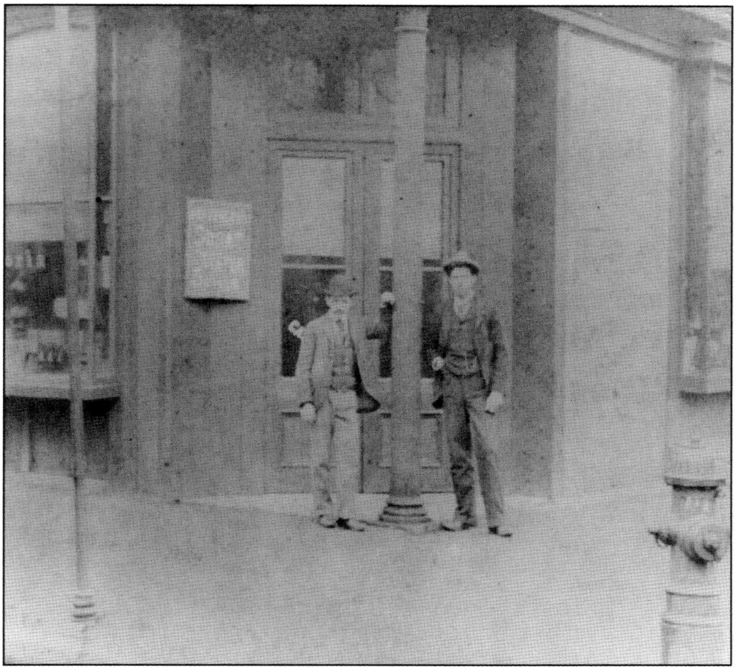

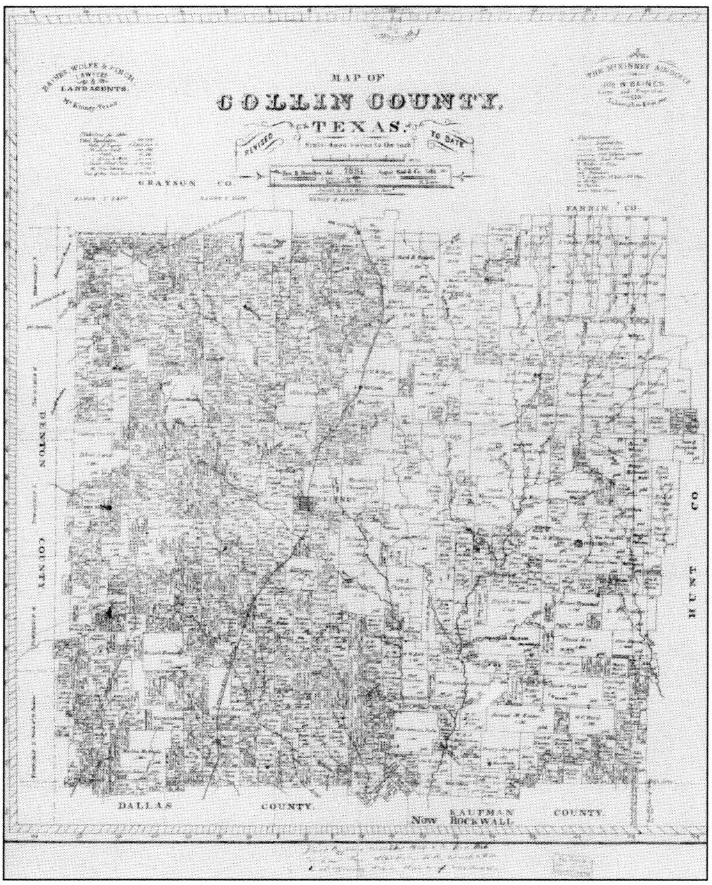

In the mid-1840s, Collin McKinney guided settlers from Kentucky and Tennessee to settle in North Texas. The county seat, McKinney, and Collin County are both named for him. Plano, south of McKinney and just north of the Dallas County line, developed on the Peters colony head-rights of Sanford Beck and Joseph Klepper (or Clepper), issued in 1850. Their names are found in the earliest abstracts of land surveys in Plano. Beck located land primarily on the east side of Main Street (present-day K Avenue), and Klepper on the west side. This 1881 Collin County map shows the most populated areas in the west half of the county, much the same as it is today. (Courtesy of Texas Map Store.)

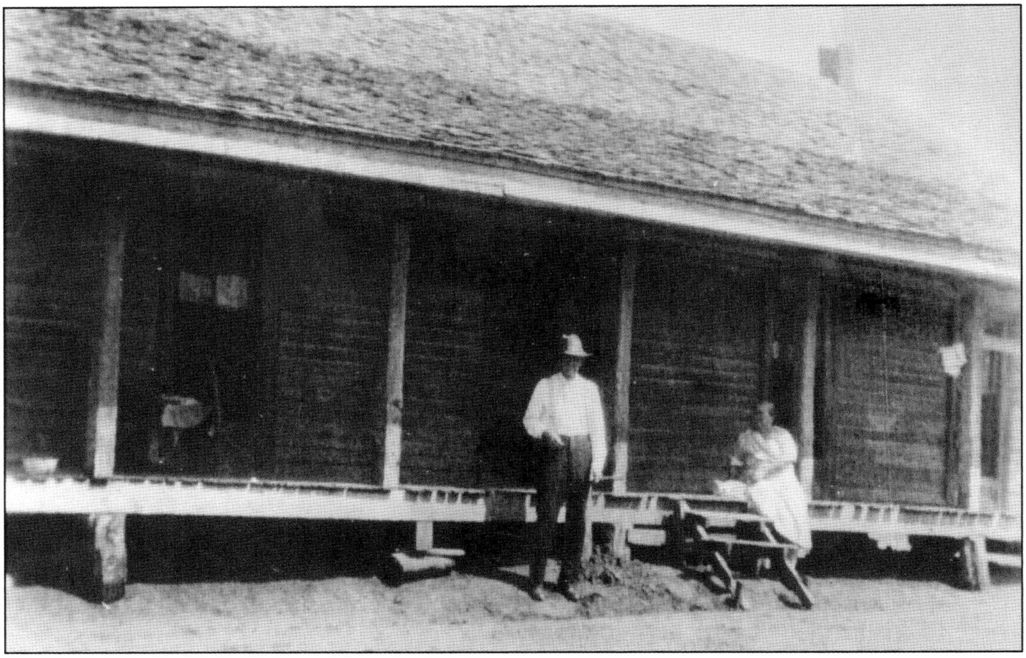

William and Ruth Forman (or Foreman) purchased the Peters colony head-right of Sanford Beck and built a cabin, which served as a stagecoach stop and post office between Dallas and McKinney. William Forman was Plano's first postmaster, serving from 1852 to 1856. The Forman house, built around 1867, is the oldest home in Plano, still standing on K Avenue.

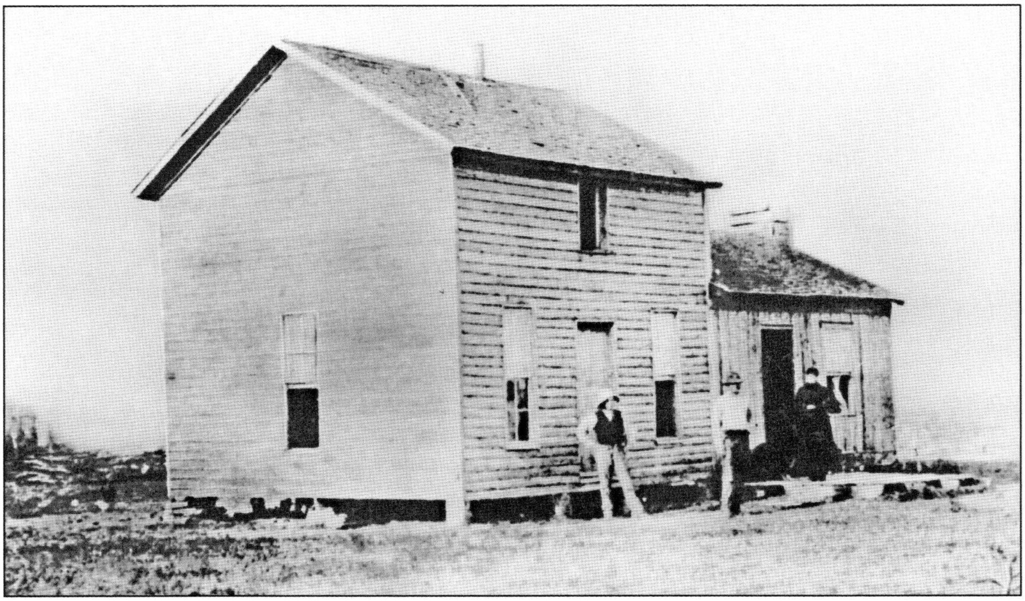

The early settlers built log cabins, which were typically one room with a dirt floor and a fireplace for cooking and heating. John Coit built this home in the 1850s, and an addition was made in the 1870s. One settler, Robert Washington Carpenter, who came to Texas in 1852, described the miles and miles of grass that reached the stirrups of his saddle, the abundance of wildlife and tillable land—"a stockman's paradise"—where longhorn cattle could be driven to market in St. Louis only 1,000 miles away. His wife, Lizzie Mathews Carpenter, kept a diary of daily life.

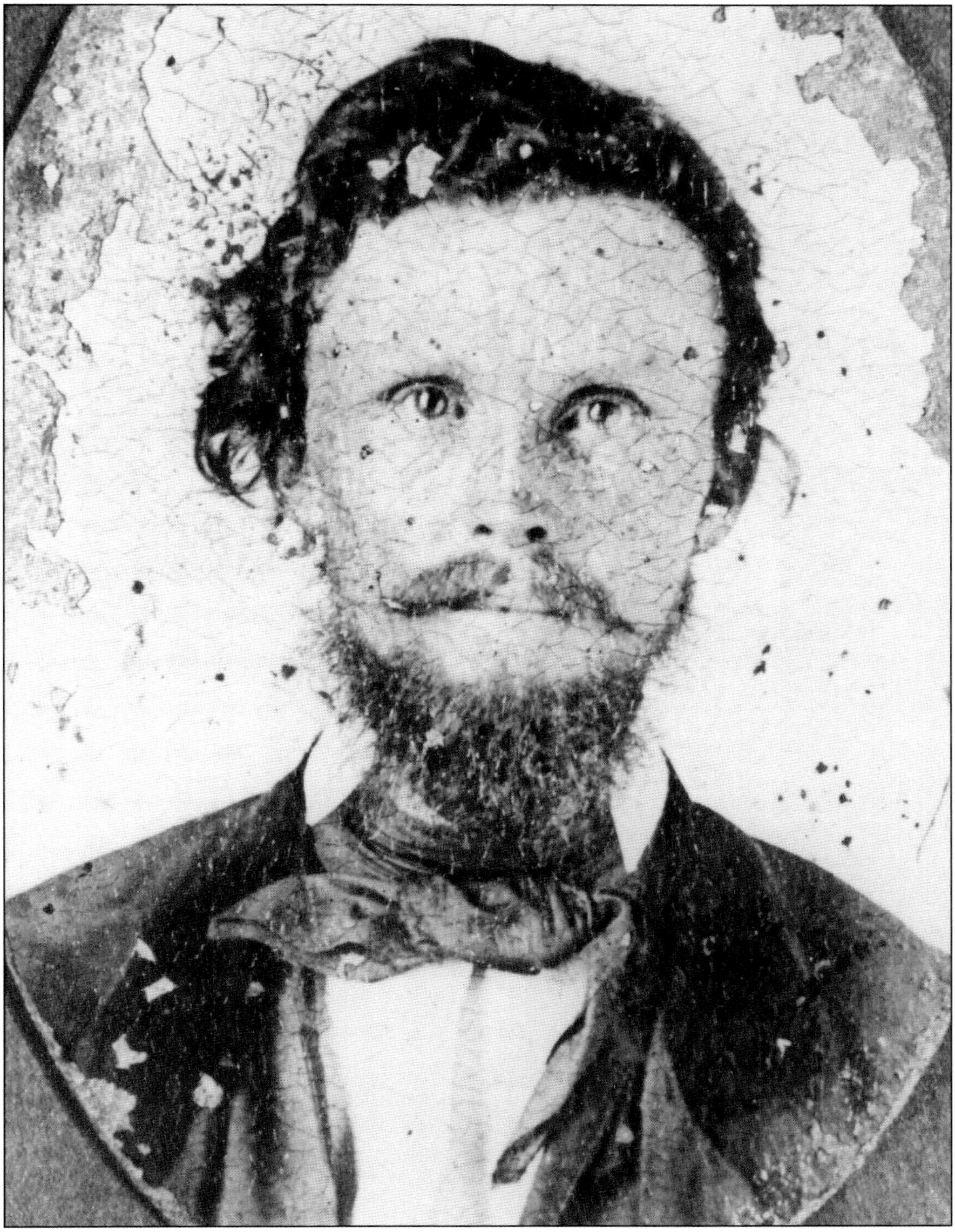

During the establishment of the post office, Forman (after the postmaster) and Fillmore (after Pres. Millard Fillmore), were considered as names for the community. Dr. Henry Dye is credited with naming the town Plano, ostensibly from the Spanish word for a grassy plain—*llano*. Dye is listed on the 1850 Collin County Census as a 20-year-old physician living with Joseph C. Klepper and his family. During the Civil War, Dr. Dye was in charge of Confederate hospitals in Arkansas where he kept a medical casebook of detailed drawings and patient descriptions, which were the subject of Dr. Billy Gurley Jr.'s book *Yankee Bullets, Southern Blood: The Remarkable Journal of Dr. Henry M. Dye, Confederate Surgeon*. Dye is buried in Bowman Cemetery in Plano.

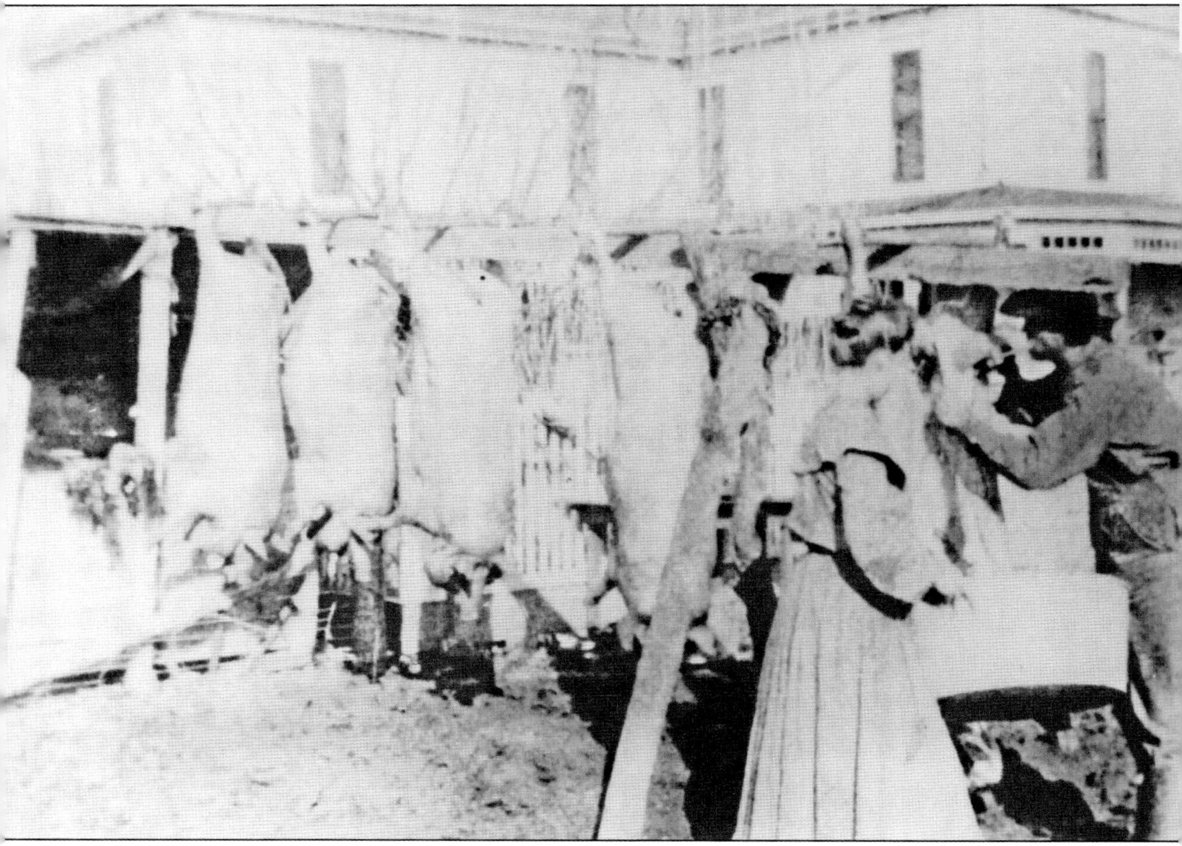

The Blackland Prairie runs from the Red River south to San Antonio and is full of the rich grass Native Americans would burn off every winter, leaving the soil fertile and black. Elm, cottonwood, pecan, and oak trees grew along the wooded creek bottoms and the early pioneers lived off the land, planting vegetable gardens and corn, wheat, and cotton crops. They made their own bread and churned butter from the milk of longhorn cows. Wild berries and nuts were gathered from orchards planted by settlers such as the Formans. Squirrels, deer, bear, and bison were hunted, along with wild hogs living along the creeks. Hog-killing time was cause for celebration at John Henry Rasor's place in the early 1900s. Here, Mittie Bush Rasor and Bill Rasor help string up the hogs.

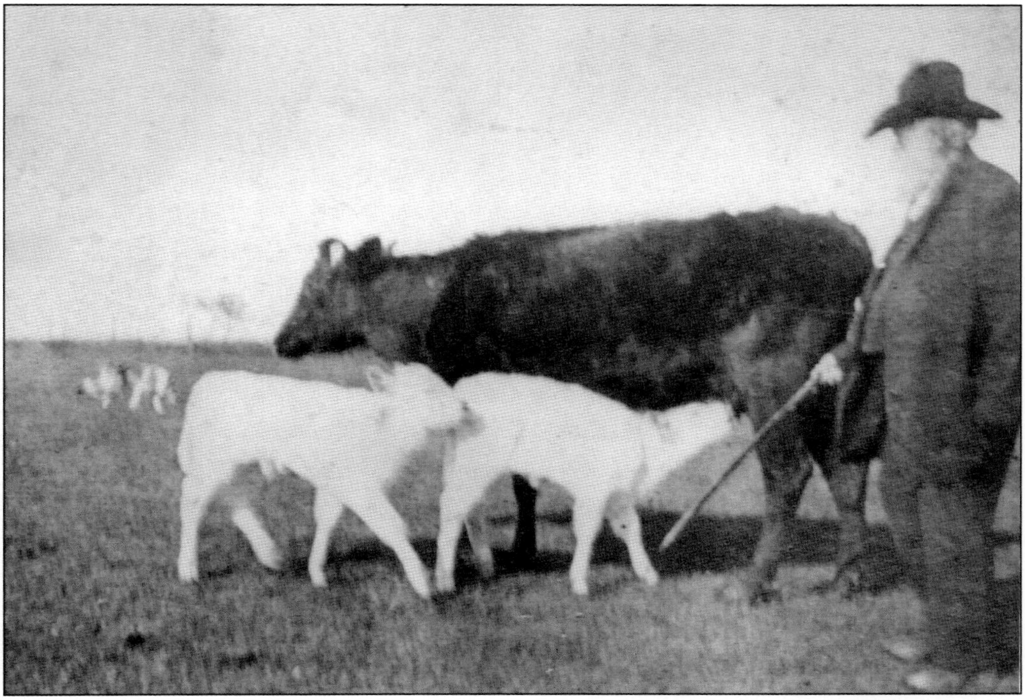

John Haggard II brought his 18-year-old son, Clinton Shepard "C.S." Haggard, shown here, to Texas after the death of his wife, Mourning Quisenberry Haggard. They settled on White Rock Creek in 1856 and invested in cattle, horses, and mules. C.S. Haggard married Nannie Kate Lunsford, and they had nine children. The family farm grew to over 2,000 acres. The Haggard family showed an interest in education from the beginning, first joining with other families to establish the Haggard School in 1848, then supporting the establishment of Add Ran College, the forerunner of Texas Christian University (TCU). On the 1860 Collin County Agricultural Census, C.S. Haggard is listed as owning one of the most valuable farms and growing wheat and oats. A park, school, and public library are named for Haggard's many contributions to the community. When Ross Perot brought the corporate headquarters for Electronic Data Services (EDS) to Plano in the 1980s, he paved the way for the North Dallas Tollway to cut through the 150-year-old Haggard Farm. In 1987, the farm was awarded the Texas Family Land Heritage Award and other Haggard farms still exist along Parker Road, Custer Parkway, and Alma Drive in Plano. (Right, courtesy of Rodney Haggard.)

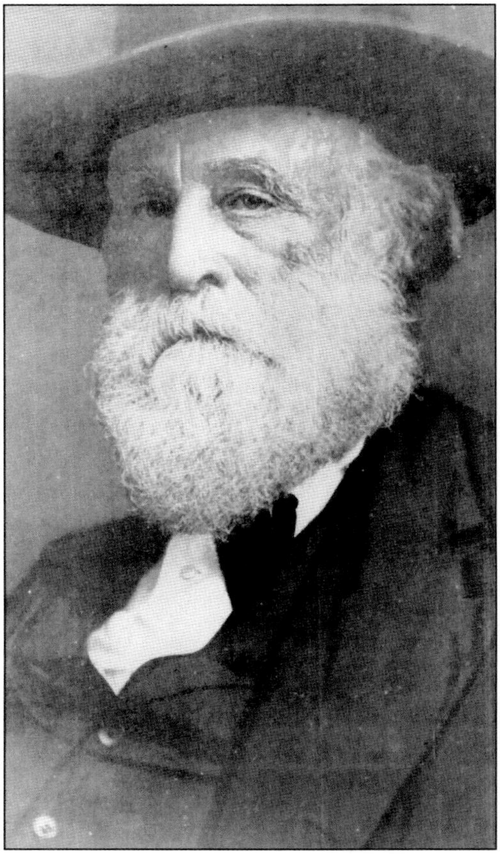

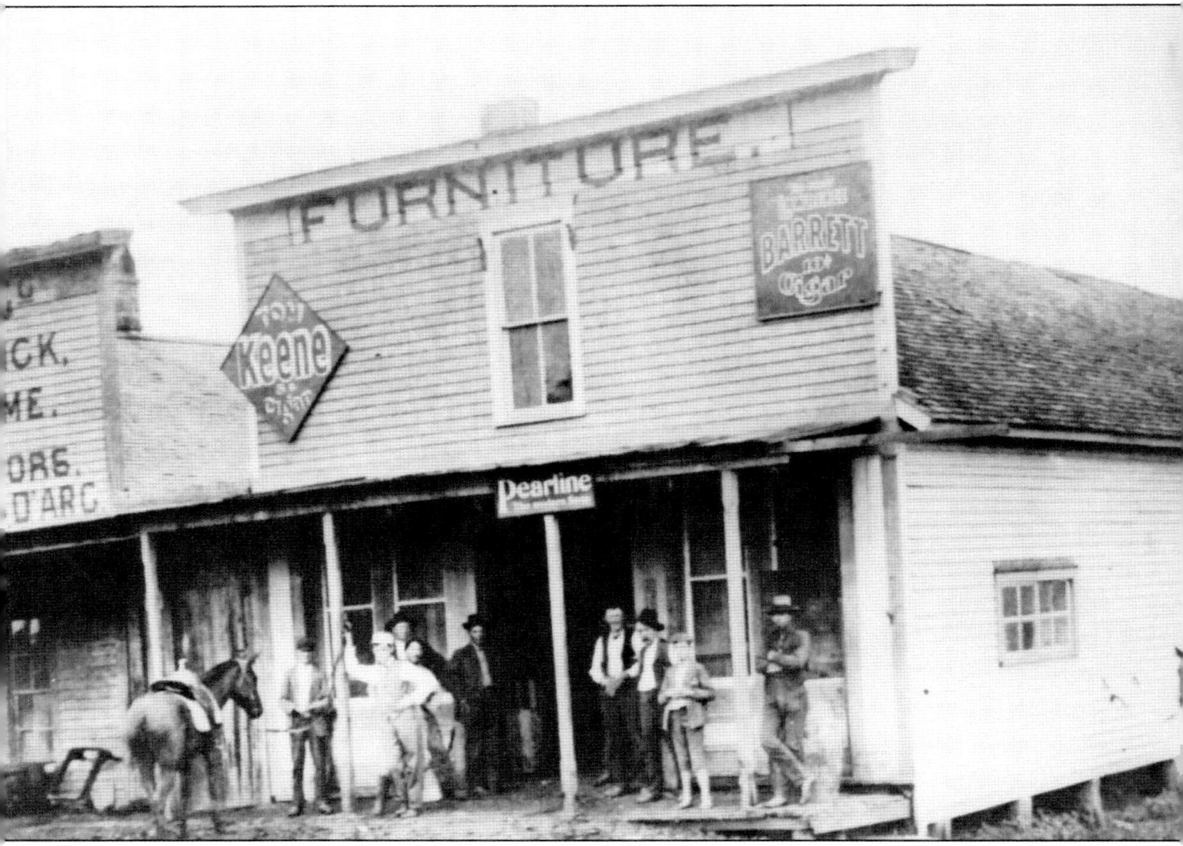

Most early settlers had little cash. They grew crops for sustenance and owned livestock for meat and milk. Trading livestock was one way to get money for staples they could not produce, like salt, sugar, and coffee. Many settlers bought on credit from stores like Carlisle Grocery, the largest grocery store in the early years of Collin County and seen here in 1910. Pearline soap, custom-ground coffee, and live chickens could be bought at Carlisle's. After the harvest, farmers would return to settle their accounts. During the Depression, bad economic conditions forced the store to close.

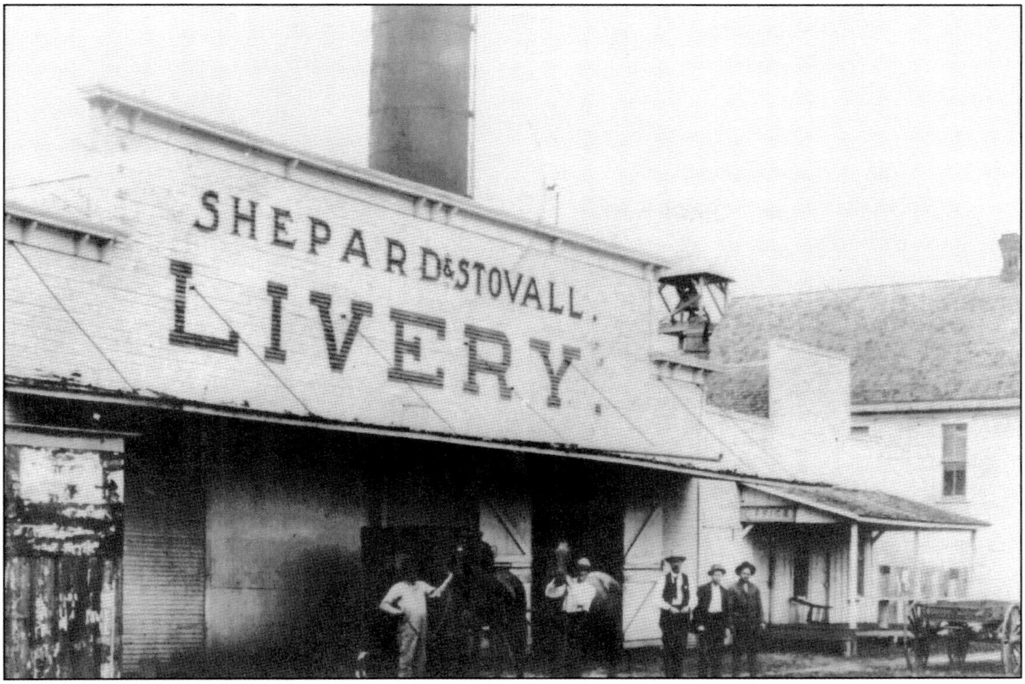

In the late 1800s, horses were the most common mode of transportation. When people came through town, they boarded their horses at the livery stable. A blacksmith was usually nearby to shoe horses, repair wagon wheels, and shape iron as needed. Buggies and wagons could be rented from the livery stable. Mail carriers like "Old Bart" Popperwell (below, around 1924) used horse-drawn wagons after mail service was established around 1850.

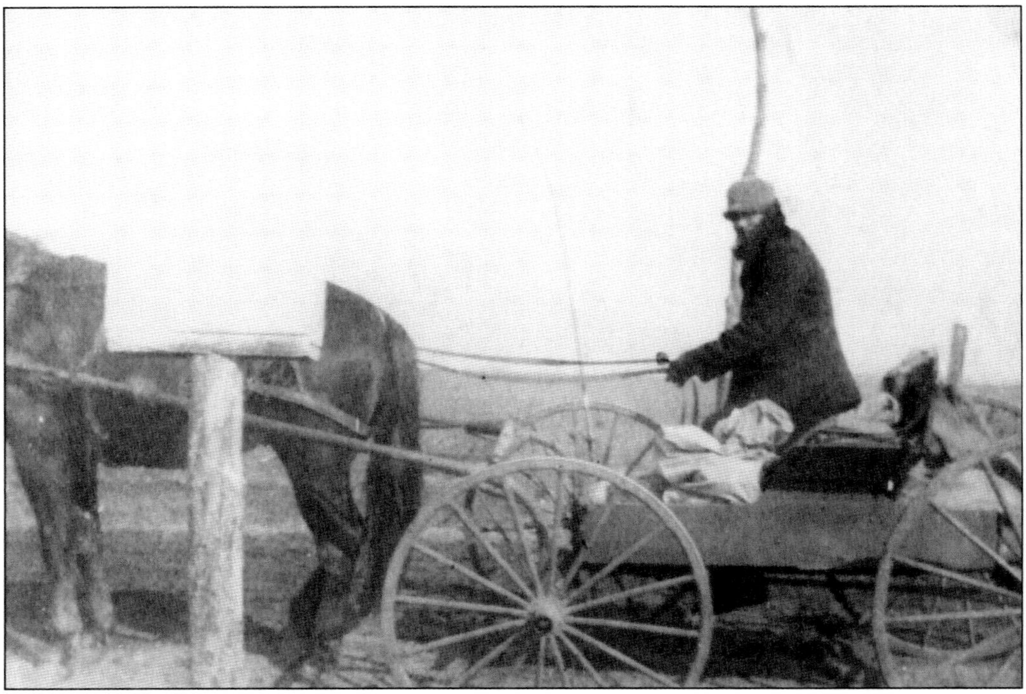

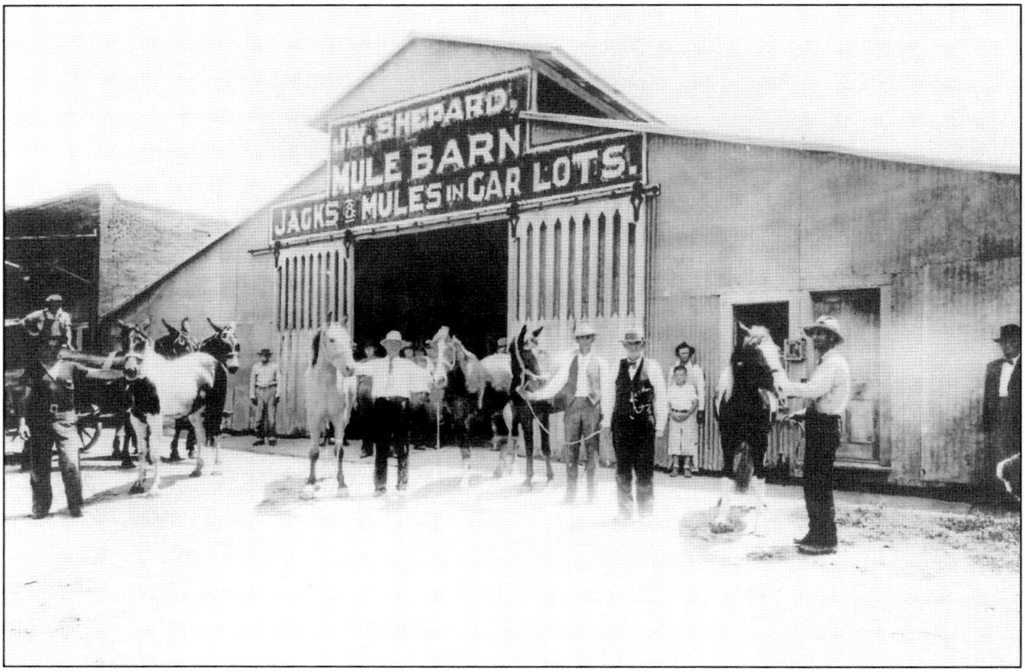

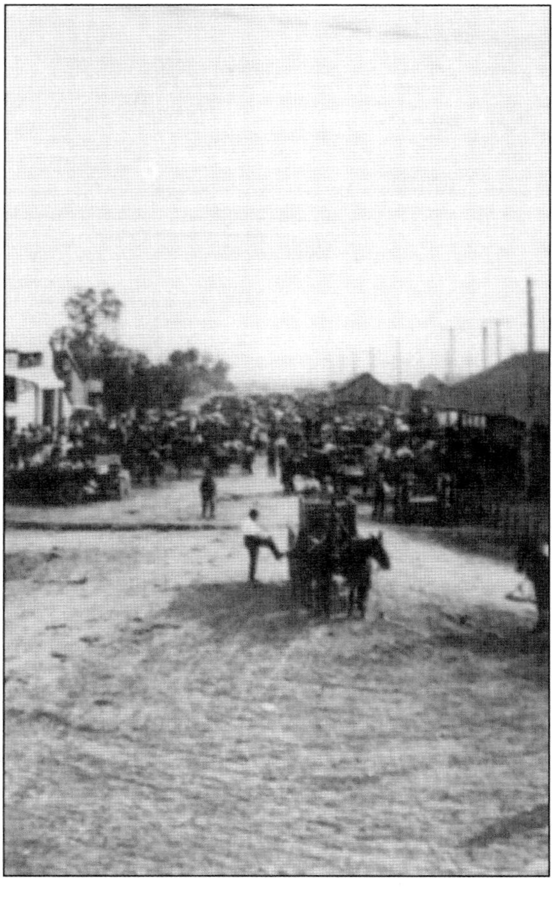

In 1866, Collin County was the leading producer of mules west of the Mississippi River, in large part because of the breeding efforts of C.S. Haggard and his son-in-law, Joseph William "J.W." Shepard, who had a large ranch west of present-day Preston Road, near Park Boulevard, and a mule barn in town next to the Masonic Lodge. The barn was the center of activity on Second Monday Trade Days, with mules sold to the highest bidder in the jockey yard (pictured on the left). The mules, used to pull plows and heavy machinery in farming, were very intelligent, and they also had more stamina and could carry more weight than a horse of equal size. C.S. Haggard brought a legendarily large mule from Kentucky to Texas known as Mammoth Jack. (Left, courtesy of Peggy Mitchell.)

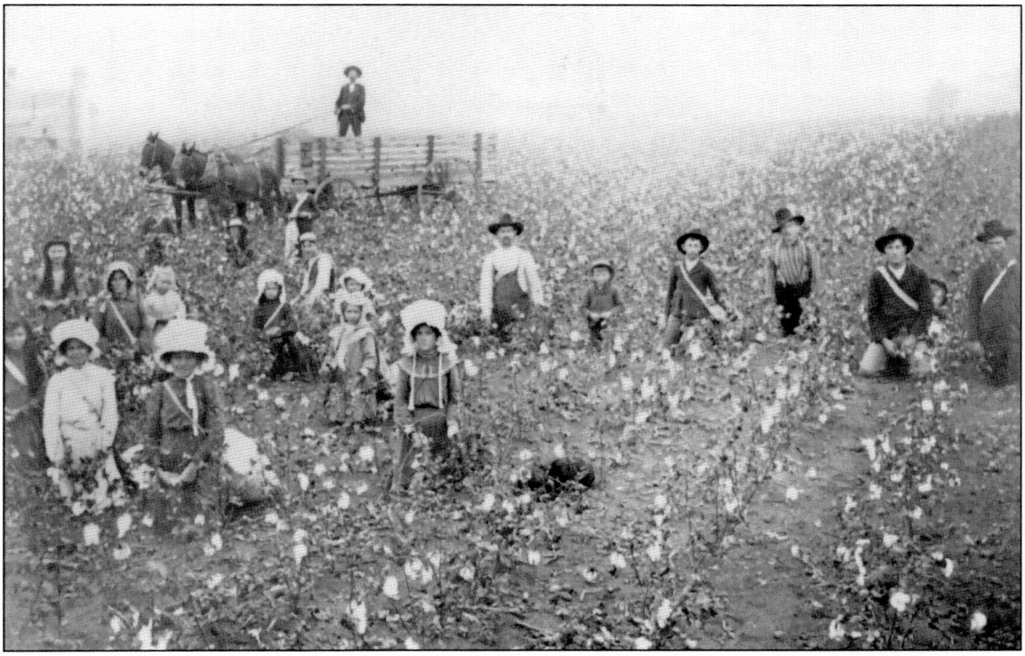

The fertile soil of the Blackland Prairie was ideal for crops. From the 1850s through the end of the Civil War, farmers grew corn, wheat, and oats to feed their families. Beginning in 1872, when the railroad came into the area, immigrants from the Deep South started moving to North Texas and growing cotton. While drought claimed other crops, farmers learned that cotton could be grown with less water and could actually grow on dry land. Some of the newcomers bought their own farms, but many worked as tenant farmers or sharecroppers, plowing, planting, weeding, and harvesting in return for a share of the crops to feed their families. By 1874, Plano's population had grown to 500. (Above, courtesy of Rodney Haggard.)

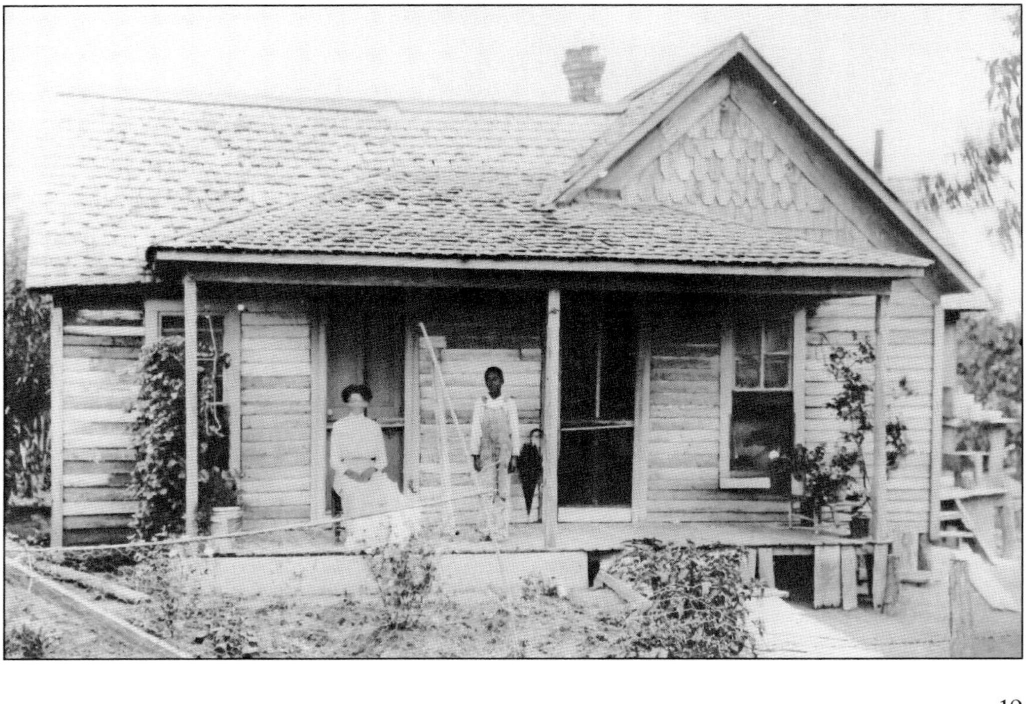

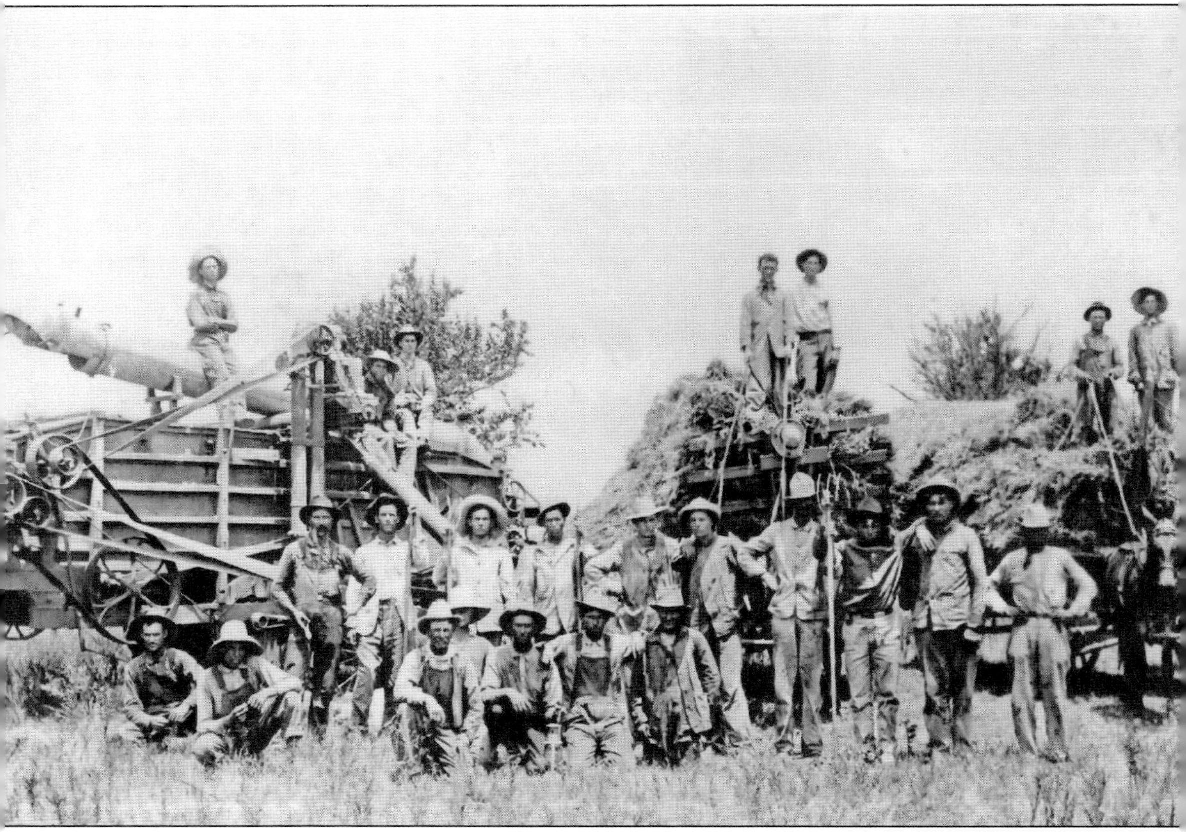

In 1874, William Henry Lafayette "W.H.L." Wells, his brother James M. Wells, and some other men journeyed across American Indian territory to buy 120 acres in Plano for $8 an acre. The Wells family is important to Plano's history; in 1987, a Texas Family Land Heritage Award recognized the family's 100 years of ownership. The original farmstead on Coit Road was built for $1,500 in 1888 with cypress hauled in from Marshall, Texas, and is still in the family. An elementary school is named in honor of the Wells family. (Courtesy of Rodney Haggard.)

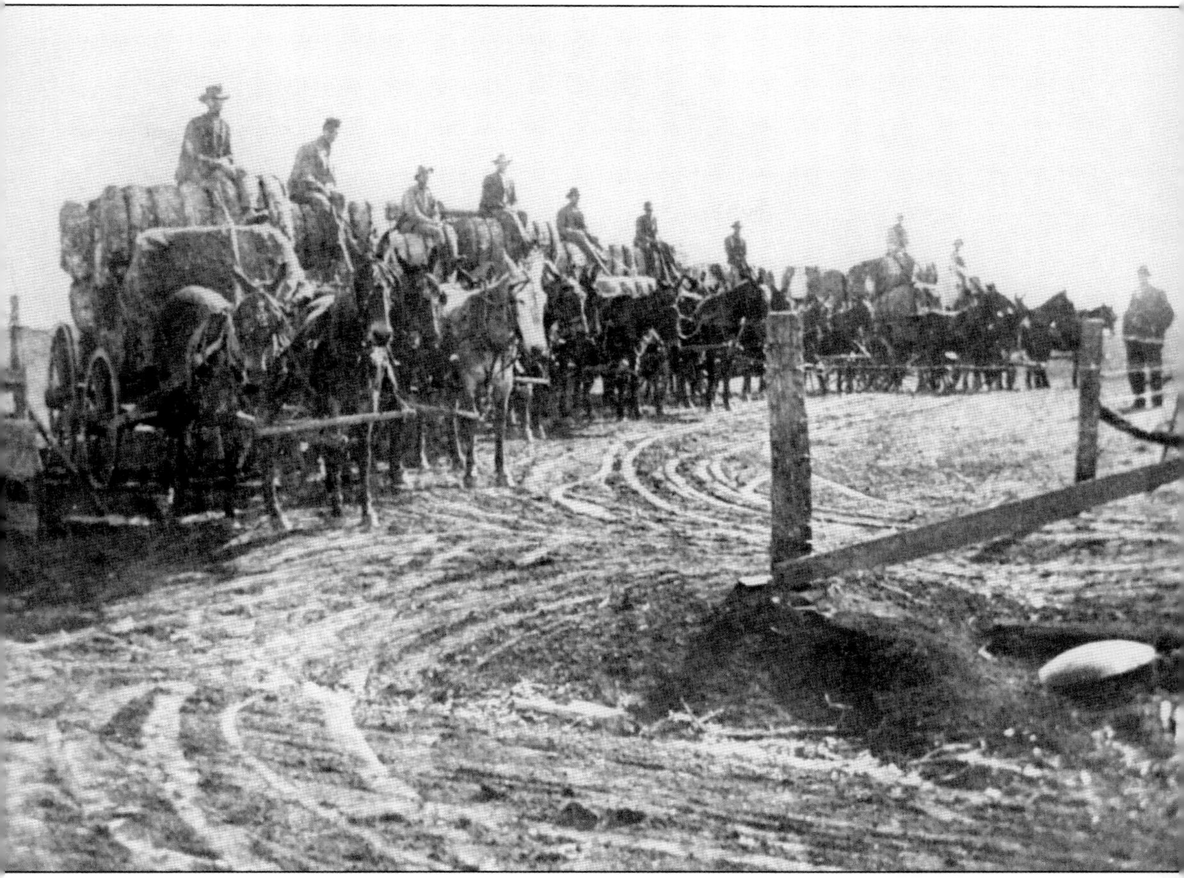

The John Henry Rasor family was important in the early cotton industry. Rasor's nine sons would fill these nine wagons with cotton to take to the cotton gin. The Rasors had giant silos, barns, feedlots, and a blacksmith. The family ran the entire operation, which became one of the largest in the area, covering almost 4,000 acres. The Rasor's ranch was centered along what is now Independence Parkway, between Hedgcoxe Road and McDermott Road in Russell Creek Park. At its height, the farm's borders stretched roughly from Hedgcoxe Road to Highway 121 and from Preston Road to Alma Road. Rasor Elementary in Plano is named after John Henry Rasor.

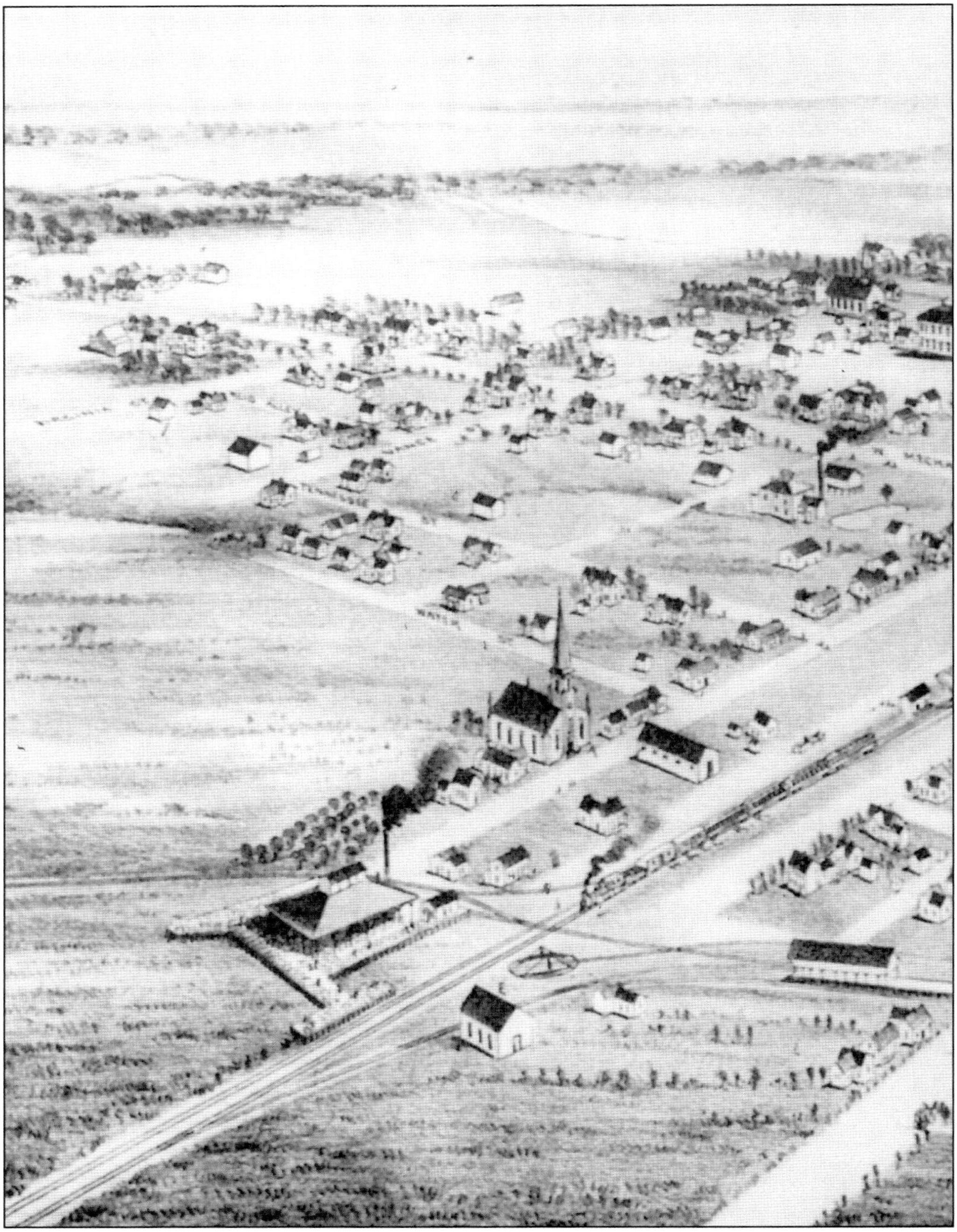

With the arrival of the Houston and Texas Central Railroad (H&TC) in 1872, Plano was linked to Dallas and the market outside Texas. Cotton became the main product shipped out of North Texas and within a few years, St. Louis, Arkansas, and Texas—or Cotton Belt—intersected with the H&TC south of Plano's business district, allowing cotton to be shipped north, south, east,

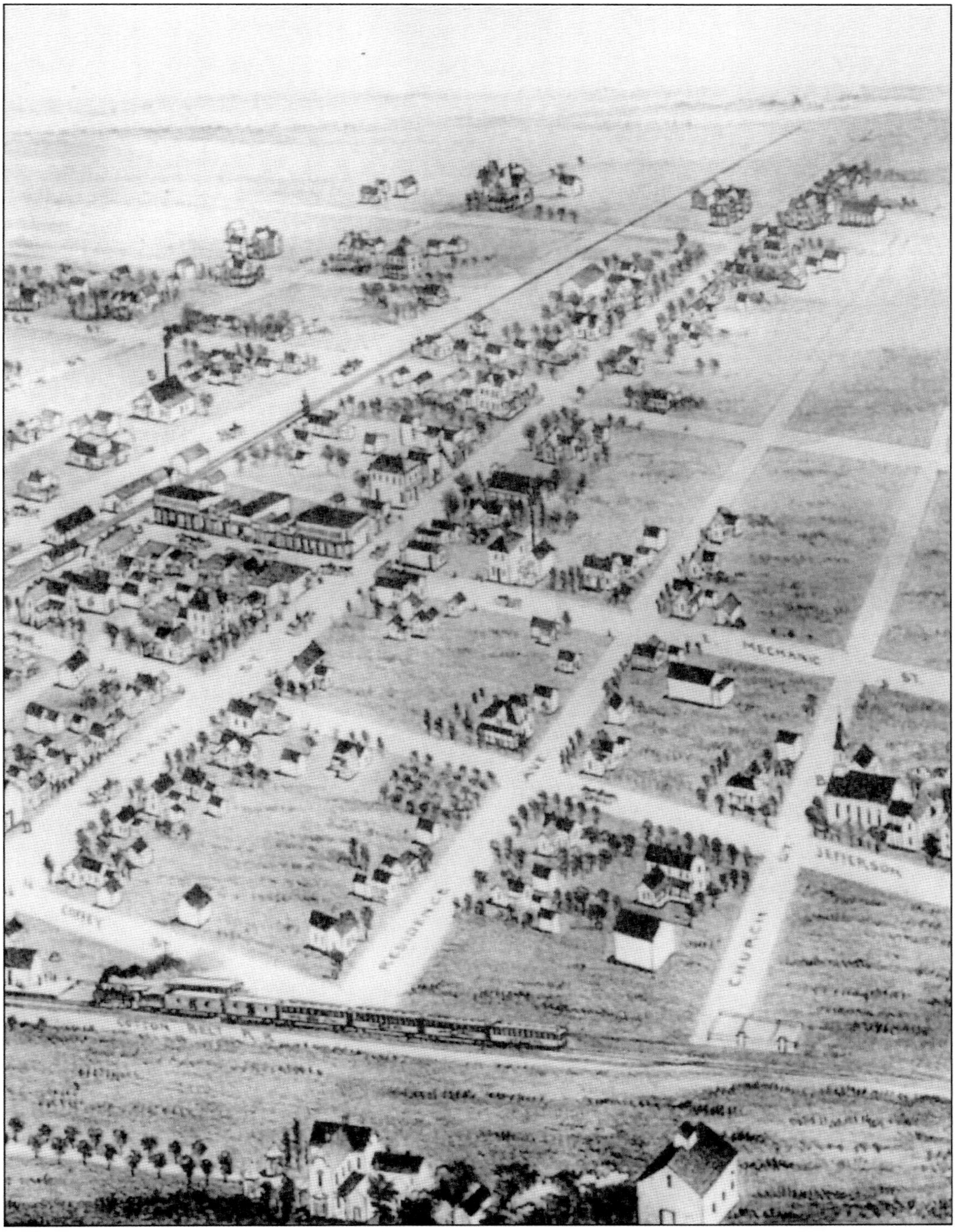

and west. The arrival of the railroad helped cotton emerge as an important cash crop. Cotton ginned in Plano could be milled in Plano or McKinney before being shipped out. Plano's economy depended on the cotton industry for almost a century. This bird's-eye-view illustration of Plano in 1891 shows the vibrant community crisscrossed by the railroads.

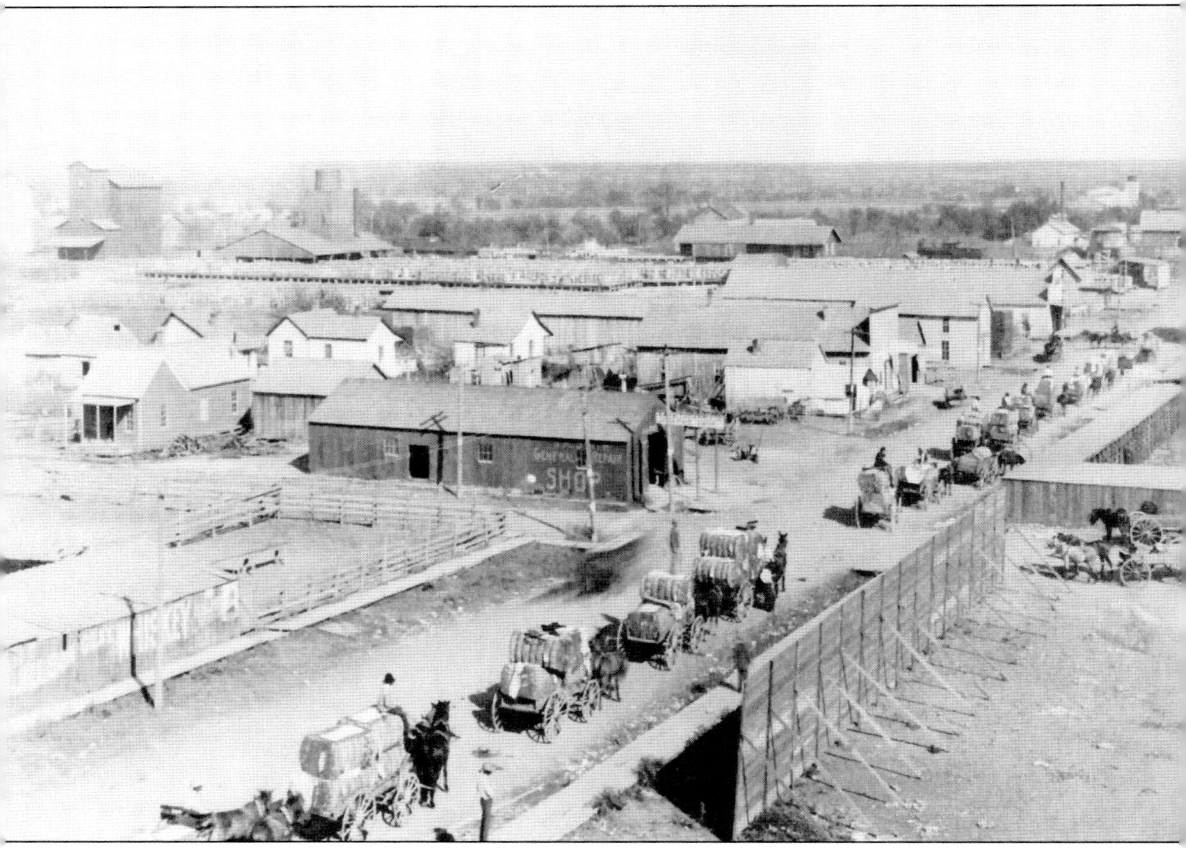

The cotton gin, invented by Eli Whitney in 1793, revolutionized the production of cotton by speeding up the process of separating the hulls and seeds from the cotton. Likewise, a steel plow was more durable and cultivated better than previous wood or iron plows, and a reaper cut down on the time needed to harvest the crops. Farmers were also able to shift from human-powered to animal-powered farming, spurring the shift toward manufacturing, as fewer people were needed to farm and the rest turned to factories for work. The development of barbed wire allowed farmers to build fences on the prairie, where there were not enough trees to build the conventional fences necessary to impede livestock from endangering crop production. All of these inventions greatly advanced agricultural productivity. Here, droves of farmers line up to take cotton to McKinney. By 1890, Plano had its own cotton compress south of town near the intersection of the two railroads. (Courtesy of Rodney Haggard.)

Two

Spritual, Educational, and Social Legacy

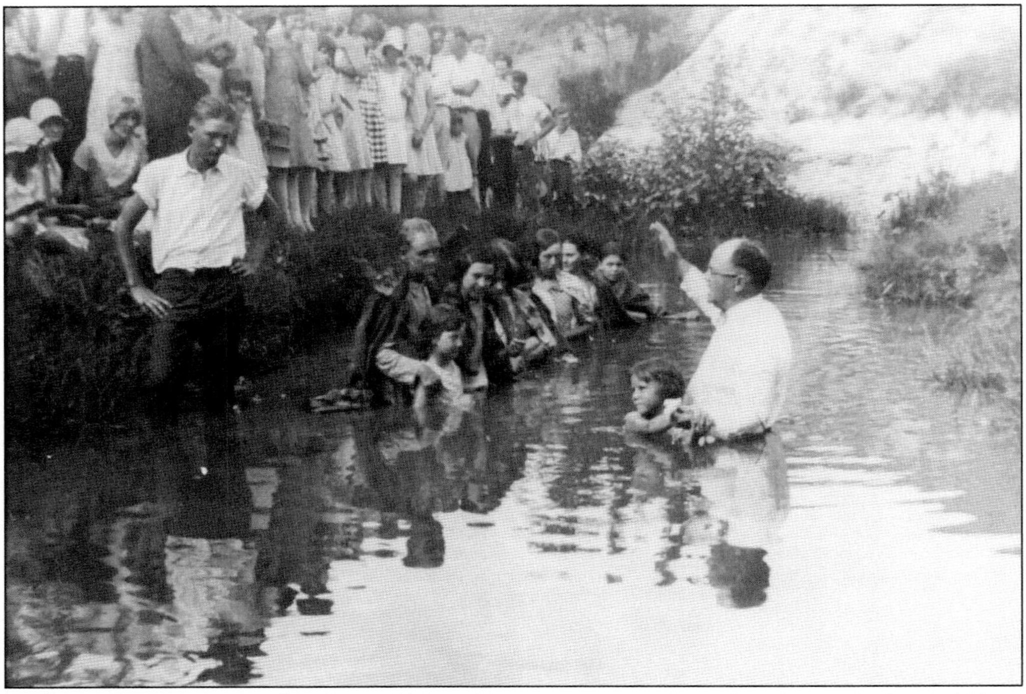

In the early years, spiritual and social life in Plano was centered on churches and schools. There were five churches in the area by the late 1800s, many of which began in the homes of the pioneers. Baptisms took place in nearby waters, like in this c. 1929 photograph taken at White Rock Creek.

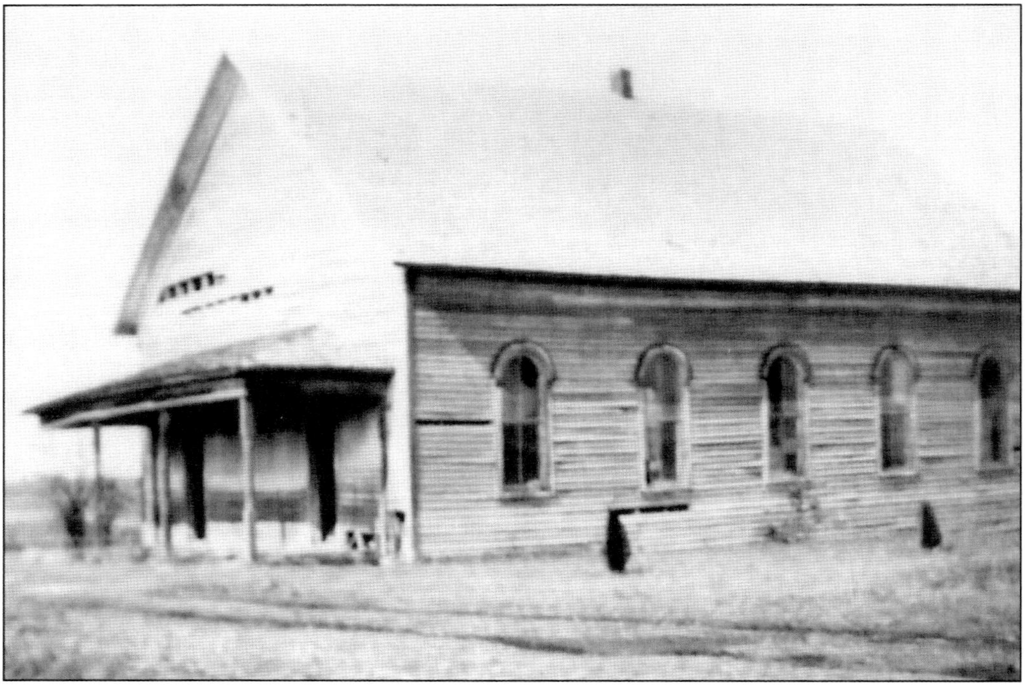

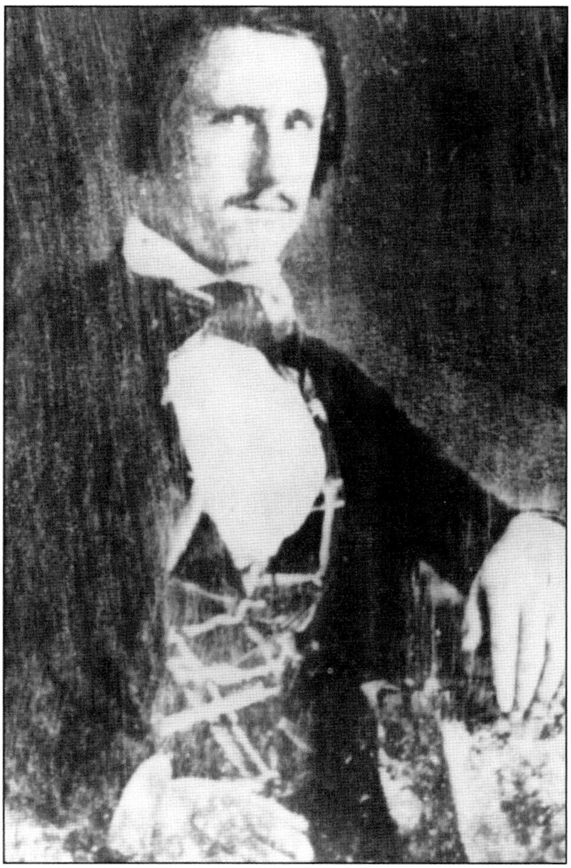

Organized in 1848, Rowlett Creek Baptist Church is believed to be the earliest Baptist church in Collin County. It is named for Daniel Rowlett, who located his land grant along the creek in 1836. Adjacent to the church, near the present intersection of Sam Rayburn Tollway (Highway 121) and Custer Road, the Rowlett Creek Cemetery has the largest number of Peters colonists buried in Collin County. The earliest marked grave is that of Alfred Harrington in 1862. Three ancestors of Pres. Lyndon B. Johnson are buried in the cemetery: his great-great-grandfather, John S. Huffman; his great-grandfather, Dr. John Smith Huffman Jr., a Peters colonist (pictured on the left); and Dr. Huffman's daughter, Ruth Ament Huffman, Johnson's grandmother. (Above, courtesy of Joy Gough.)

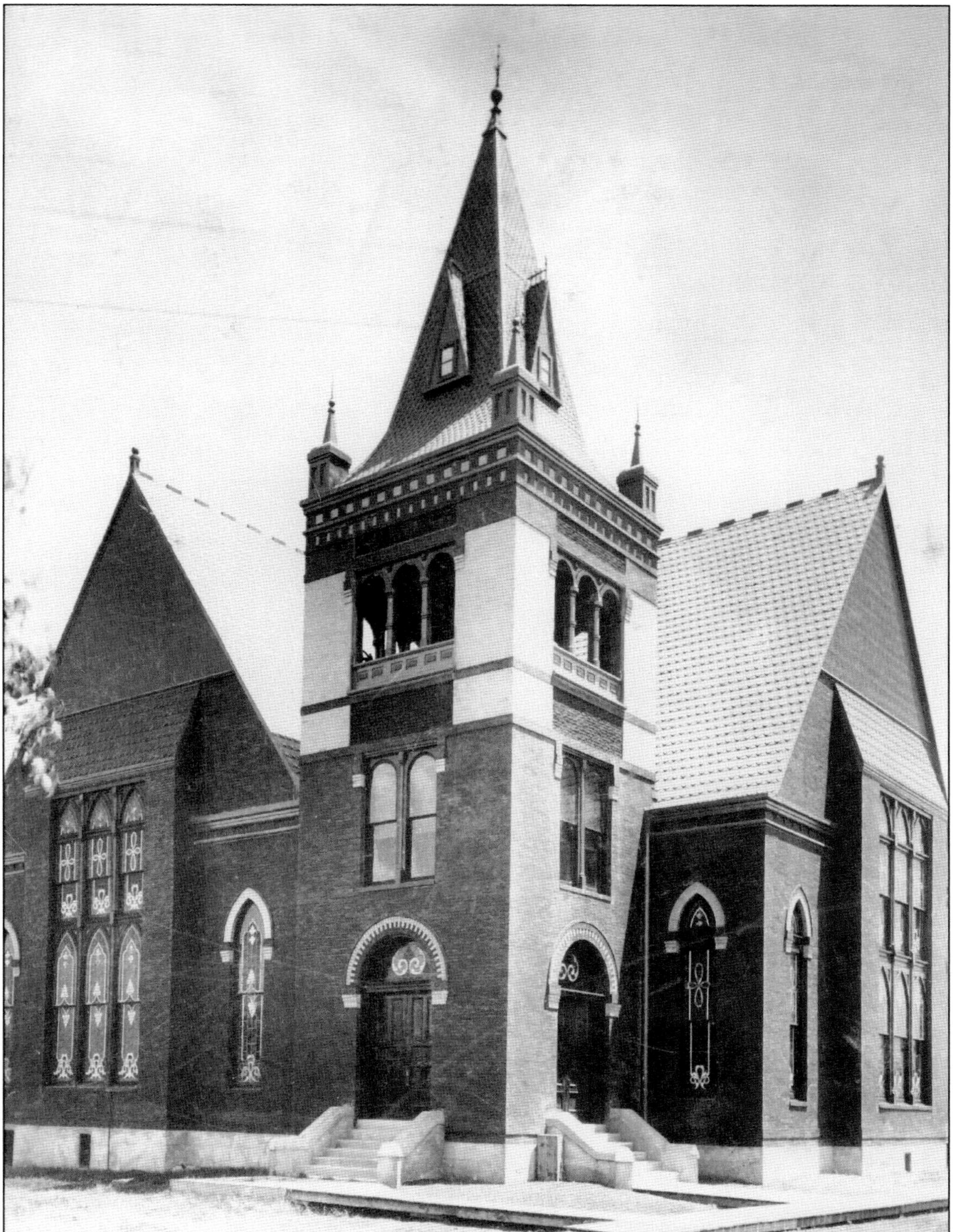

First Baptist Church, founded in 1875, is located at 1300 East Fifteenth Street and is one of the oldest churches in Plano still located on its original site. In its early days, the Baptist settlers met at the farm of Sam Young near the present intersection of State Highway 121 and Independence Parkway. In those days, the men kept vigil in case of an Indian attack, keeping their guns ready nearby. In 1853, the Spring Creek Baptist Church met in a schoolhouse on Jacob Routh's property near Plano Road and Renner Road. It was not until the railroad was built that the country Baptist church moved to town.

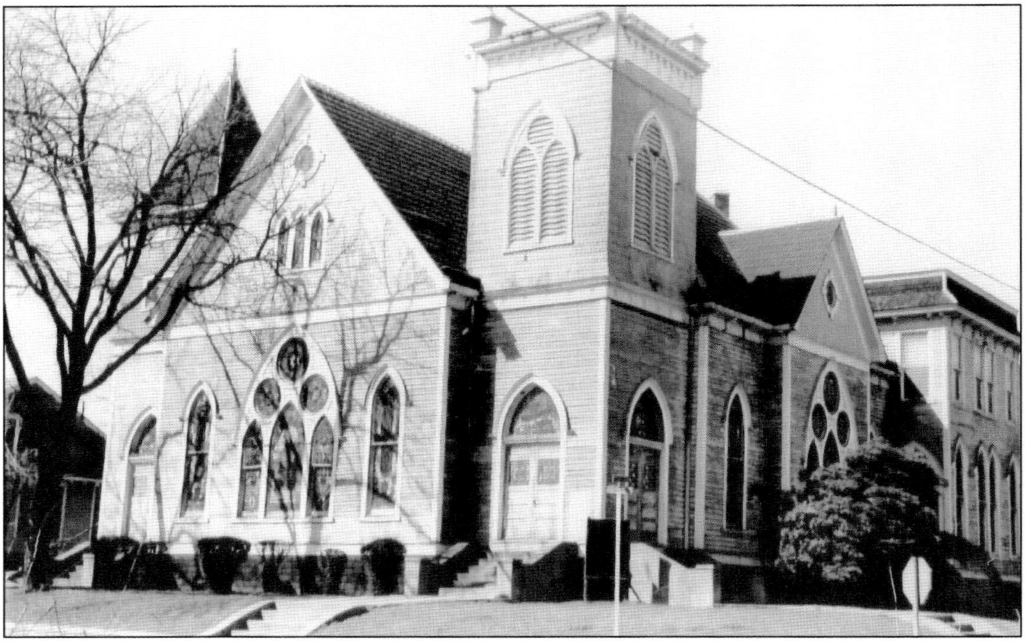

Written church records from the First Christian Church of Plano date as far back as 1857, when a few people met in the small frame building at the Spring Creek schoolhouse. The church was formally constituted in 1860 and continued worship in its country home until 1873, when a new church was erected in town on College Hill (now Sixteenth Street). The church building consisted of one large room with a center aisle separating men and women. A fire destroyed the church, and in 1899, the congregation moved to its present location at Fifteenth Street and H Avenue. This building was razed in 1952, but the bell, stained-glass windows, organ, and cornerstone were saved for use in the new chapel, dedicated in 1951. The church celebrated is first centennial in 1960, and the present sanctuary was dedicated in 1986.

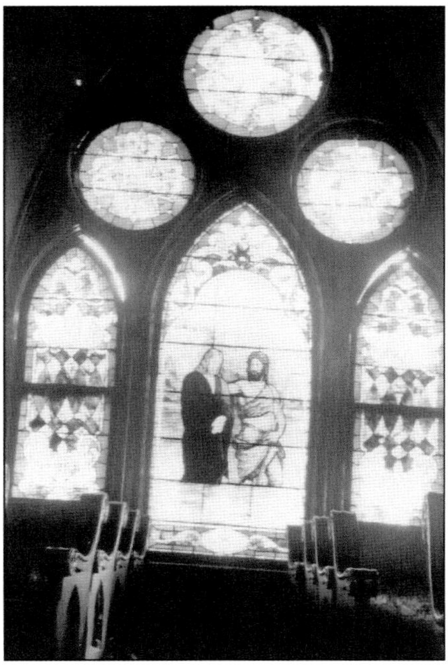

After being struck by lightning in 2001, a new education building was constructed. The chapel was renovated and dedicated in 2006, again saving the stained-glass windows. The original stained-glass windows celebrate the offerings of early founders like the Haggards, Bishops, Saiglings, Andrews, Barnetts, Bowsers, Smoots, Oglesbys, and Carpenters. The church celebrated its 150th anniversary in 2010. (Courtesy of Henry Hays and Peggy Mitchell.)

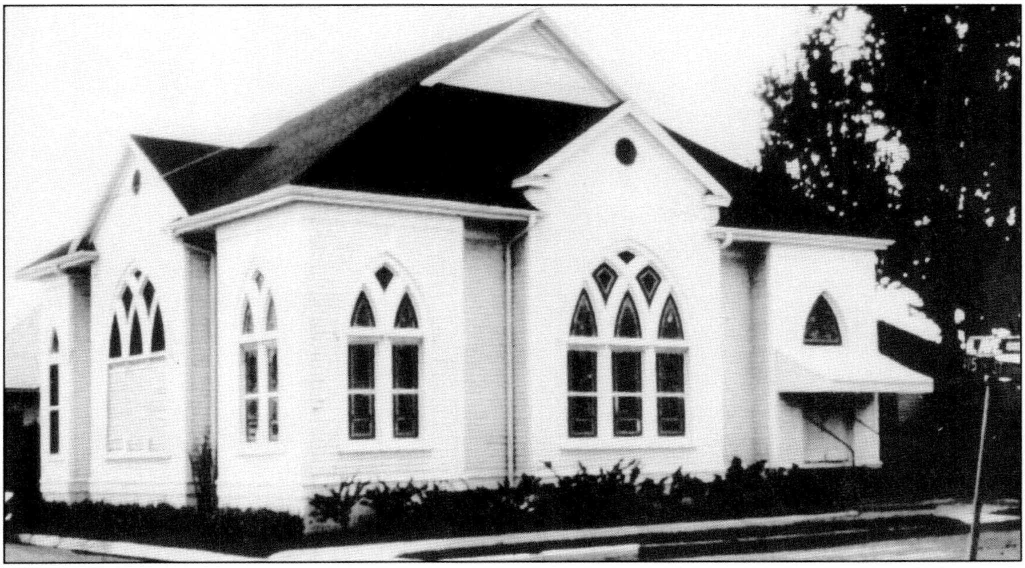

First United Methodist Church was founded in 1847 at the log cabin home of Joseph and Elizabeth Russell, four miles north of Plano. The church was part of the Dallas circuit from Dallas to Bonham and was visited every two weeks by traveling preachers. In 1946, the cornerstone of the church was opened; bibles, books, and articles dated the organization of the Plano congregation to 1847. In 1968, after several moves, the church built a new sanctuary on Eighteenth Street, with men, women, and children carrying the stained-glass windows and other furnishings. In 2002, the church moved to East Spring Creek Parkway for more visibility and congregational growth.

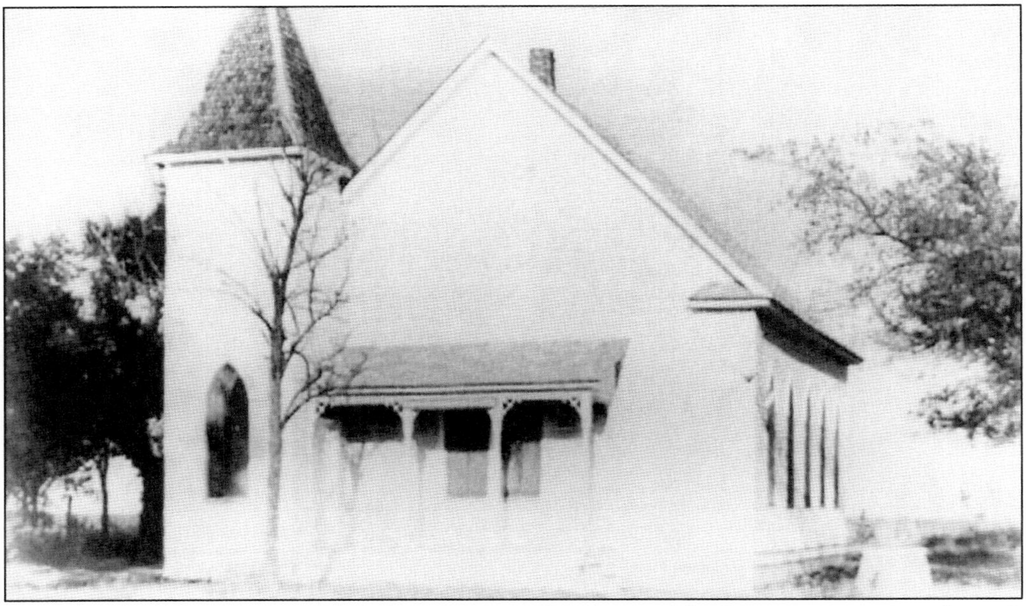

In 1903, a Methodist country chapel was organized and named for Fannie Harrington, the wife of John Harrington, in recognition of her tireless efforts to provide visitation, transportation, and clothing for children so they could attend Sunday school. According to *Plano, Texas: The Early Years*, they affectionately said of Fannie, "If she didn't get to heaven, there isn't any use of anybody else trying." Fannie Harrington Chapel was at the corner of present-day Custer Road and Legacy Drive until it was torn down in 1963.

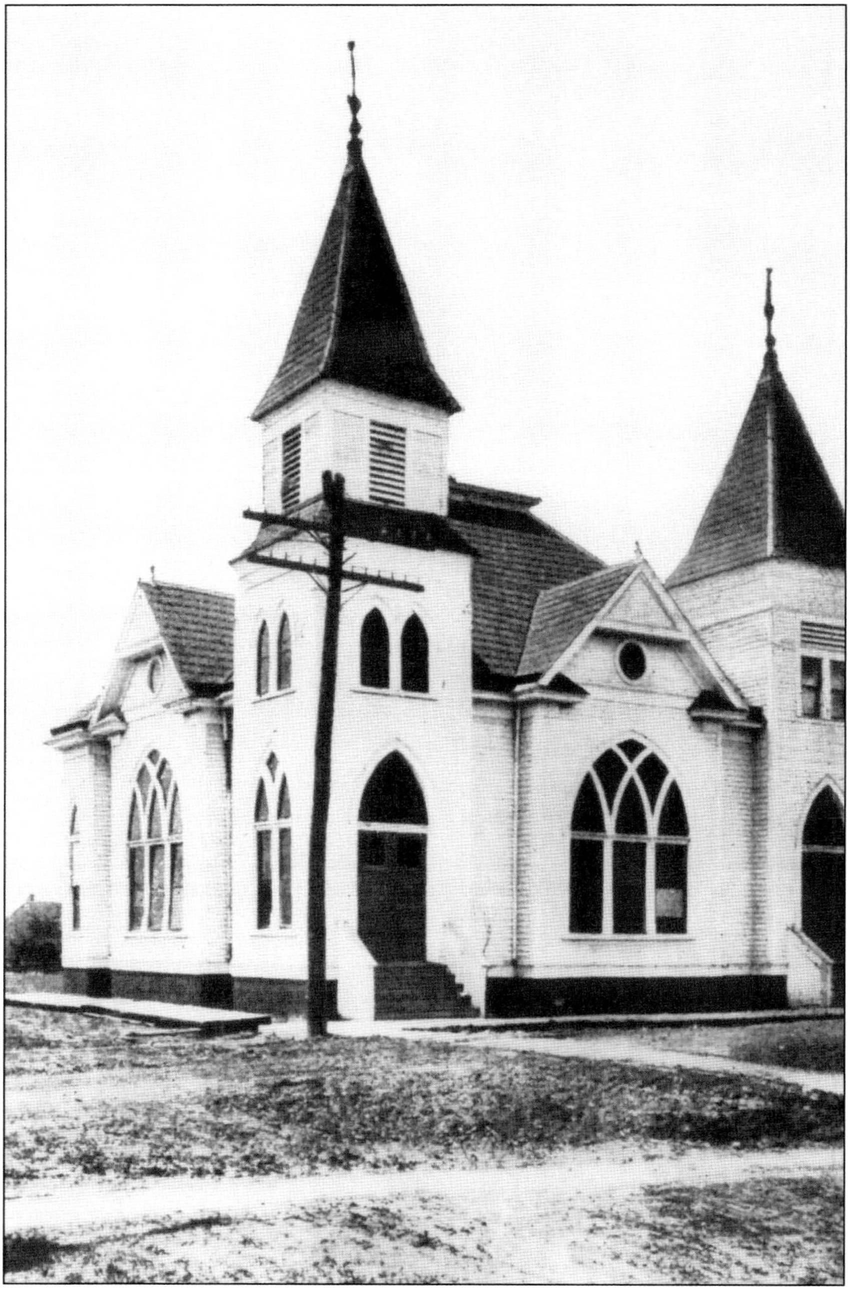

First Presbyterian Church was originally organized as the Cumberland Presbyterian Church of Plano in 1871. Services were held in a grove or in the church building erected by the Baptists at Jacob Routh's farm on Spring Creek. Dr. Henry Dye was the primary founder of the church and donated the property for its first building on Main Street when the congregation moved to Plano in 1873. After his death, the church lapsed into inactivity for several years. Still under its original name, the congregation built a new structure in 1897. The old Presbyterian Church burned in 1938, and the congregation rebuilt and installed memorial windows in the new church. In 1966 and 1967, larger facilities were required, and a new church was built on Jupiter Road, where it remains today.

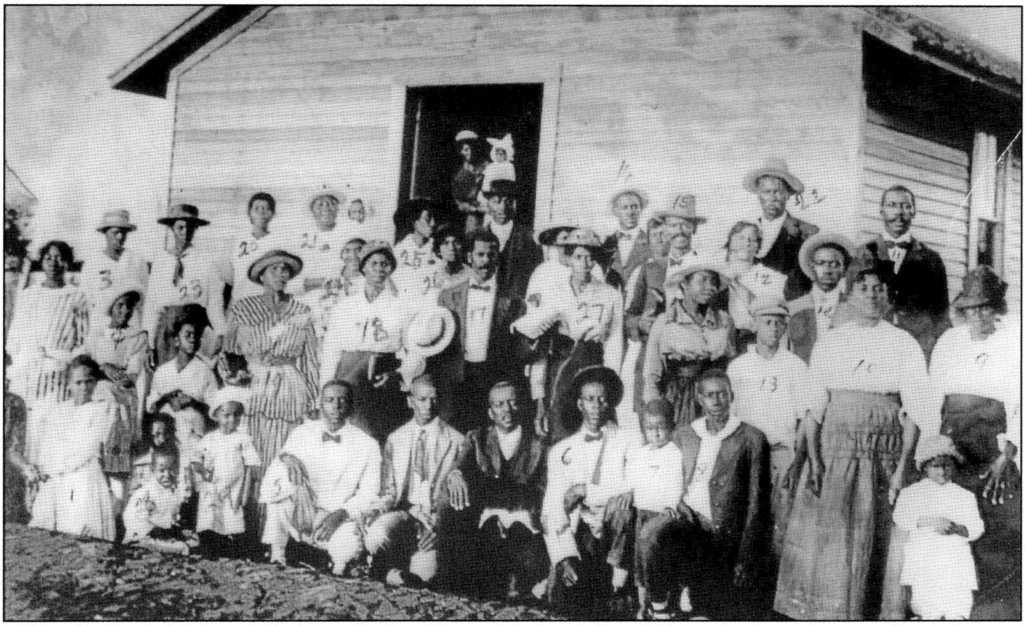

Before the Civil War, many slaves moved to Plano carrying the names of their masters. In the 1860s, Andy Drake, the first free African American in the area, came to work for Silas Harrington. Drake, the patriarch of one of Plano's largest African American families, is buried in the Pioneer Cemetery on H Avenue in the Douglass community. Many African Americans worked as tenant farmers and sharecroppers, and in the 1890s some came to town to work in the mills and cotton gins while others started their own businesses. Their children attended schools held in local churches, first in the Shiloh Baptist Church, from its founding in 1884 to 1894, and the Methodist Episcopal Church after that.

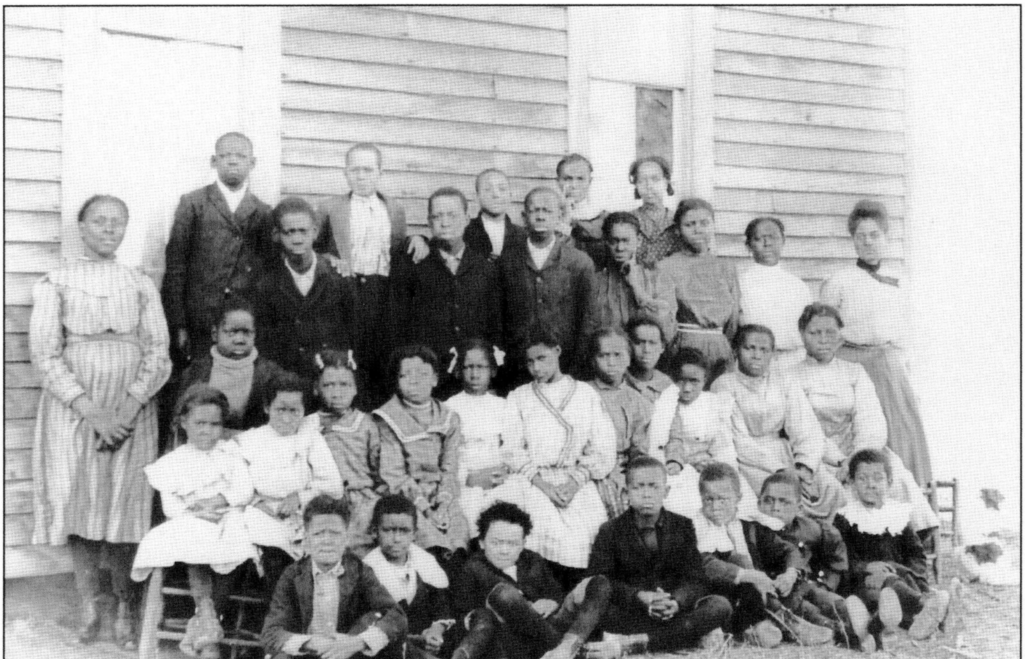

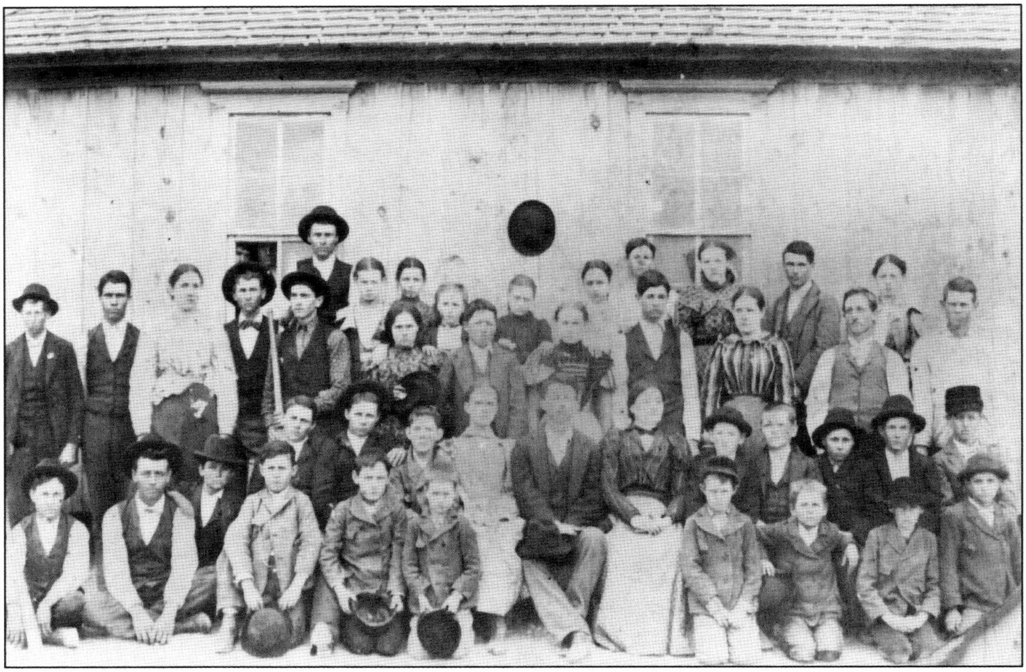

Early schools were started on farms with the support of neighbors. Early examples were the Haggard Schoolhouse, built on the C.S. Haggard farm in 1848; the Spring Creek School, started on George W. Barnett's land in 1857; and M.C. Portman's School. By 1880, county funds were made available for schools and the Plano Institute was opened by Princeton graduate W.F. Mister in 1882 on the site of the current Cox Administration Building. The County-Line School is seen here around 1898.

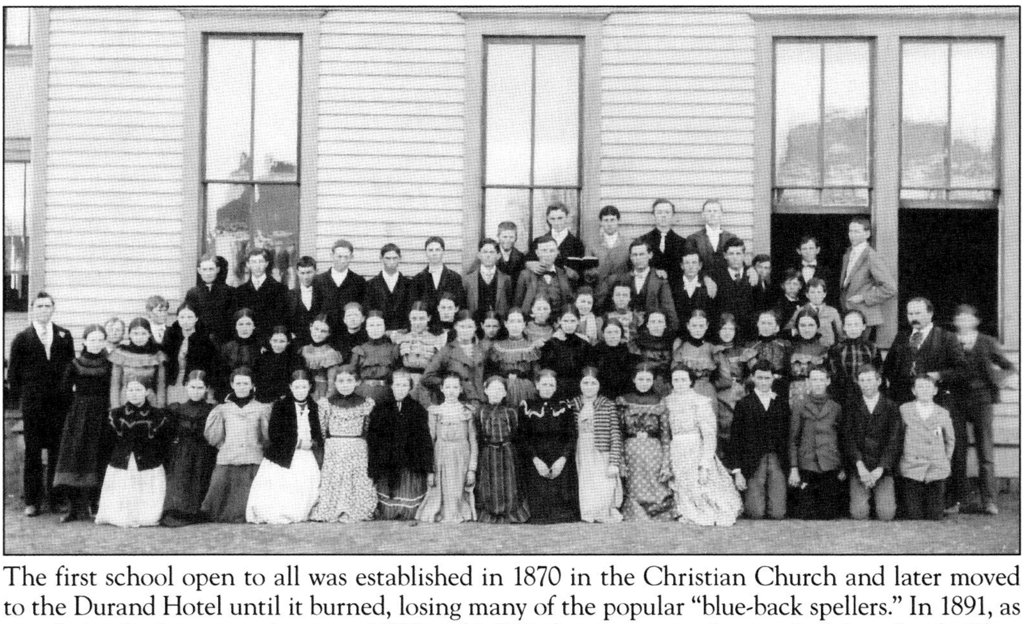

The first school open to all was established in 1870 in the Christian Church and later moved to the Durand Hotel until it burned, losing many of the popular "blue-back spellers." In 1891, as population had grown to between 1,200 and 1,500, the city assumed control of the schools. They then bought the property on present-day H Avenue and Sixteenth Street. Seen here is a Plano High School class from around 1898.

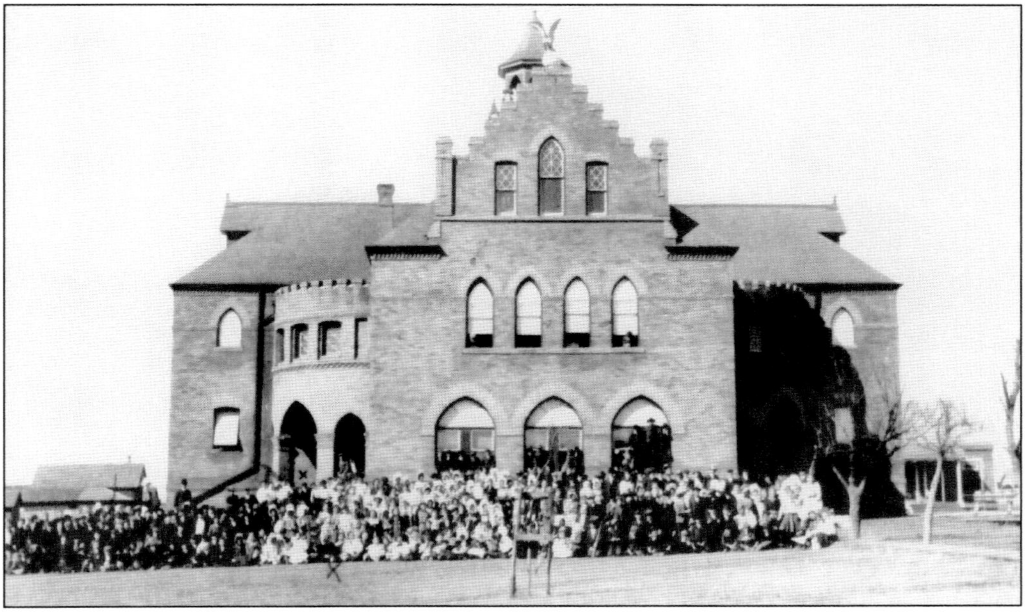

In 1899, the school separated from the city, establishing the independent public school system in Plano. Following fires of wood frame buildings in 1894 and 1903, the Plano Public School opened in a red brick, three-story building called the "Spanish school" for its architectural style. In 1904, Mayor Fred Schimelpfenig donated a small frame structure on the school grounds to house music, art, and elocution classes.

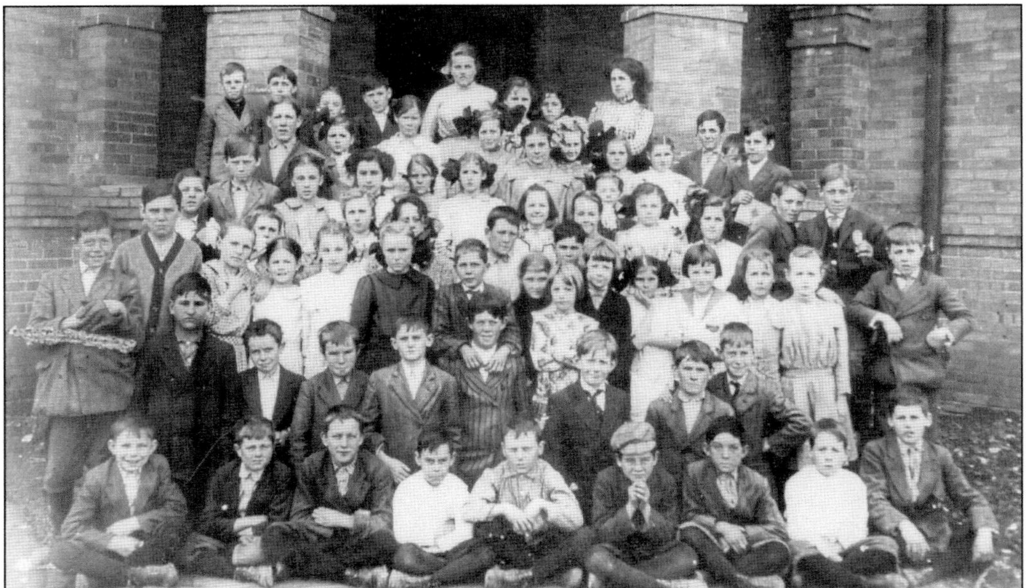

All Plano children between the ages of 8 and 16 were eligible for public school benefits. But students had to provide their own books and stationery and could be suspended if they did not have supplies. According to the Cox School Museum, school was not free, as early annual school reports list tuition at the primary level as $1.50, $2.50 for grammar (fifth grade through seventh grade), and $3.50 for high school classes. Pictured is Kruger Chaddick's schoolroom in 1911. (Courtesy of Rodney Haggard.)

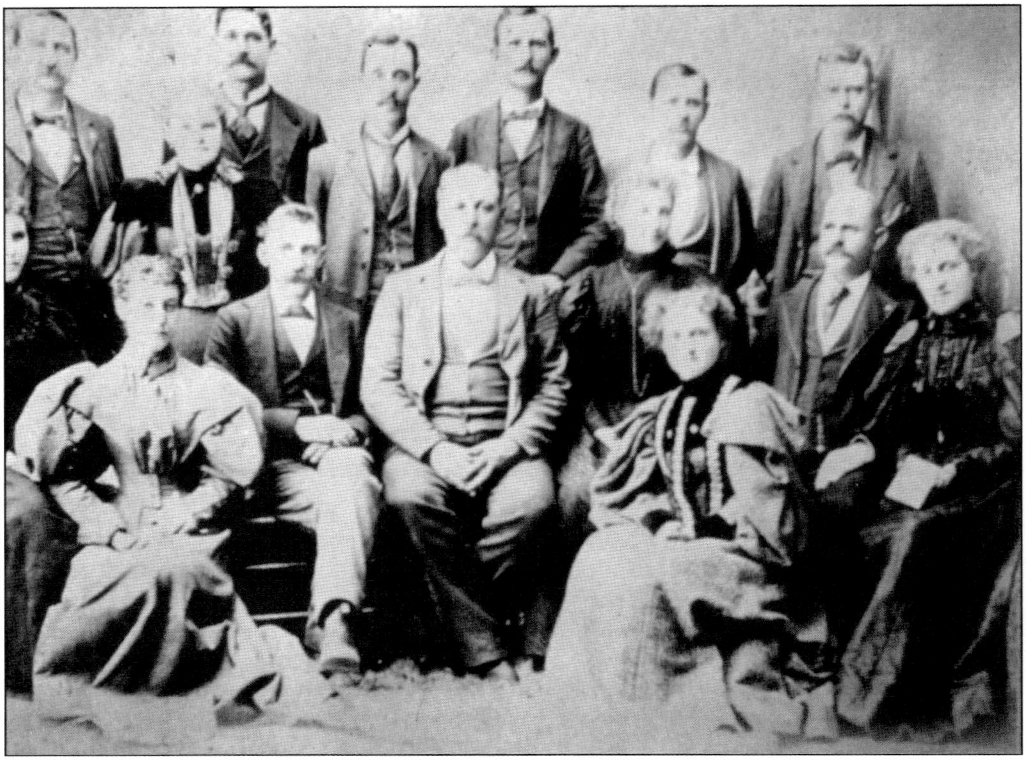

An official board of education was charged with management of the Plano School in 1899 with the beginning of the public school system. Names such as Mendenhall, Schimelpfenig, Davis, Hendricks, Harrington, and Wyatt served on this early school board and as faculty. These families have schools named in their honor today, and the voters elect the seven-member school board. The district currently employs about 4,000 teachers, and the overall staff tops 6,800.

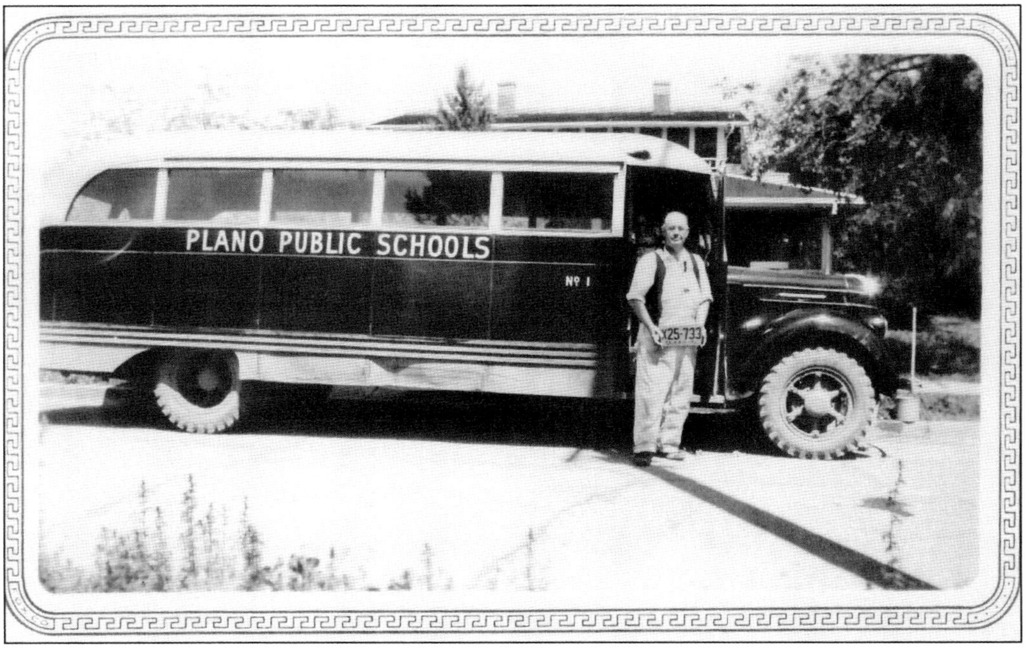

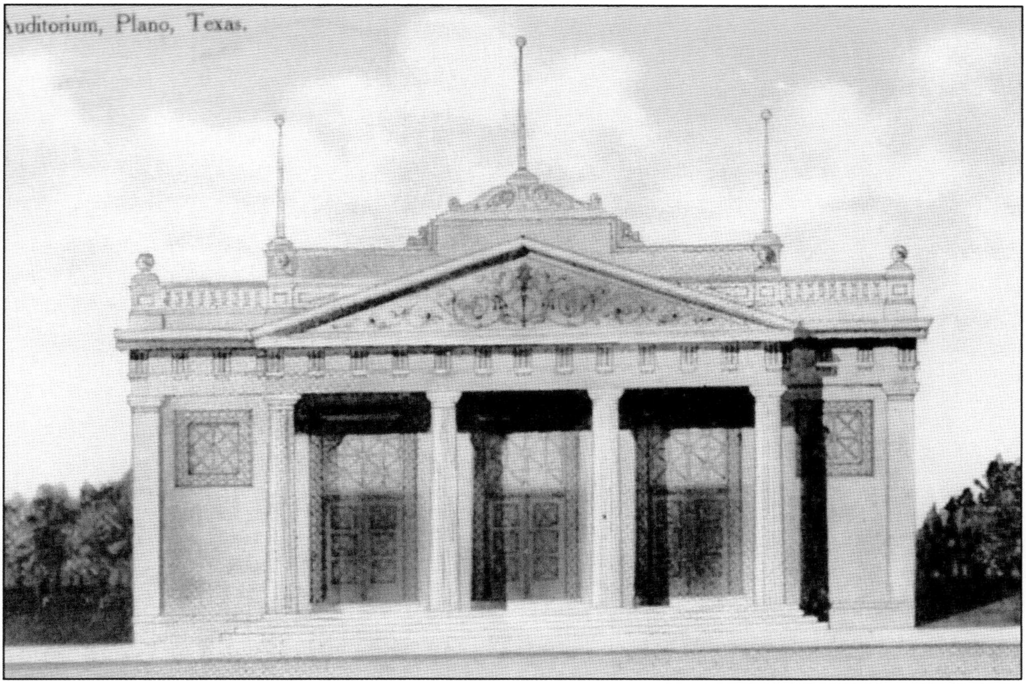

The civic auditorium (above) was built next to the school in 1909 to serve as a gymnasium and auditorium. The auditorium was used for public gatherings and school functions. It was replaced by a federal Works Progress Administration (WPA) project in 1938 to provide work for the unemployed during the Depression. The new building (below) still stands and is known as the Courtyard Theater for Performing Arts. After World War II, Plano's school system began to grow in prestige and size. In 1952, Plano received accreditation from the Southern Association of Secondary Schools and Colleges. In 1964, the schools were integrated, adding elementary and high school students from the Douglass School, built in the 1950s. In 1975, the district had grown to an enrollment of almost 15,000 students, with one high school, three middle schools, and 13 elementary schools. Today, there are 68 schools enrolling 55,000 students. (Above, courtesy of Peggy Mitchell.)

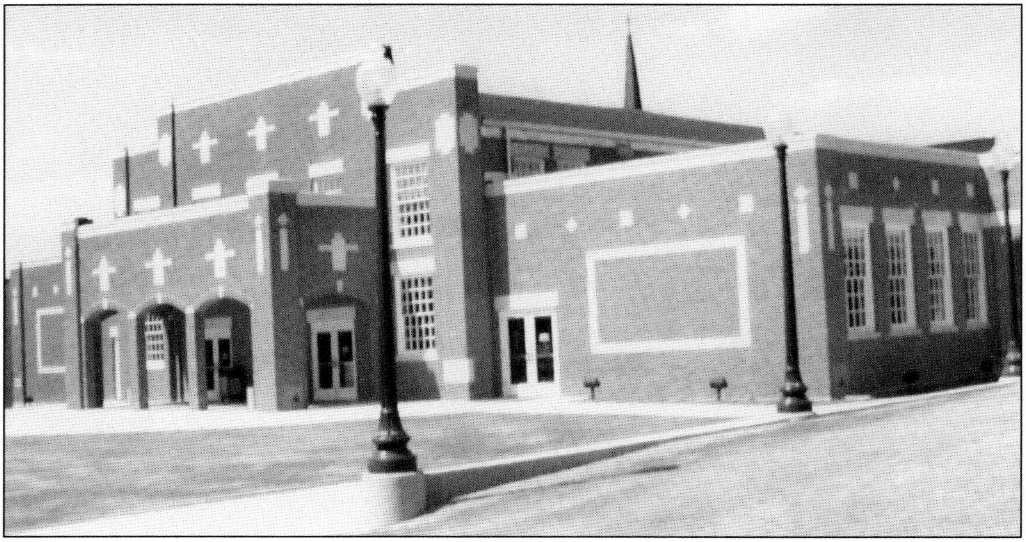

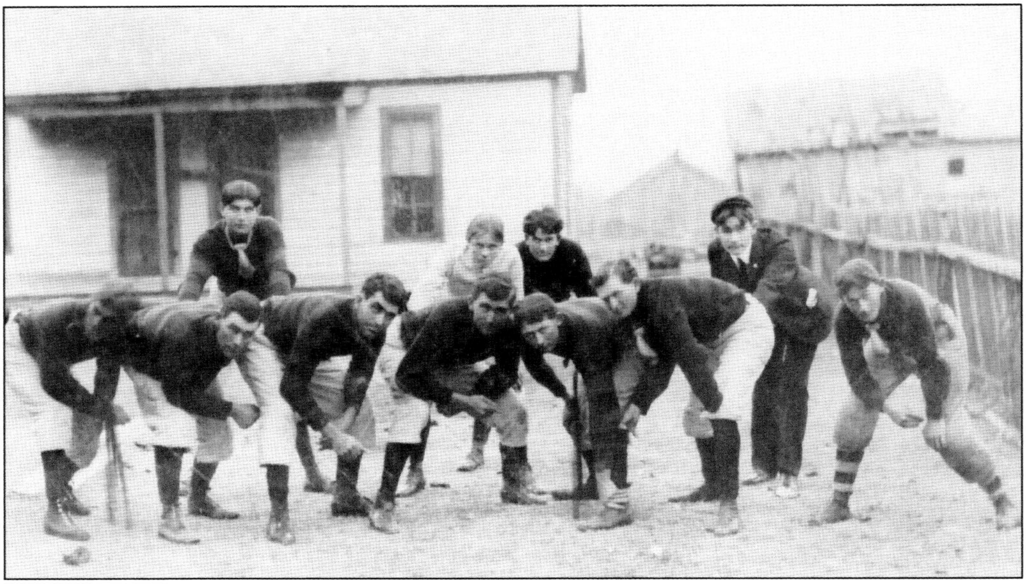

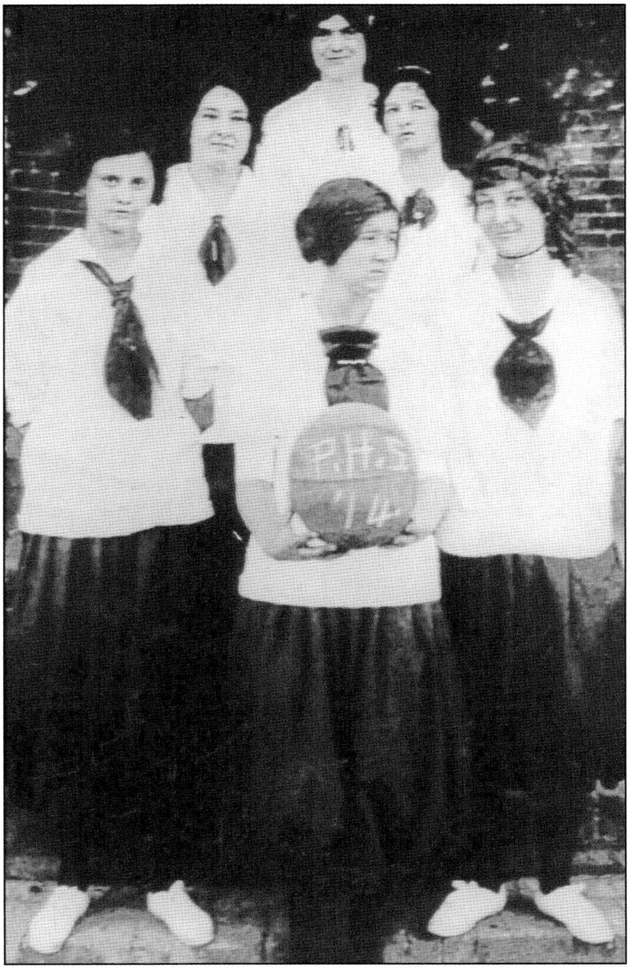

The Plano Wildcats competed in football, baseball, basketball, track, volleyball, tennis, soccer, and golf. The first football team (above) played in 1900. In 1971, the school rose to the AAA ranks, and a year later to AAAA, still managing to go to the state football tournament. Plano teams have consistently been rated highly in sports. Due to rapidly increasing school enrollment in the 1980s, Plano veered from the typical US school system by separating 11th and 12th grades from the high school to a new senior high school level. Now, three high schools, the Plano Senior High Wildcats, the Plano East Panthers, and Plano West Wolves, each have over 1,000 graduates each year.

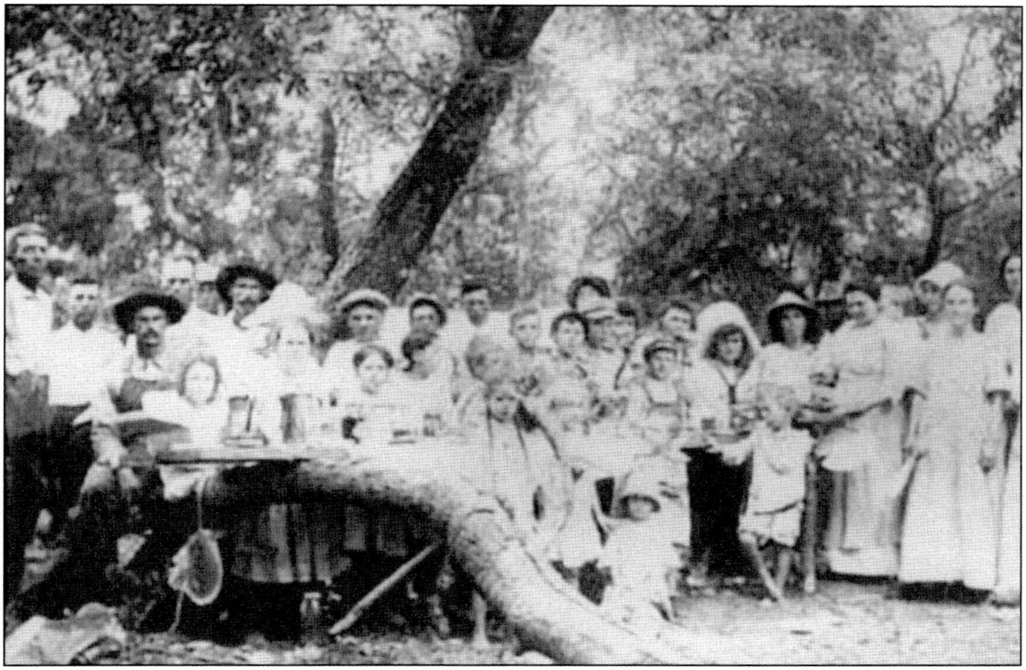

Early social life was centered on the church, fraternal organizations, and clubs formed by both men and women. Plano was a social community, celebrating everything from birthdays to weddings, anniversaries, and christenings with family and friends. Women formed study, knitting, canning, and needlework clubs, and men played dominoes and held dances. In 1884, Louise Ernestine "L.E.R." Ramner, the wife of mayor Fred Schimelpfenig, lent her personal book collection to the community, starting the earliest library service. She formed the Juvenile Missionary and Aid Society for Girls to promote reading, reciting, and singing. She was also instrumental in establishing a Temperance Hall to rid the town of saloons and liquor. The couple's descendants continue to serve Plano in many capacities, with schools, parks, and a library named in their honor. The interior of their beautiful home (right) reflects the culture the Schimelpfenig family instilled in Plano for more than a century. (Right, courtesy of Rodney Haggard.)

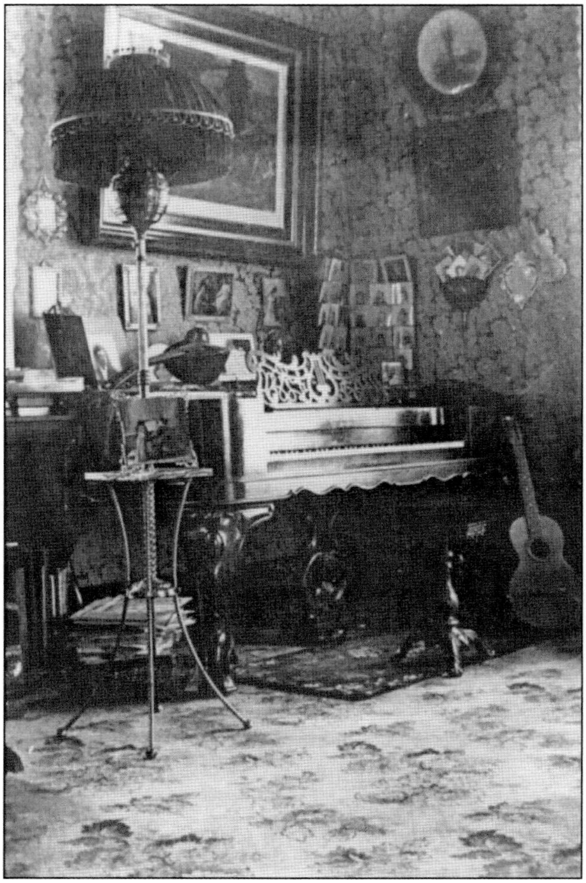

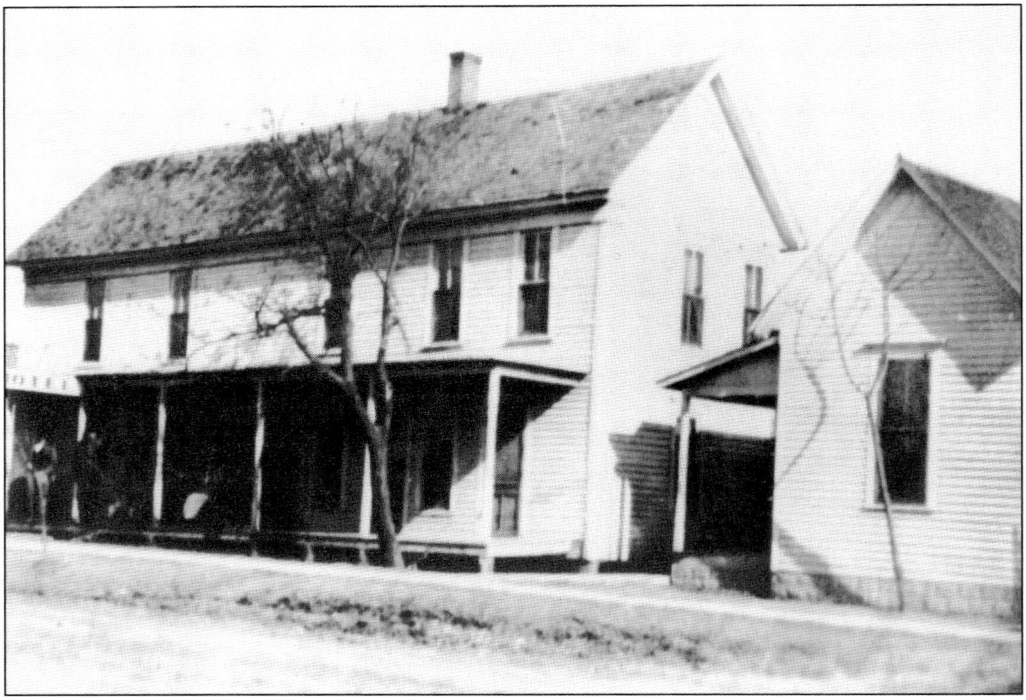

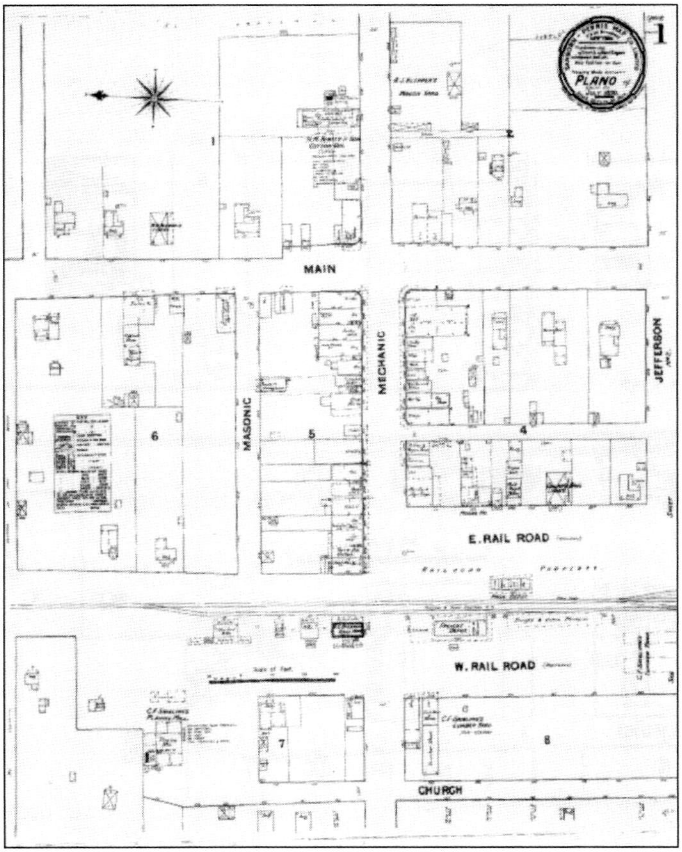

The earliest fraternal organization in Plano was the Masonic Grand Lodge of Texas, Lodge No. 235, chartered in 1859. Originally above the Gossum Storehouse on the southeast corner of modern-day Fifteenth Street and K Avenue, the lodge fell on difficult times and was disbanded in 1888. Lodge No. 768 was granted a charter in 1894 and is still south of Fifteenth Street on J Avenue. Originally built as the Moore House Hotel, it catered to rail travelers on the Houston and Texas Central Railroad and is seen on this 1890 map. Originally built on E. Rail Road as the Moore House Hotel, it was later named the Commercial Hotel, before the Plano Masonic Lodge purchased it. (Left, courtesy of Sanborn Map Company, Sanborn Library, LLC.)

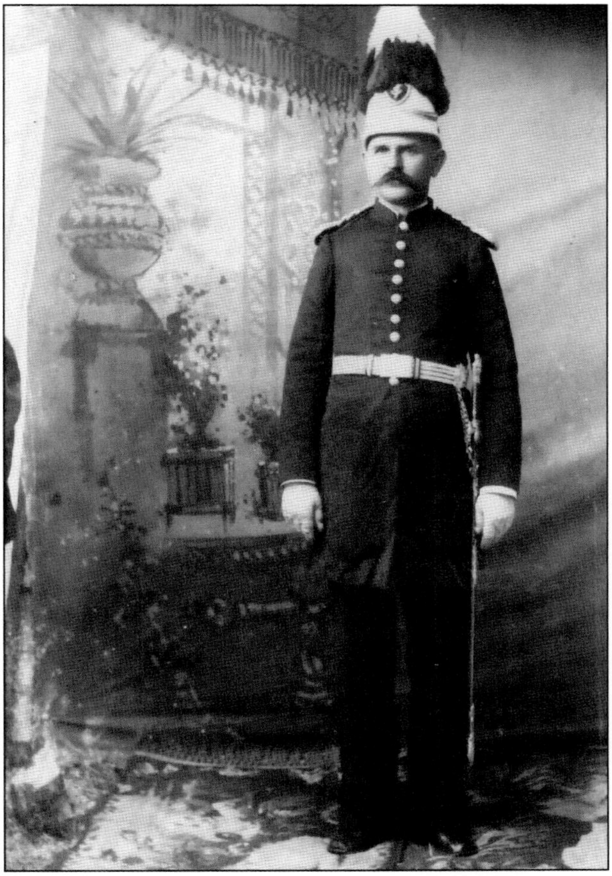

An International Order of Odd Fellows Lodge was in existence as early as 1870. These men cared for the sick, widows, and orphans, holding a picnic every year and inviting lodges from other towns. Here, Olney Davis poses in his lodge uniform. Davis was a prominent businessman, civic leader, and mayor of Plano. He became the first president of the board of trustees for the Plano School System in 1899. His home, pictured in the 1891 photograph below, still stands on Eighteenth Street and is now used for offices and the ArtCentre of Plano.

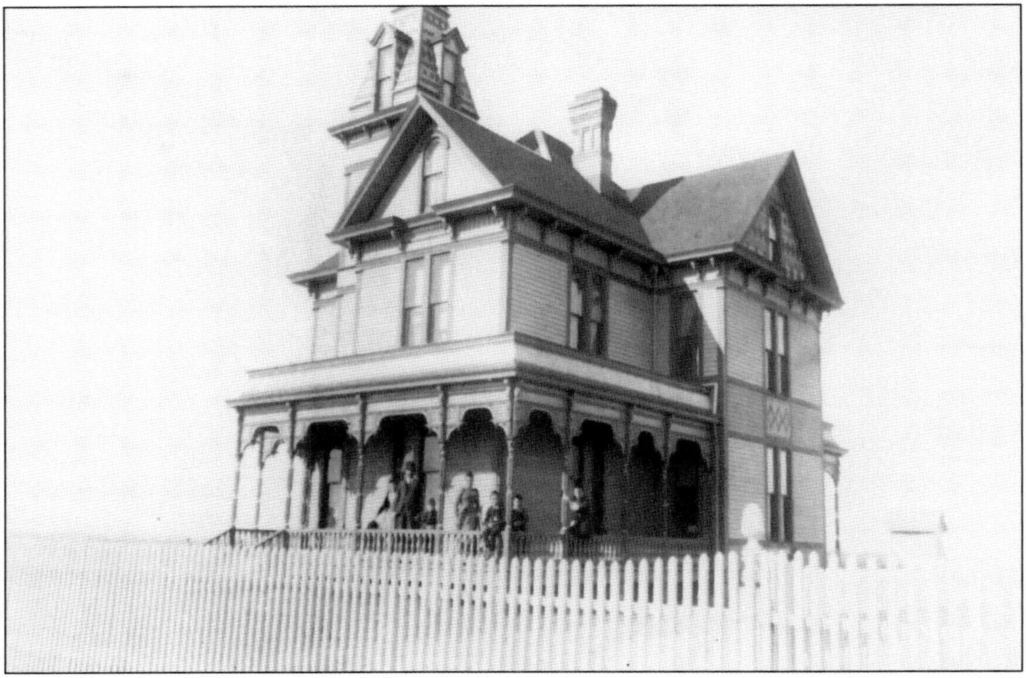

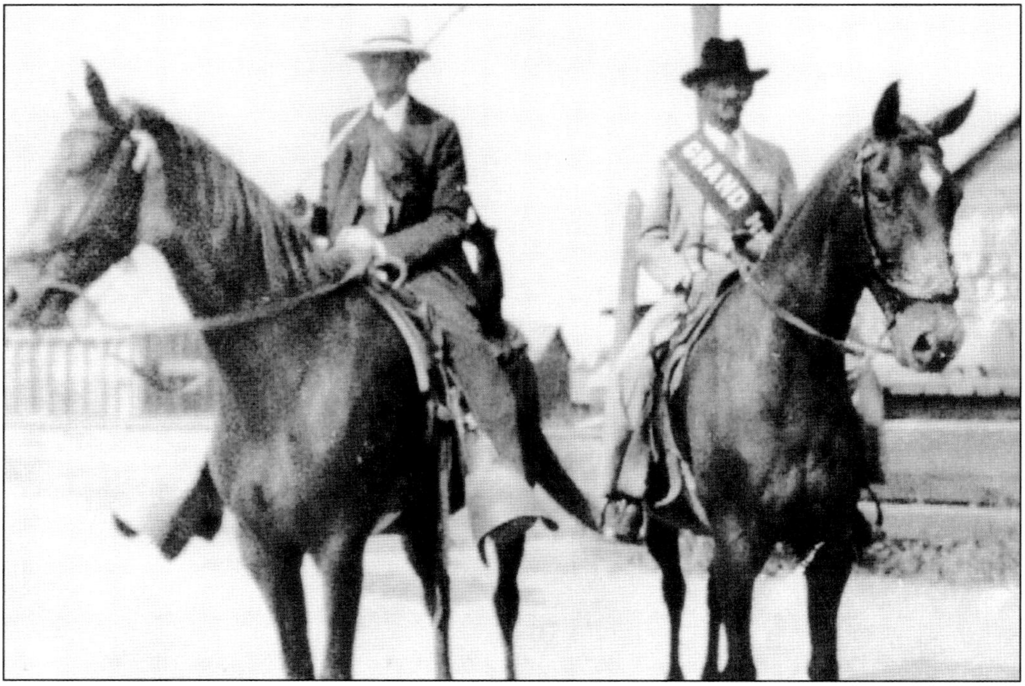

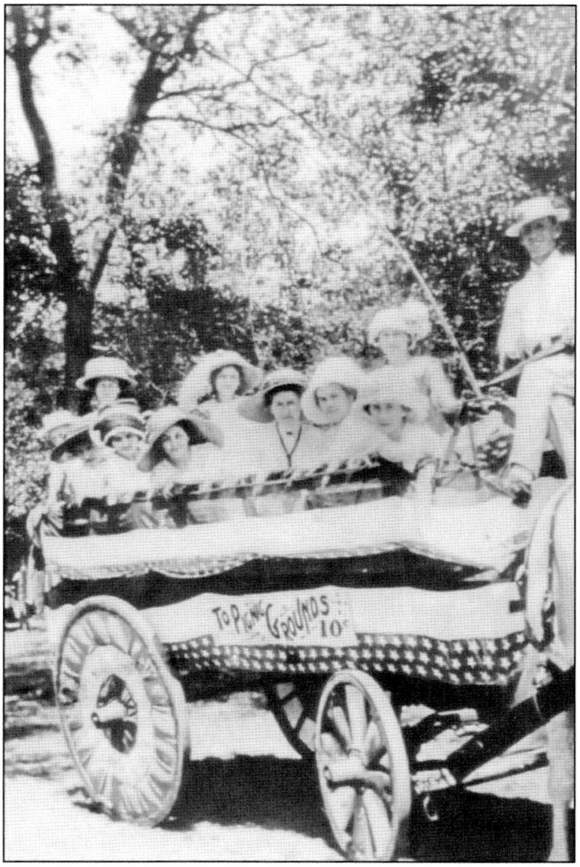

Grand marshal W.H.L. Wells (right) leads the Old Settler's Day parade in the 1920s. Wells was a Confederate veteran who came to Plano after the Civil War. His homestead still stands on Coit Road, and his farm was honored by the Texas Department of Agriculture for a century or more of farm operation by the same family owners.

Shown here in the early 1900s, George Good's wagon heads to the Settlers Picnic, a late summer event, which usually started with a parade gathered at the Shepard Mule Barn across from the old depot and went through downtown to the City Park (now Harrington Park) on Spring Creek. There was typically music, dancing, and a carnival. Once, the opening festivities included hot-air balloons. Decades later, Plano became known for its Balloon Festival, held every September since 1980. The Old Settlers reunion continues today at the Haggard Party Barn with descendants of the early pioneers.

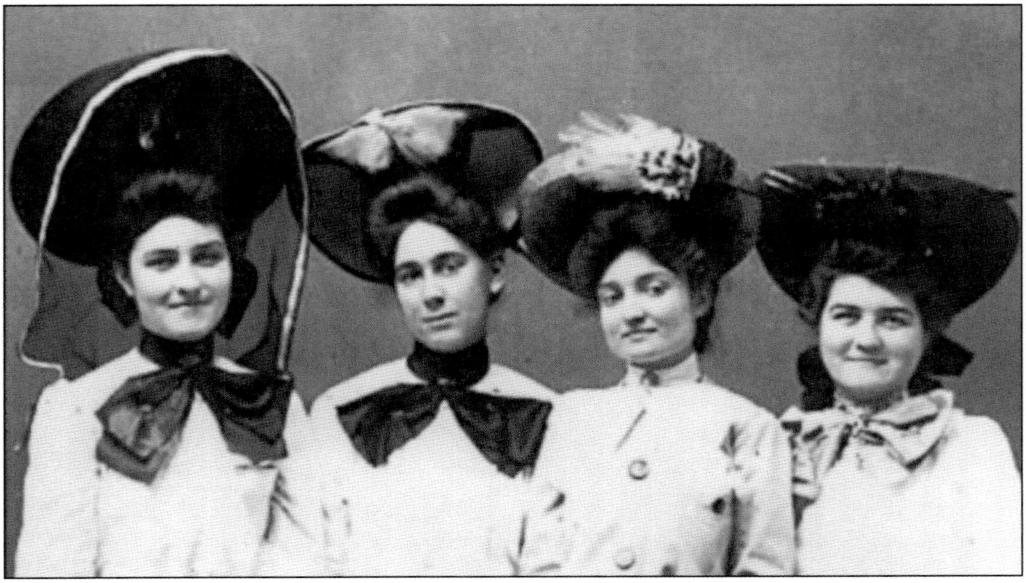

Here, Olney Davis's girls sport their fancy hats and party dresses lovingly stitched with pleats and embroidery. Clubs for ladies became popular around 1900. One of the first was organized in the home of Mary Catherine Haggard Shepard. Below, the women are gathered to study and enjoy the Southern hospitality of their hostess. In 1910, the Mothers' Club, the forerunner of the Parent Teacher Association, was formed. In 1921, Lizzie Armstrong Aldridge was the first PTA president.

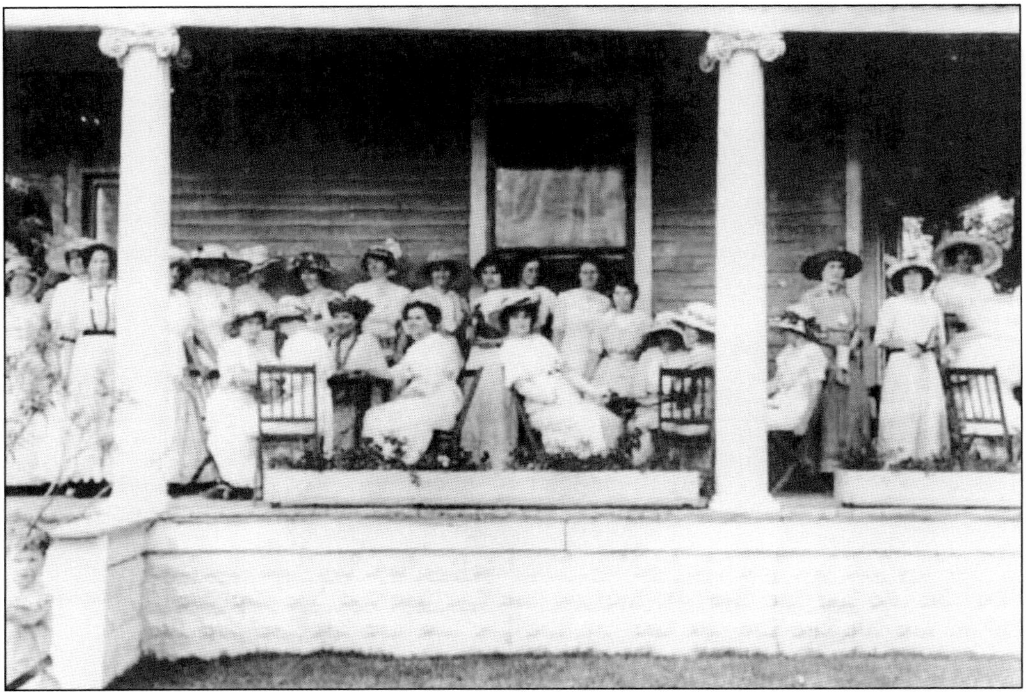

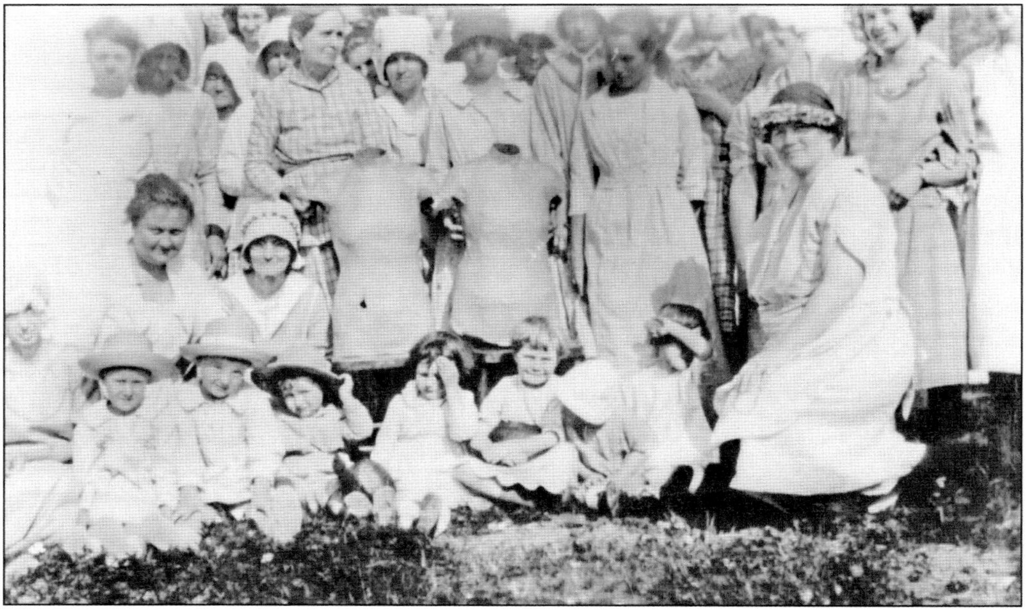

In 1917, the Girls Knitting Club made washrags and mufflers for the men away in the war. The 1924 Bethany Home Demonstration Club shown here met in a clubhouse built just south of Bethany cemetery (now Custer Road near Legacy Drive), where they canned fruits and vegetables. Ladies also enjoyed playing in bridge clubs in the 1920s.

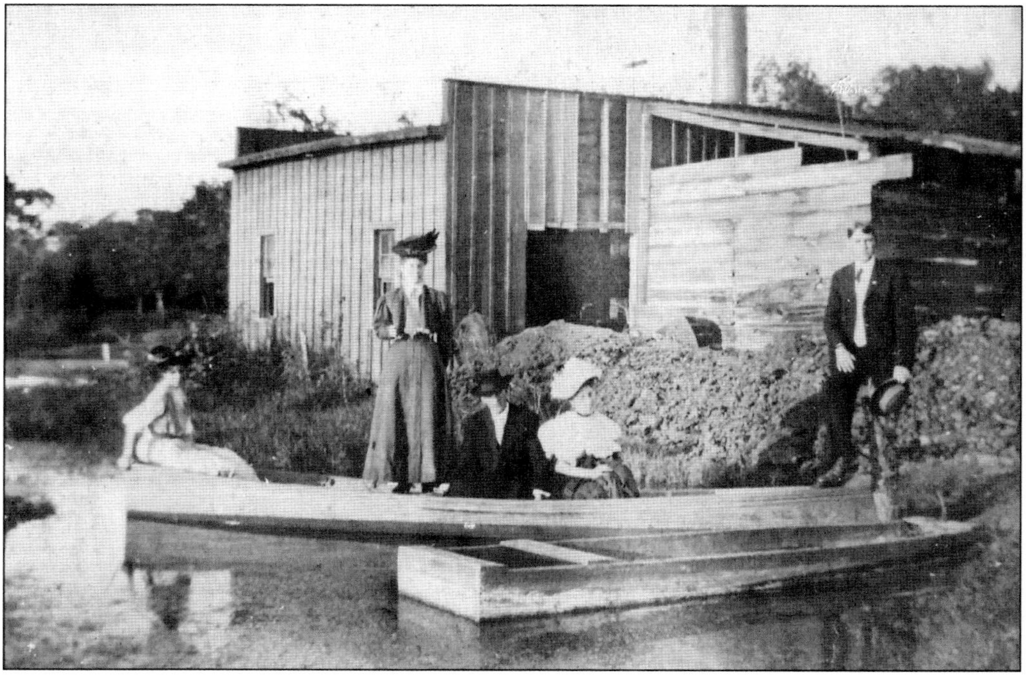

In 1897, the Plano Fishing Club was organized. Members dammed up Spring Creek to make a small lake, building a boathouse and other recreational facilities. The fishing club deeded the property to the City of Plano to be used as the source for Plano's first water supply that year, and the city developed it as Harrington Park. Here, from left to right, Pattie Hudson, the Garrett girls, a Mr. Mays, and Gee Hudson take a boat out in the lake. (Courtesy of Cynthia Hudson Reed.)

Three

Early Mercantile and Community Development

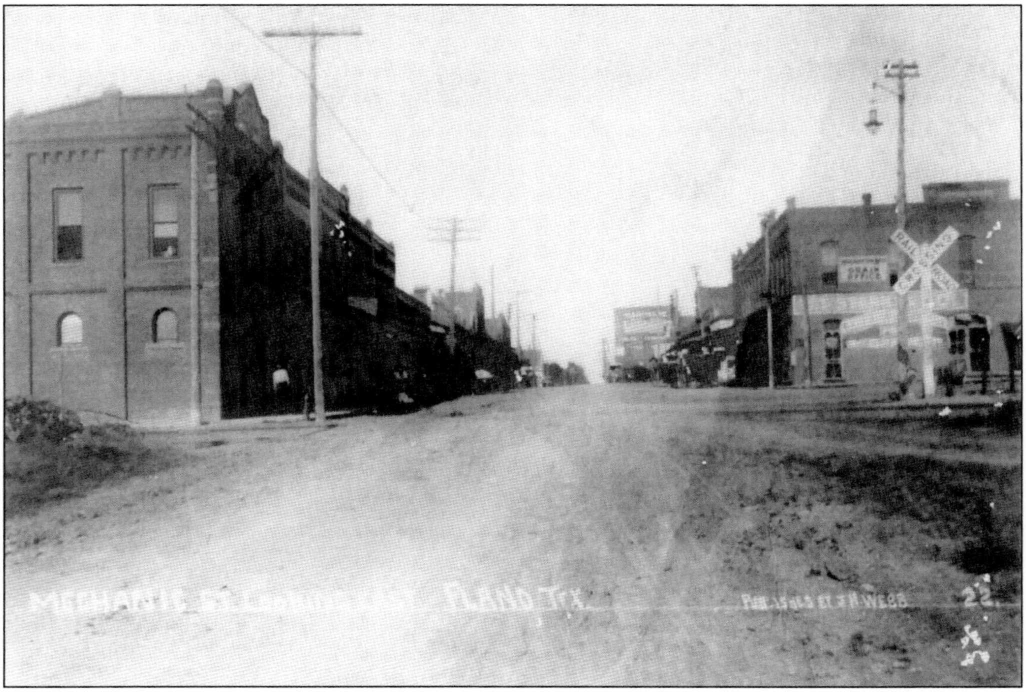

Businesses sprang up around the old stagecoach stop on Highway 5 and then along Mechanic Street in the 1870s when Plano became a stop on the Houston & Texas Central Railroad. In 1873, the town incorporated with a mayor, five aldermen, and a councilman. By 1890, the town of almost 1,500 people was thriving. This view looks east from the railroad toward Main Street, showing Plano's original business district. (Courtesy of the Heritage Farmstead Museum.)

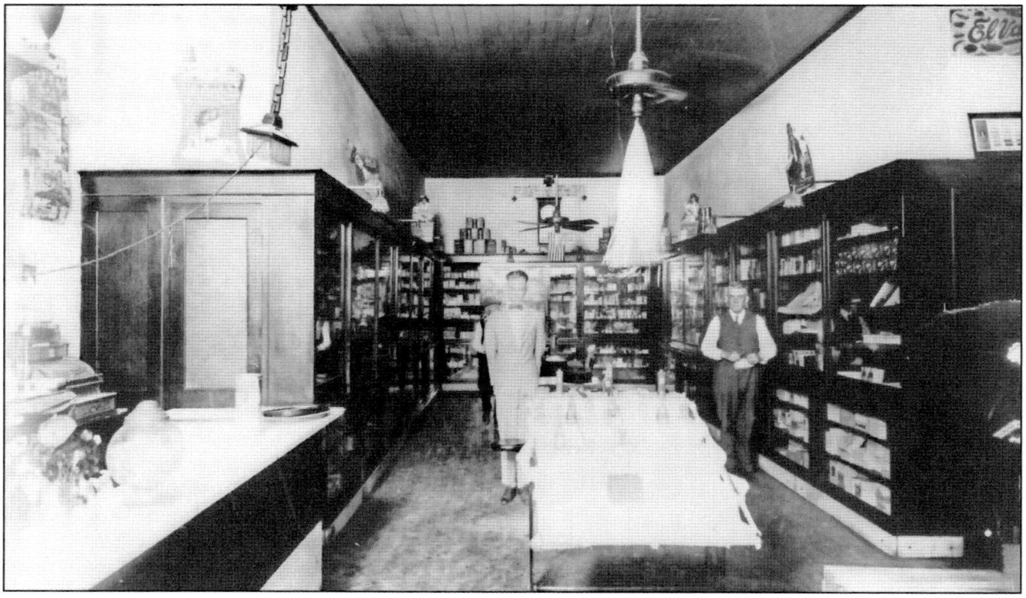

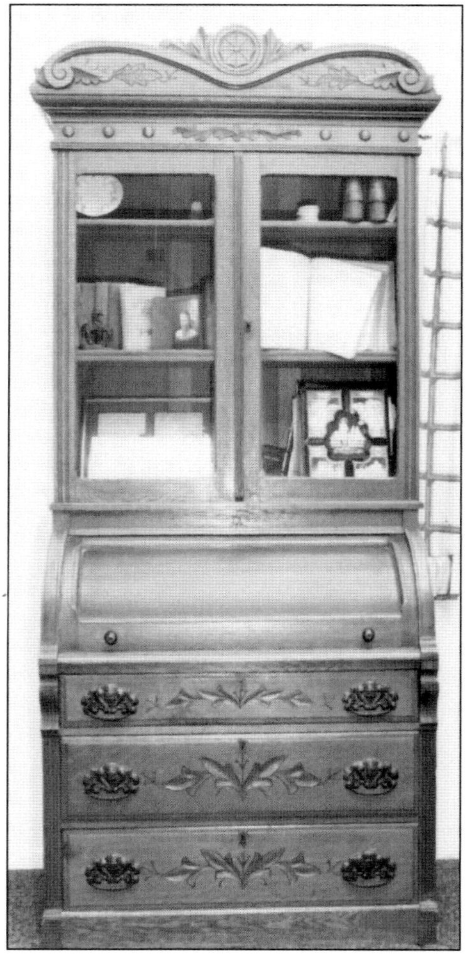

Silas Harrington came to Collin County with his brother Alfred in 1848, locating his Peters colony head-right of 320 acres northwest of the soon-to-be town. His son, Silas Marion Harrington, was a graduate of the Philadelphia College of Pharmacy and opened Harrington's Pharmacy in 1881 on the east side of the alley on Mechanic Street (now Fifteenth Street). Harrington Pharmacy, narrowly escaping the great fire of 1895 that destroyed most of the business district, continued in business for almost a century.

Andrew Wetsel came to Plano in 1873 and worked with his father, Peter, at a furniture and cabinet shop on the south side of Mechanic Street until his father's death in 1877. Wetsel was also Plano's first undertaker, a natural adjunct to the furniture business, as early as 1870. Wetsel built fine furniture, some of which is now in museums. He manufactured doors, windows, and scrollwork using his foot lathe, which he referred to as a "one-boy power" motor, alluding to the fact that children would pump the old treadle-like machine. The Wetsel name is listed among the finest craftsmen in Texas during that period.

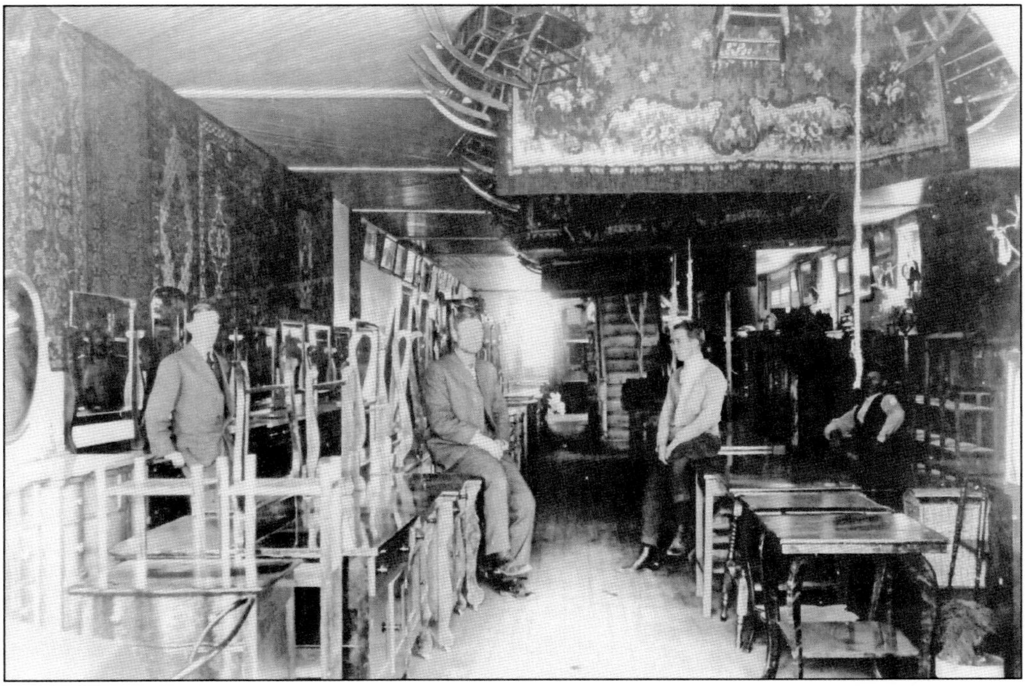

In 1892, Wetsel sold his furniture and undertaking business to the Harrington family. Silas Harrington's son, Edwin Omar, or E.O, operated the family funeral parlor and furniture store on the northwest corner of Mechanic and Main Streets. The store operated from 1893 to the 1980s as Harrington Furniture and Undertaking. E.O. Harrington's name is still commemorated in mosaic tile at the entrance to the landmark, which had previously served as an early grocery, a saloon hall, a cigar shop, sleeping rooms, and a printing shop.

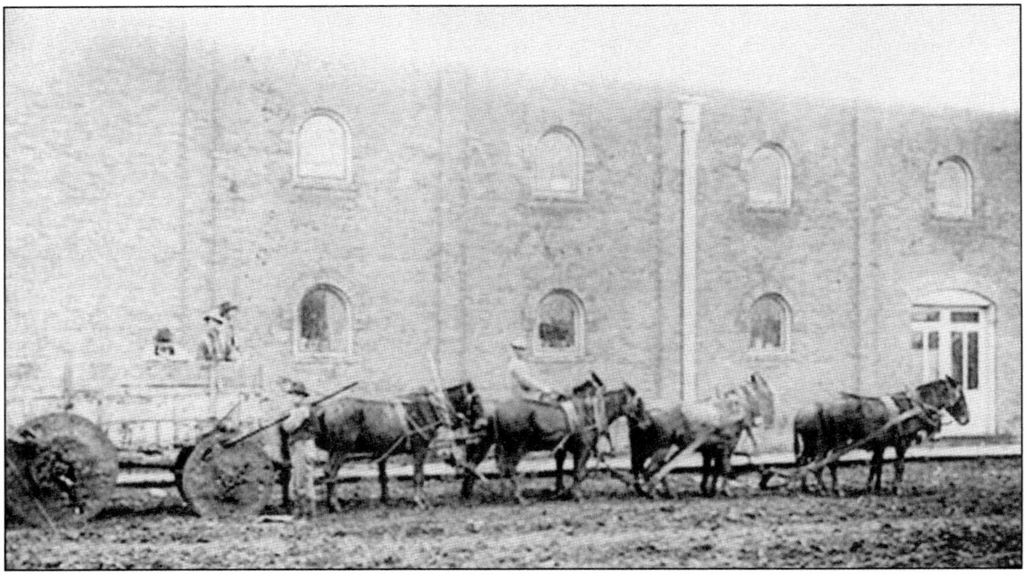

A team of eight mules has trouble pulling a wagonload of furniture over the rough roads outside Harrington's Furniture. The Main Street through Plano was virtually impassable in the rainy season due to the black clay soil, which stuck to wagon wheels in wet weather. According to *Plano, Texas: The Early Years*, the main highway through Plano was known as the worst road in Texas.

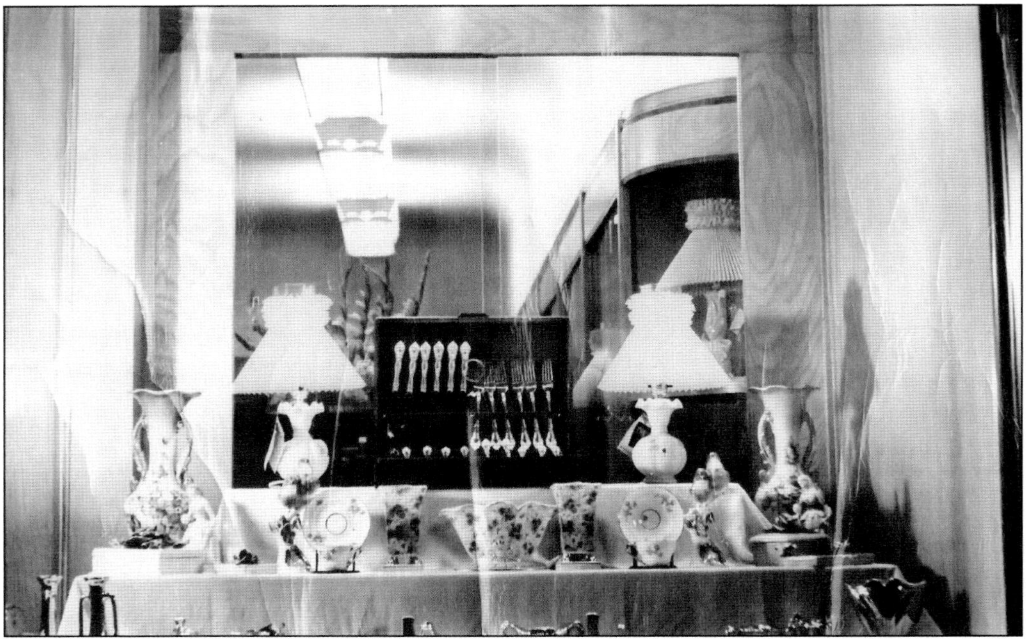

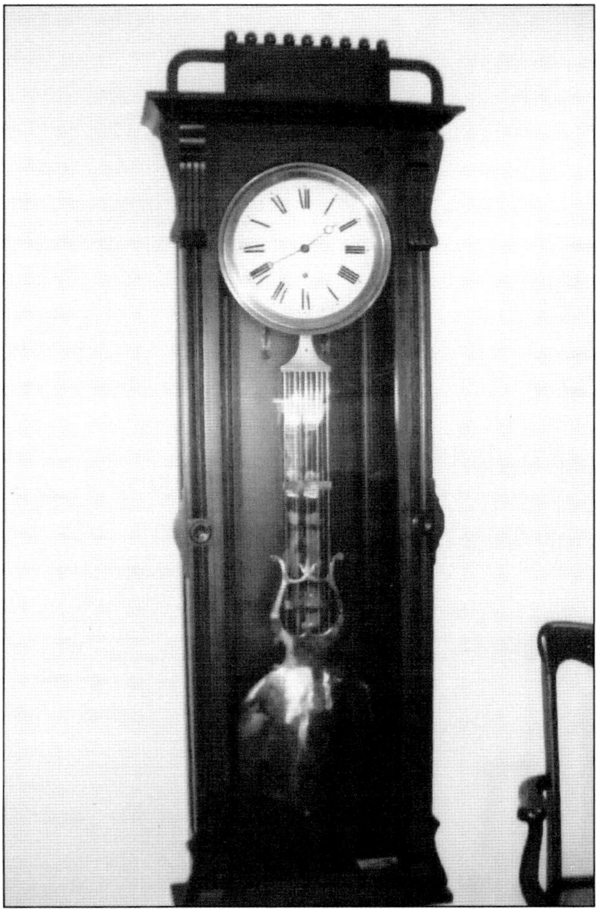

Located on the south side of Mechanic (later Fifteenth Street) for over 75 years, Weatherford's Jewelry Store is an integral part of Plano's history and still remains in the original owner's family. Arch Weatherford set up a small watch repair service in 1898. He was dedicated to personal service and offered the finest linens, diamonds, watches, crystal, lamps, and Lenox china. Many of the clocks, icons of the early Weatherford's Jewelry Store, are still in the family. (Photographs courtesy of Judy Moore.)

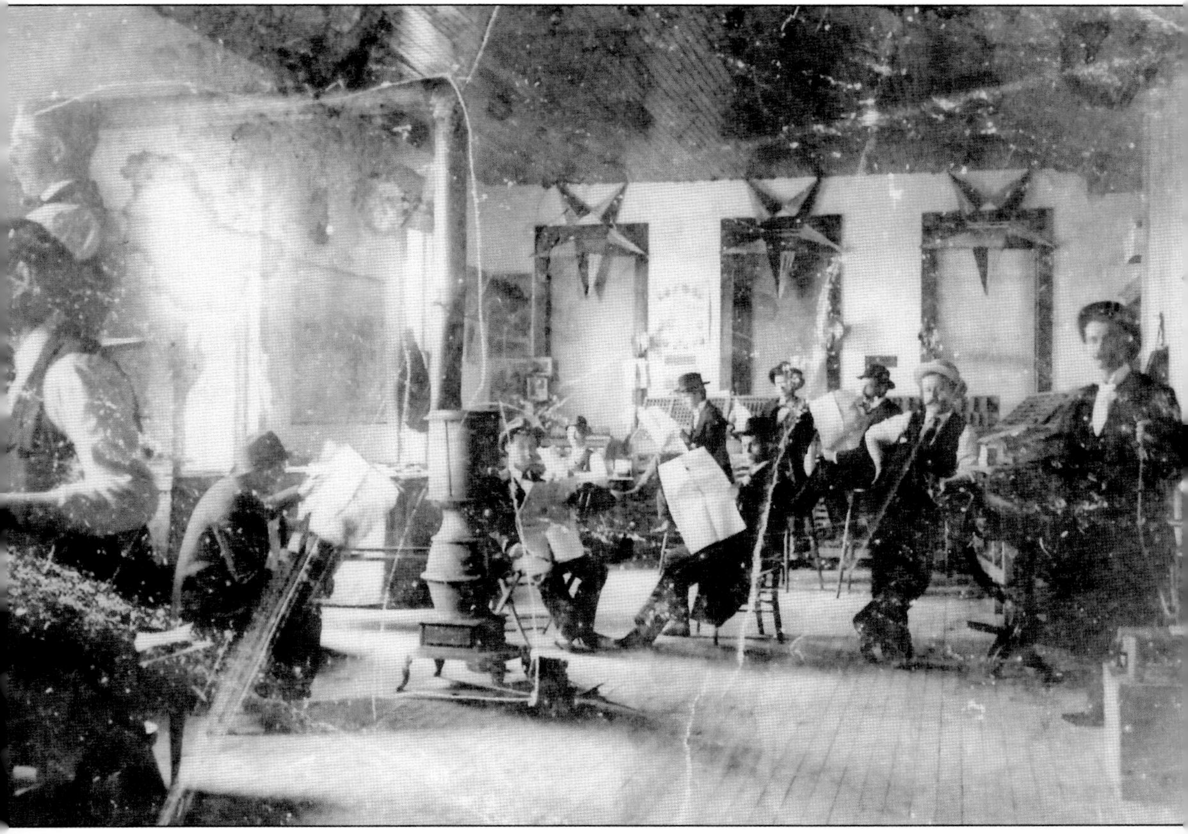

The *Plano News*, the city's first newspaper, was established in 1873 by J.C. Son and E.K. Randolph. Later, Joel Lively Aldridge owned it and used the telegraph wire service and the railroad for much of the news content. John Custer bought the newspaper in 1915 and started a classified advertisement and comic section. Charles W. Ridout purchased another paper, the *Plano Star*, in 1895. According to the *McKinney Gazette* in 1897, Ridout was a versatile writer and "yields a free lance." The *Plano Star* and the *Courier* merged and in 1935, Arthur A. Bagwill bought it, moving the printing office to a building in the middle of the block on the north side of Mechanic Street. Bagwill's daughter Louise and granddaughter Linda continued operating the newspaper for 50 years. The *Plano Star Courier* has reported major headlines in Plano's history, managing to compete with radio and television and recently creating its own Internet presence.

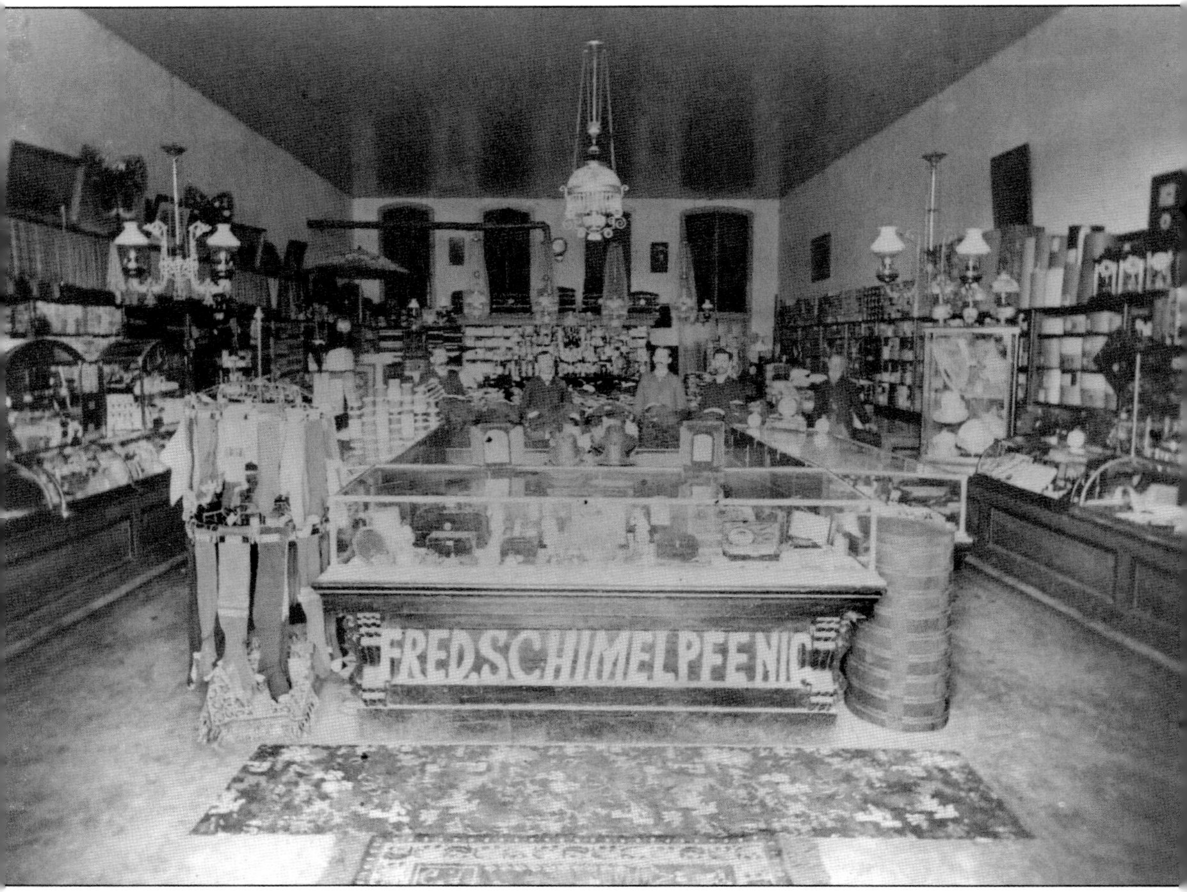

Fred Schimelpfenig came to Plano in 1878 and opened his dry goods store on the southwest corner of Mechanic and Main Streets. Schimelpfenig lost nearly everything in the fire of 1891 but purchased a lot on the north side of Mechanic Street. His friend Alex Sanger—of Sanger Brothers, predecessor to Sanger-Harris Department Stores and forerunner of Foleys and Macy's Department Stores—built his new store. The early department store featured household items and clothing for the family. The great fire of 1895 finally destroyed Schimelpfenig's business, but he became mayor in 1902 and served the city for many years.

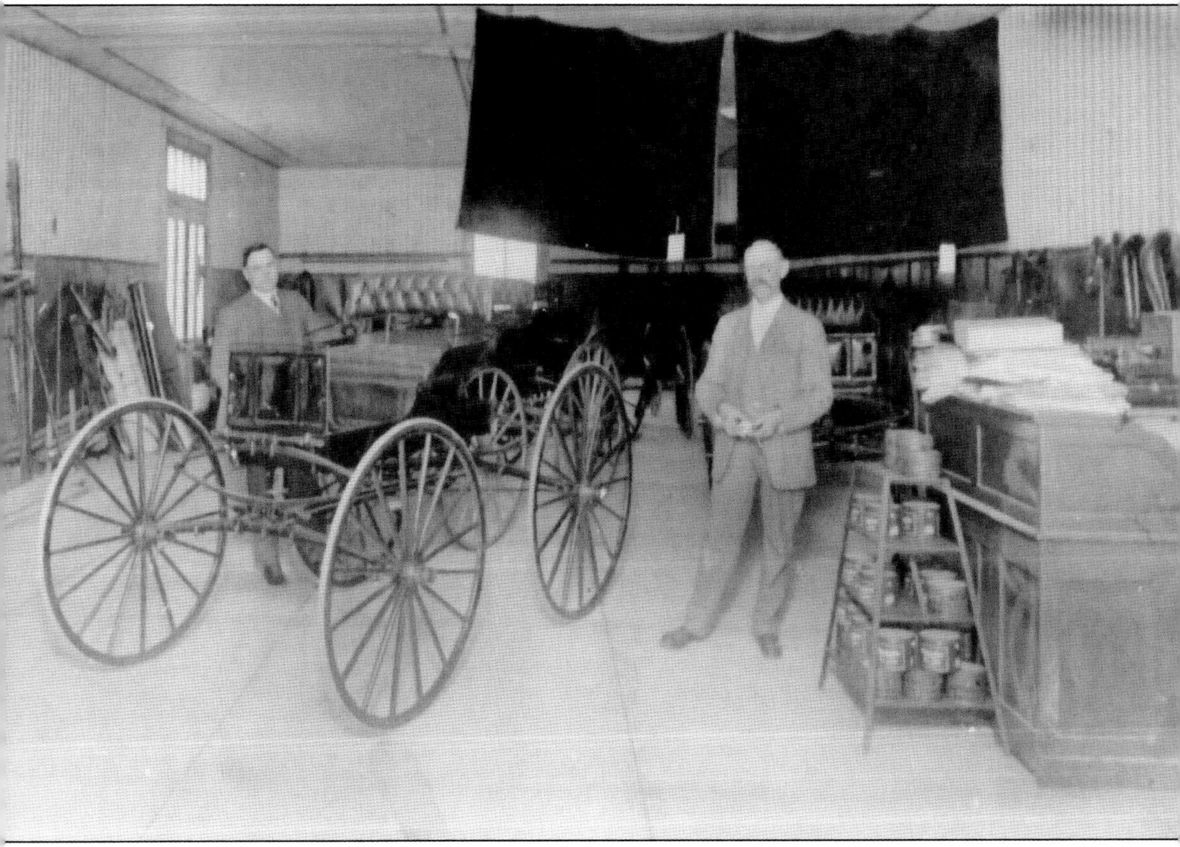

Around 1900, the horse-and-buggy days in Plano required at least crudely graded main roadways. This Concord buggy was used in early Plano until mass production of the automobile brought its price within reach of most citizens. Buggies cost as little as $25 and could easily be hitched and driven by untrained men, women, or children. Their widespread use encouraged the grading and graveling of main rural roads, and actual paving in towns to provide all-weather passage within and between larger towns. The 1885 Sanborn Fire Insurance map shows McIlhaney Richardson "M.R." Kendrick's carriage and agricultural implements shop on the northwest corner of Masonic and Main Streets. The December 25, 1897, *McKinney Gazette* described his "lively trade that has everything on wheels." (Courtesy of Rodney Haggard.)

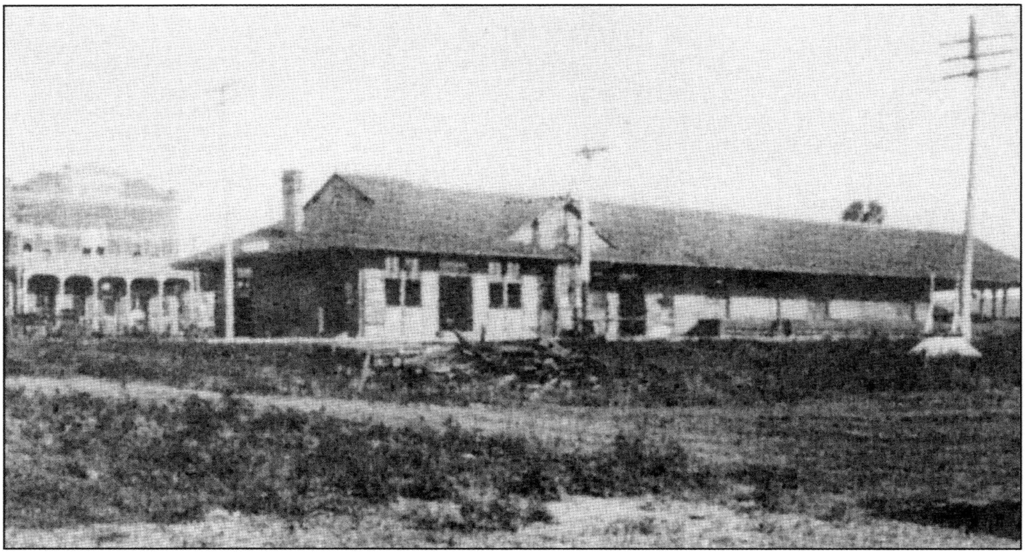

The Houston & Texas Central Railroad (H&TC) was chartered in 1853 in Houston. Bonuses and land grants of 16 square-mile sections were offered to railroads to build through Texas towns. The location of the railroad could make or break a community, and many towns became ghost towns because they were bypassed by the railroad. The coming of the railroad to the small town of Plano was due primarily to its prime location between Dallas and McKinney, two county seats. In 1873, the railroad reservation was plotted including lots, blocks, streets, and crossings. By the mid-1890s, Plano was a cotton market with two railroads crossing within its borders—the H&TC running north and south and the Cotton Belt Railway running east and west. There were also several grain merchants with flour and gristmills and two cotton oil companies at that time. The Durand Hotel, which later became the Plano Masonic Lodge, was built east of the H&TC depot to cater to railroad travelers. (Courtesy of Peggy Mitchell.)

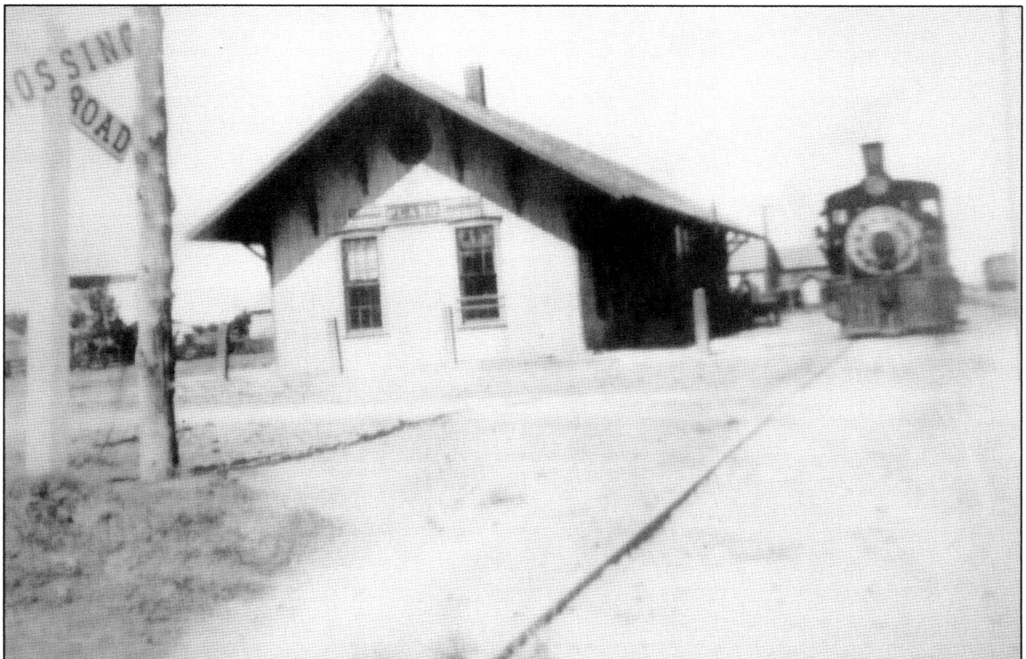

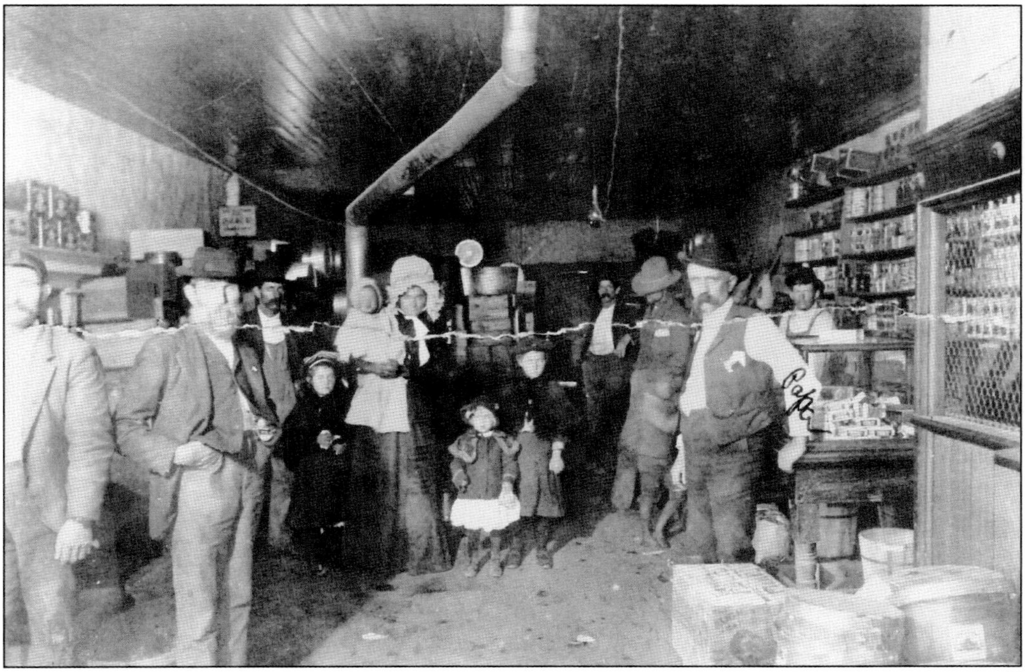

In 1889, brothers Henry B. and J.M. Carlisle opened a grocery store with staple groceries as well as grain, hay, and cottonseed. Carlisle Grocery was located on the south side of an unpaved path now known as Fifteenth Street, across the tracks from the H&TC railroad depot. Later, Manly Carlisle went into business with his father and changed the name of the store to the Plano Grocery Company. According to the *McKinney Gazette* in 1897, this was a "first class grocery store that also handled cotton and grain and shipped as much of this produce as any firm in North Texas." In the 1920s, Plano Grocery Company was the largest grocery store in Collin County. Poor economic conditions resulted in the closure of the store in the Great Depression.

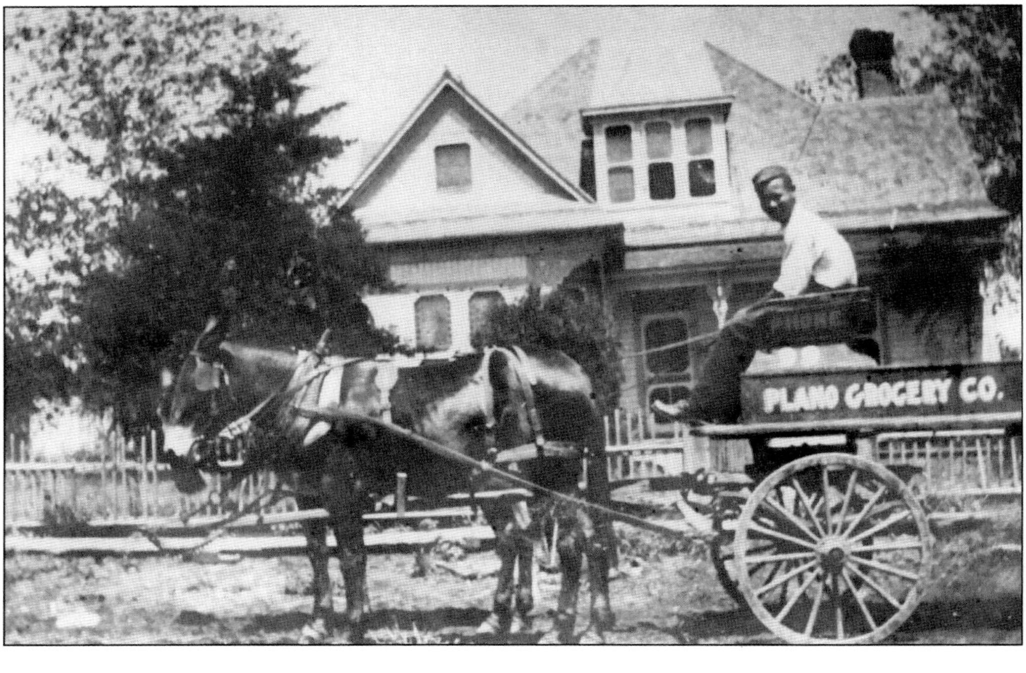

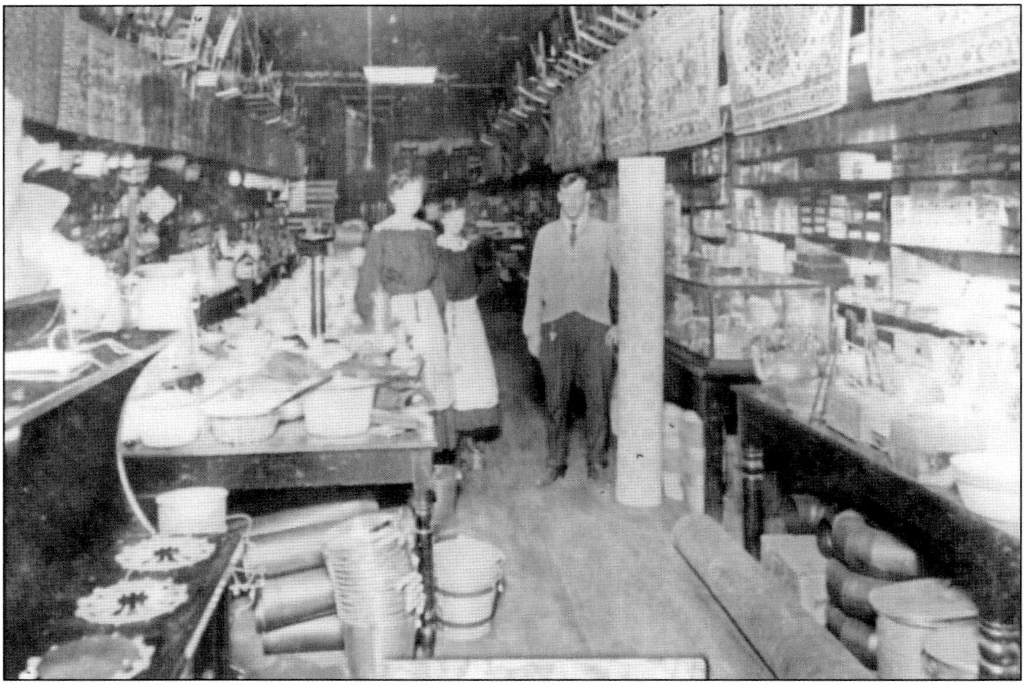

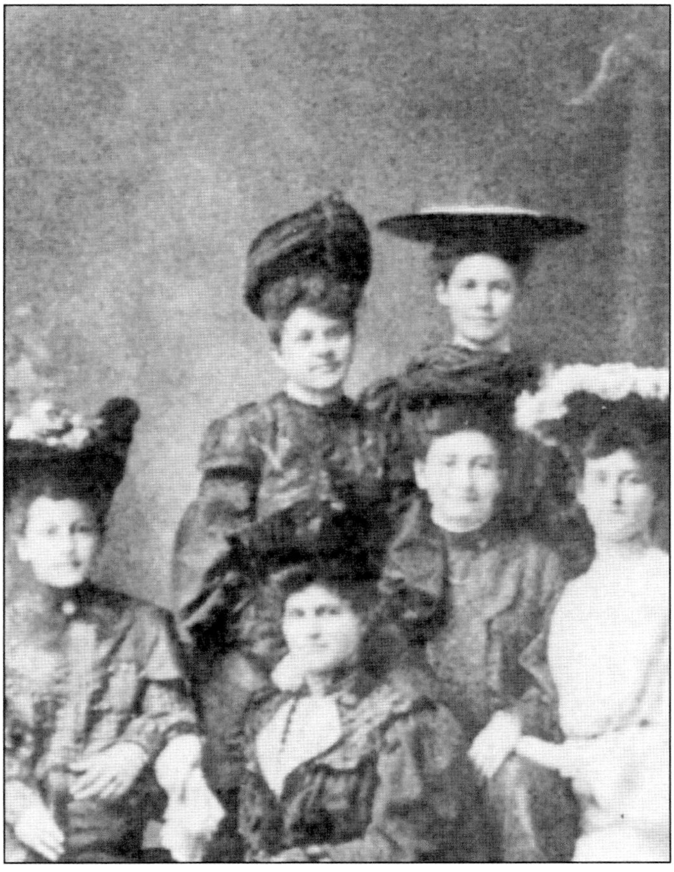

In 1893, Sidney J. Mathews established a small store on the south side of Mechanic Street, moving it across the street in 1906. According to the *McKinney Gazette* in December 1897, the store "sells most anything you want to buy . . . furniture, hardware and a millinery, with prices in keeping with the times." A popular gathering place, Mathews stayed open late on Saturdays and Second Monday Trade Days so people could visit, shop, and pay their bills. Mathews's wife was a milliner, and she and her two daughters made hats for customers. Matthews' Department Store remained in business for 52 years. Perhaps these young ladies on the way to Clara Schimelpfenig's party in 1904 bought their fancy hats at Mathews. (Above, courtesy of Rodney Haggard.)

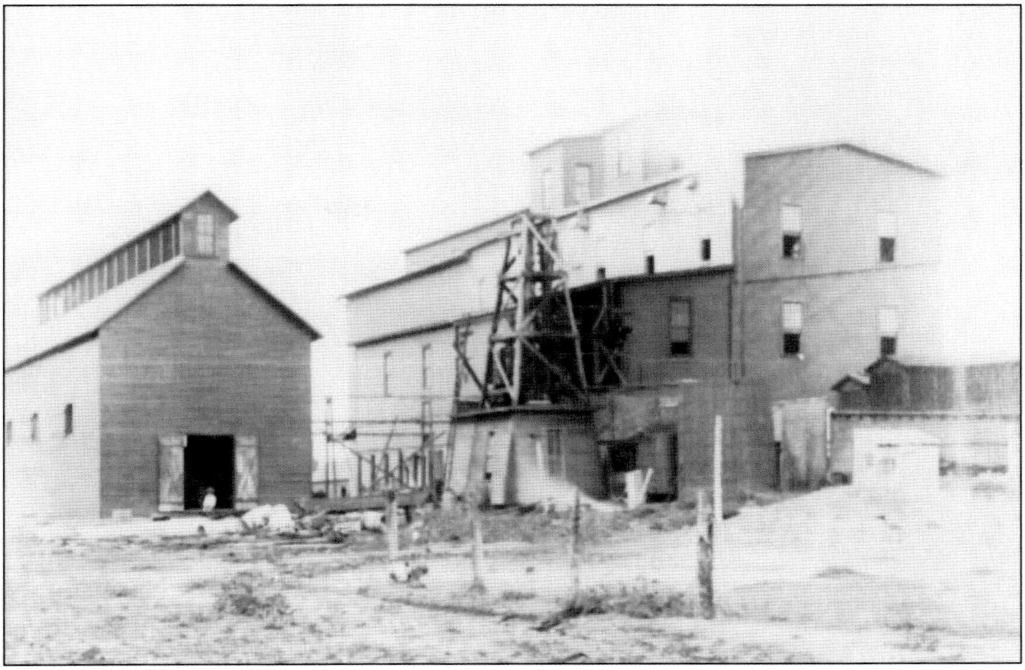

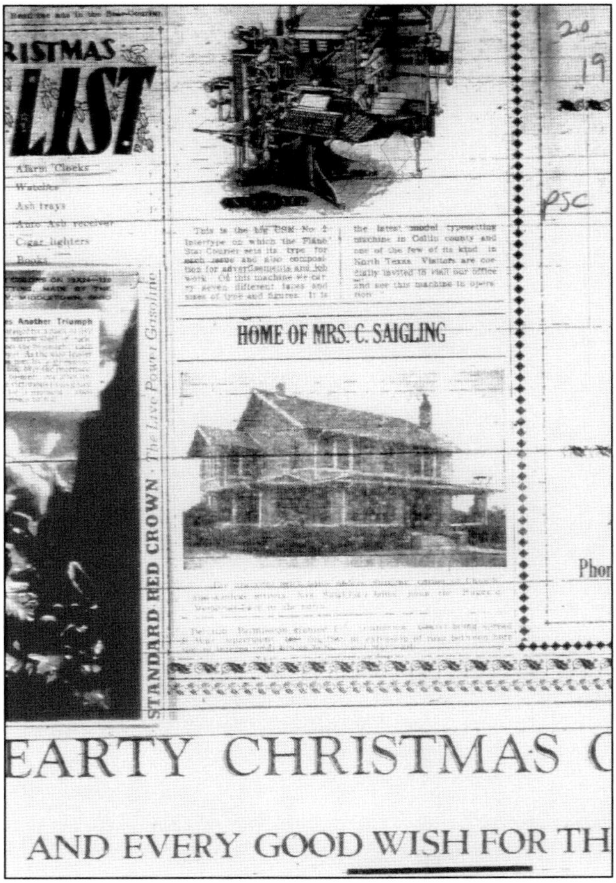

In 1895, Charles Frederick Saigling and his wife, Celestine, bought an existing mill and established Plano Milling Company—also known as the Plano Roller Mills. The mill produced flour, bran, oats, and cornmeal. Morning Glory Flour was a popular brand produced at the mill. Saigling also built an elevator for storage near the railroad. The Saiglings built the first brick house and the first, if not the only, house with a basement for the furnace. The house still stands on Sixteenth Street and H Avenue in Haggard Park. The wraparound porch pictured in this 1928 Plano newspaper was removed at some point. (Above, courtesy of Rodney Haggard.)

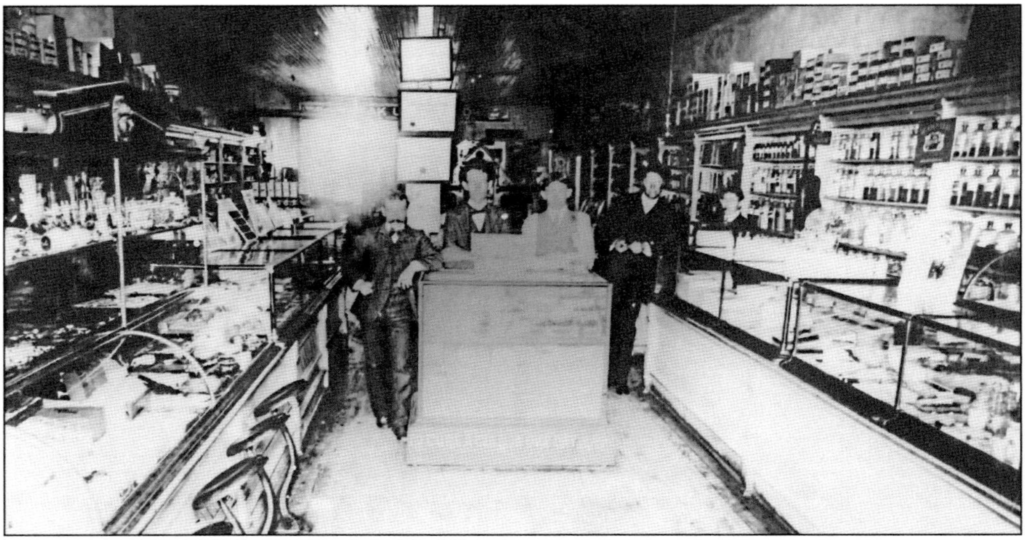

Edward A. Carpenter was born in 1871, the son of pioneer settlers Robert Washington "R.W." and Lizzie Mathews Carpenter. He graduated from the Philadelphia College of Pharmacy and bought the Schoolfield's drugstore in the W.D. McFarlin building on the north side of Mechanic Street in 1895. In 1908, Carpenter sold the drugstore to the Allen brothers, who ran it for 31 years.

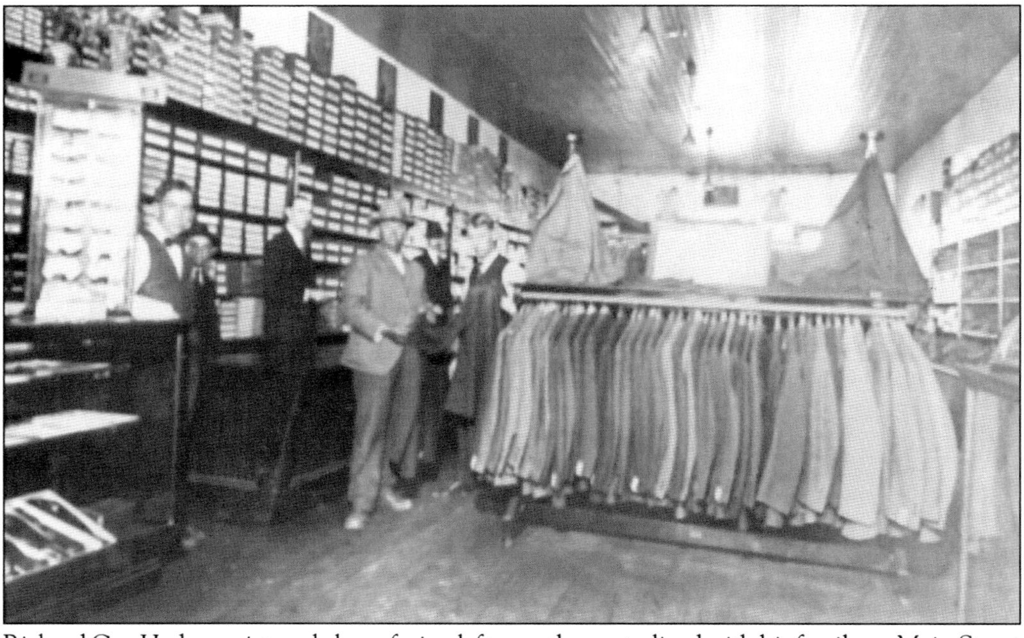

Richard Gee Hudson, pictured above facing left near the coats, lived with his family on Main Street and attended the Portman School in Plano. He worked in R.W. Sandifer Dry Goods Store and was later associated with J.G. Thompson in the "gents furnishing" business. Thompson-Hudson Company succeeded J.H. Gulledge in the dry goods business in 1918. Gee was also a popular caterer for Thompson & Company, which had one of the nicest short order and confectionery houses in Texas, carrying oysters, fish, and game in season, as well as specialty candy. Thompsons was "the place to eat in Plano," according to the 1897 *McKinney Gazette*. Gee Hudson and his brother Milton Murry "Dag" Hudson were volunteer firemen in the early 1900s. (Courtesy of Cynthia Hudson Reed.)

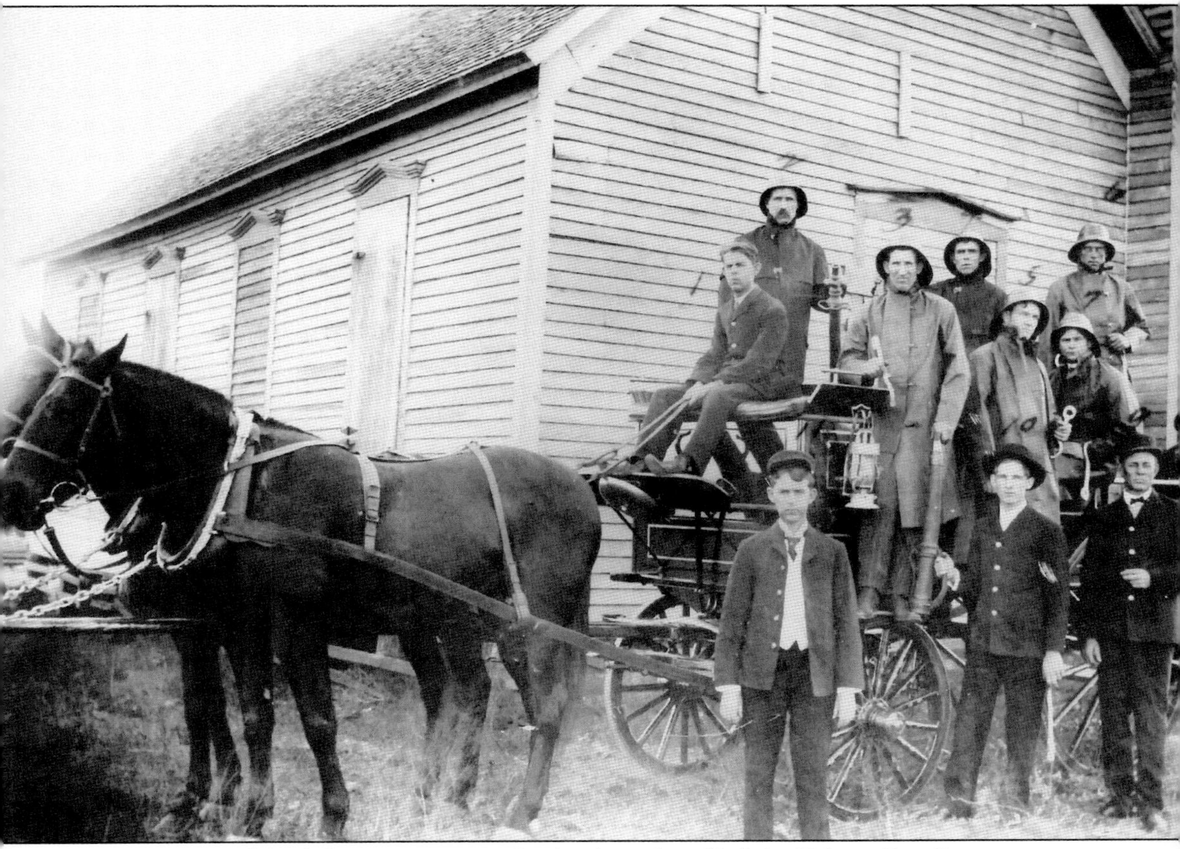

The first organized firefighting crew was a bucket brigade called the Eclipse Fire Company in 1887. After a devastating fire destroyed Plano's business district in 1881, the city faced many challenges including inadequate equipment and water supply and rough roads. The city purchased a hand-drawn wagon made by O. Davis Hook and Ladder Company. A man had to run to the fire station, pull the equipment to the fire over rough, dirt roads, fight the fire, and then pull the equipment back to the station. In 1899, the first horse-drawn equipment was put into service.

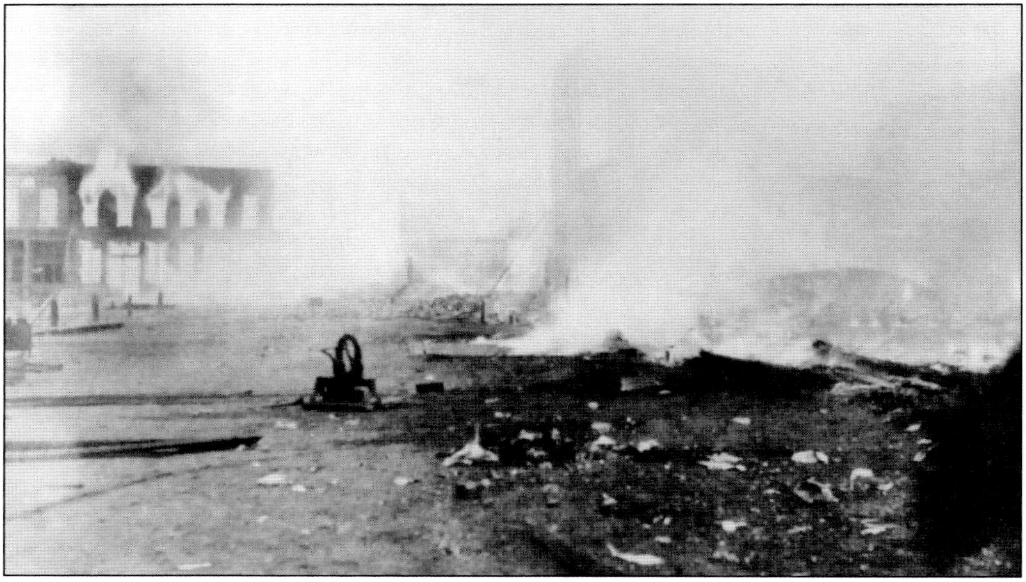

The great fire of 1895 again destroyed Plano's business district while the state fair was in Dallas. According to *Plano, Texas: The Early Years*, Nannie Kate Haggard gave an account of the 1895 fire in her diary: "As I was going out on the porch after water, I saw a great blaze of fire. Called Mr. H and he said it was over at Plano . . . the Moore Hotel, then Bowser Skiles Implement and Opera, a dry goods store of Bridgeman, Mr. George Saddler shop, Mr. John Schimelpfenig Furniture store, a grocery and notion store, the shop next to Mr. Fred Schimelpfenig and Mr. McFarland's dry goods. Mr. Chaddick's Saddler Shop, the National Bank and all the upper story occupied by Lawyers, Dentist, Doctor, Plano Star Office, all went in the flames." In early December 1895, the city marshal hired teams to remove the bricks from the burned buildings to the streets. All told, 51 businesses were destroyed by the fire. (Courtesy of Rodney Haggard.)

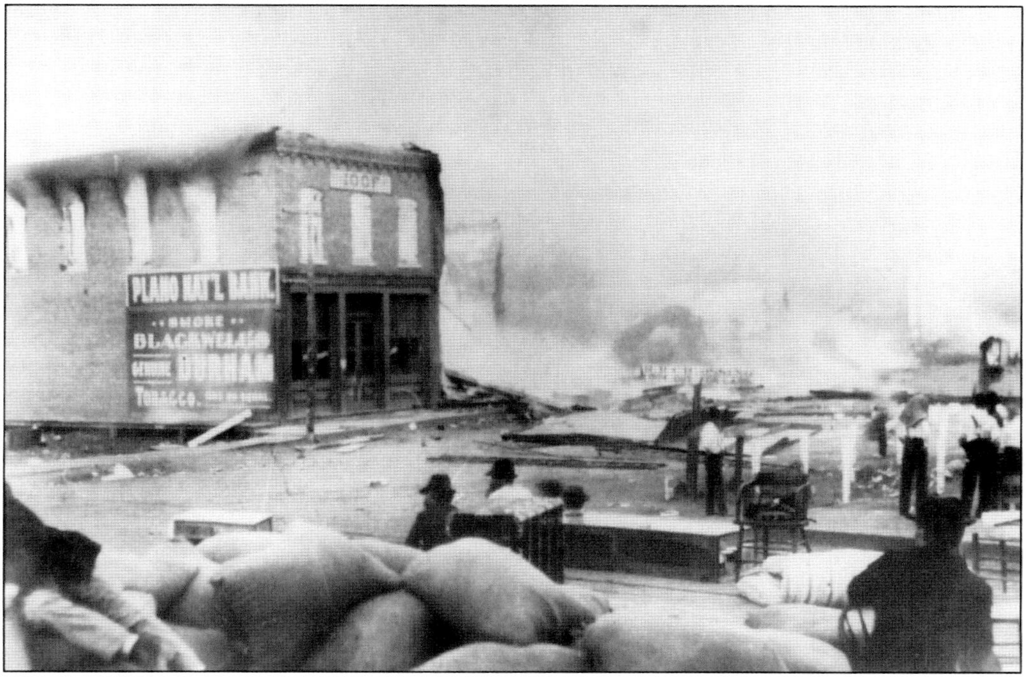

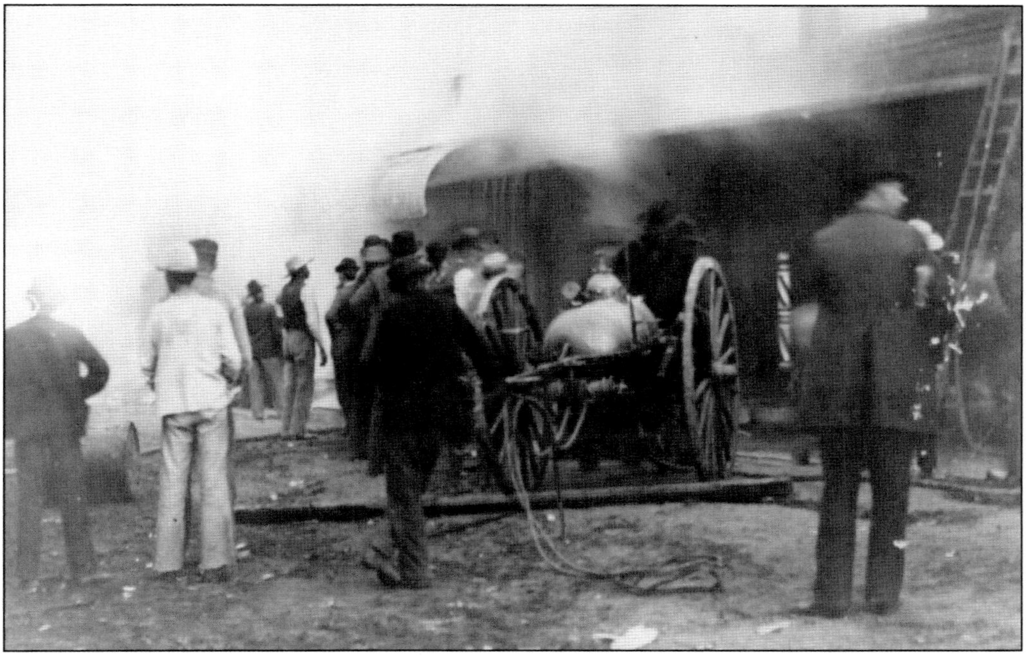

In the 1895 fire, the Plano "Fire Boys" used the hook and ladder wagon and the Holloway Chemical Engine while the male citizens of Plano formed a bucket brigade from the big well at Main and Mechanic Streets to fight the fire. On the south side of Mechanic Street, the fire was stopped at the west side of the alley, just a few feet from Harrington's Pharmacy, which was then located on the east side of the alley. The Dallas Fire Company sent a steam pumper on an H&TC car to help Plano, but there was not enough water to run that type of pumper at the time. (Courtesy of Rodney Haggard.)

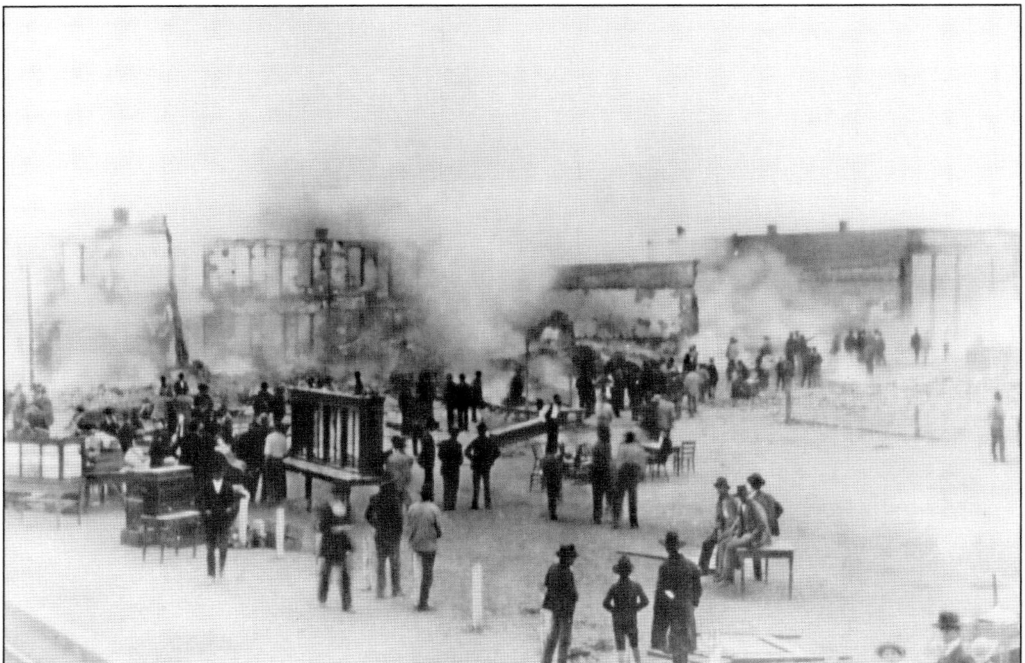

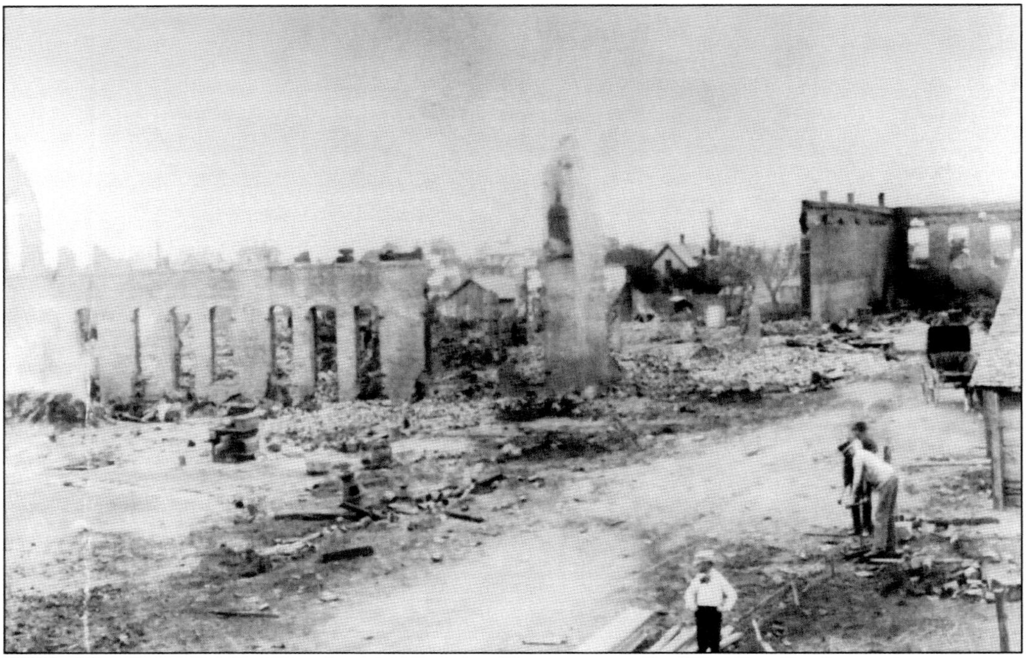

Joseph Penrose (J.P.) Spillman had come to Plano in the 1870s. He bought property on Railroad Street across from H&TC depot, where he had a livery stable in the 1890s. He also purchased property east of the bank, pictured here totally destroyed. After the fire of 1895, he reconstructed these buildings and rented them out. W.D. McFarlin constructed a new building just east of Spillman's. 1915, after several large fires destroyed the flourmill, a cotton gin, and three buildings owned by Spillman, the fire department changed from horse-drawn wagons to motorized equipment. A committee from the fire department met with the city council and offered to donate $350 toward an automobile fire truck if the council sold one team of horses and a wagon, with the proceeds going toward a truck. (Courtesy of Rodney Haggard.)

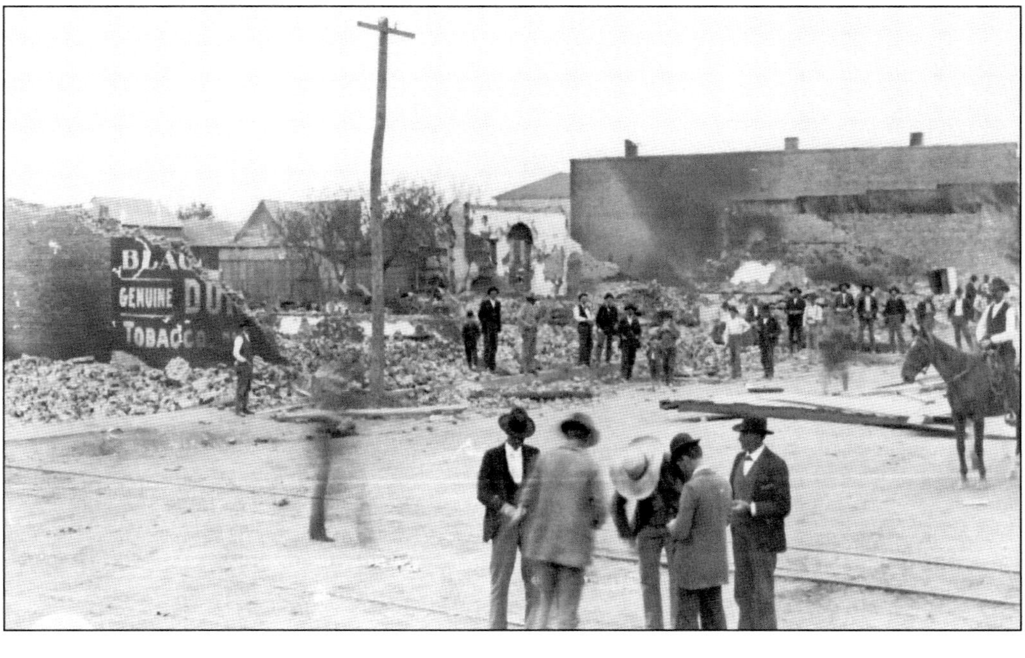

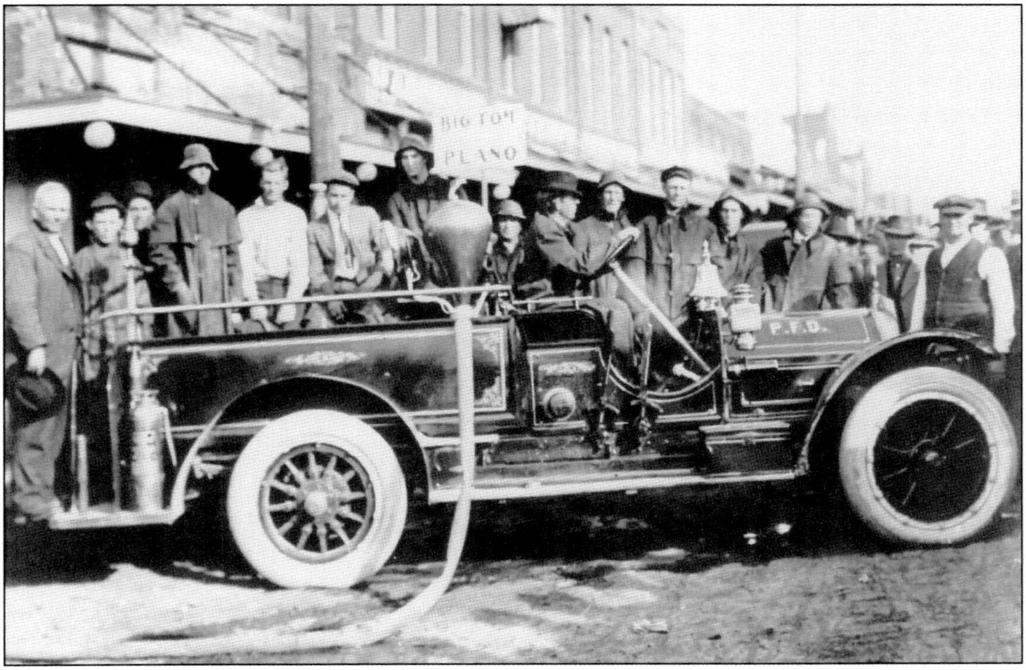

A Thomas Flyer automobile was purchased, and the firemen and citizens of Plano built the first automobile fire truck, calling it "Big Tom." A pump and hose bed was mounted on the chassis, enabling the fire department to boost its pressure to fight fires. It served until 1930. Another Thomas Flyer auto was purchased in 1917 and converted into a fire truck with a chemical tank, giving the city two engines with a combined pumping capacity of 1,100 gallons of water per minute. In 1923, the city council held a bond election to build a new fire station and city hall. The new station was a two-story brick building on Mechanic Street east of Main Street. The lower floor on the west side included the city hall, the jail, and a workshop for the fire department. The east half was for the two fire trucks. The upper floor was for fire department meeting and sleeping rooms. This building served the fire department until 1966. (Courtesy of Rodney Haggard.)

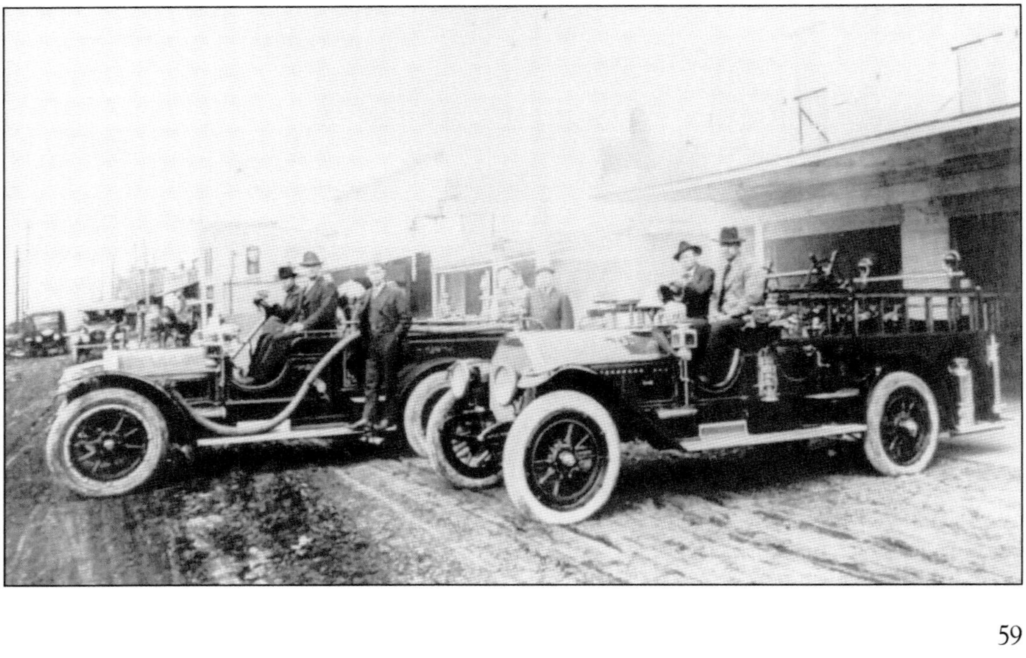

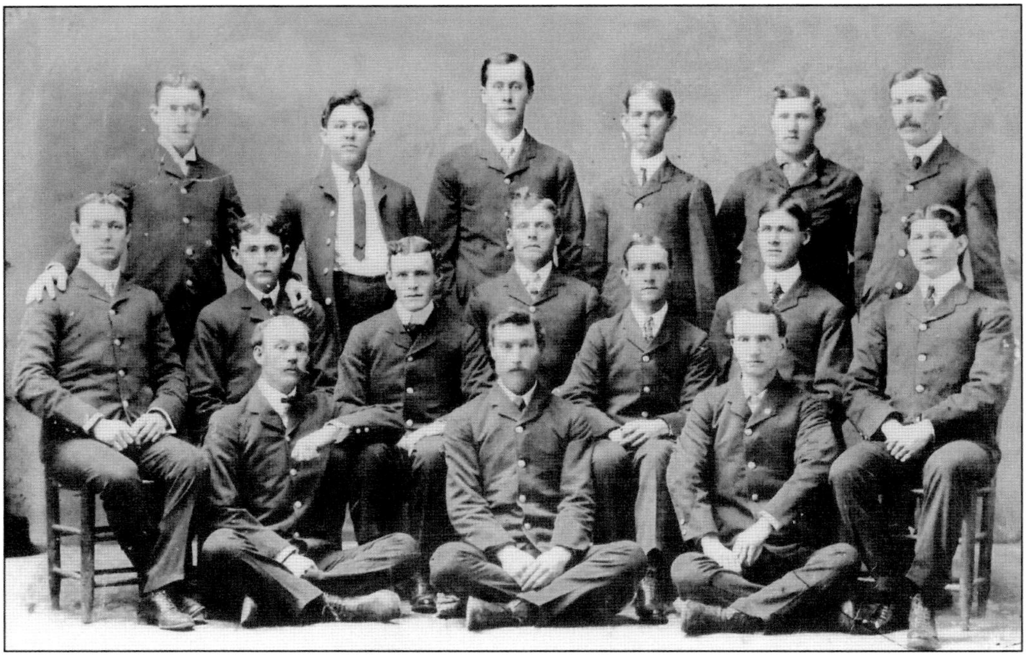

According to the December 25, 1897, *McKinney Gazette*, Plano was a thriving little city second only to the county seat in size and importance. "After the devastating fires reduced it to ashes, Plano has risen, Phoenix-like, grander and more substantial than ever. The citizens have rebuilt of sound brick and stone, one and two story and now the town presents a better appearance than ever before. No undertaking is too large for these progressive citizens, attested by the fact that a $40,000 waterworks system has just been completed, a new city hall erected and other public improvements of a solid character."

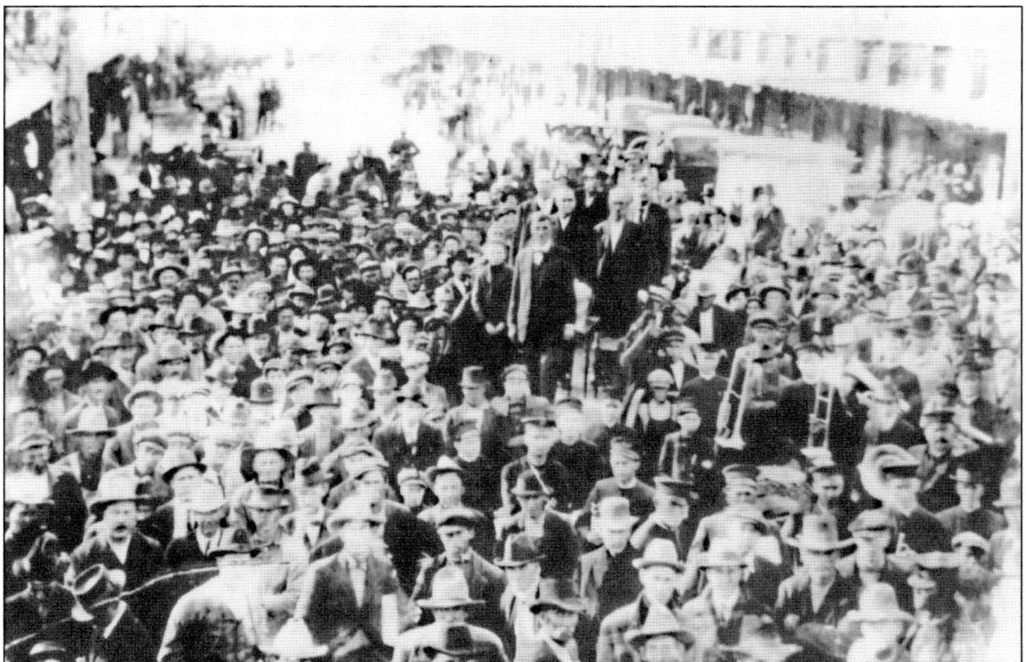

Four

Twentieth-Century Business District

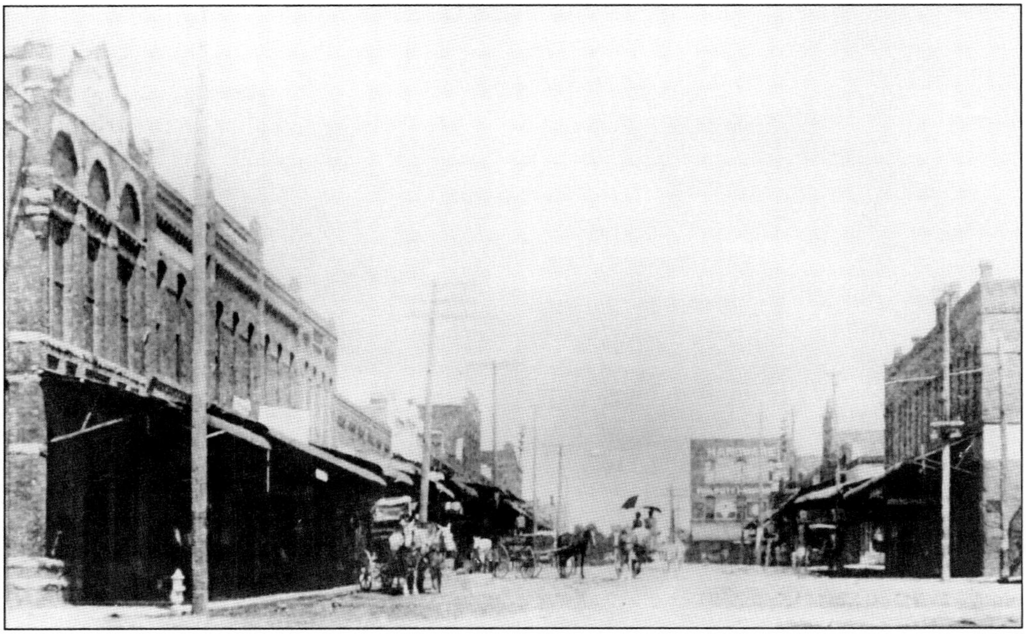

By 1900, Plano officially had a population of only 1,304. The strong community spirit enabled Plano to persevere after the fires destroyed the downtown area and the railroad spurred growth in agricultural production and trade. The town also emerged as an education center in 1899 with a new public school system. In 1908, the Interurban railway provided commuter service through Plano every hour. The business district changed as the automobile came on the scene, but greater Plano was still an agrarian community through the mid-1900s. (Courtesy of Rodney Haggard.)

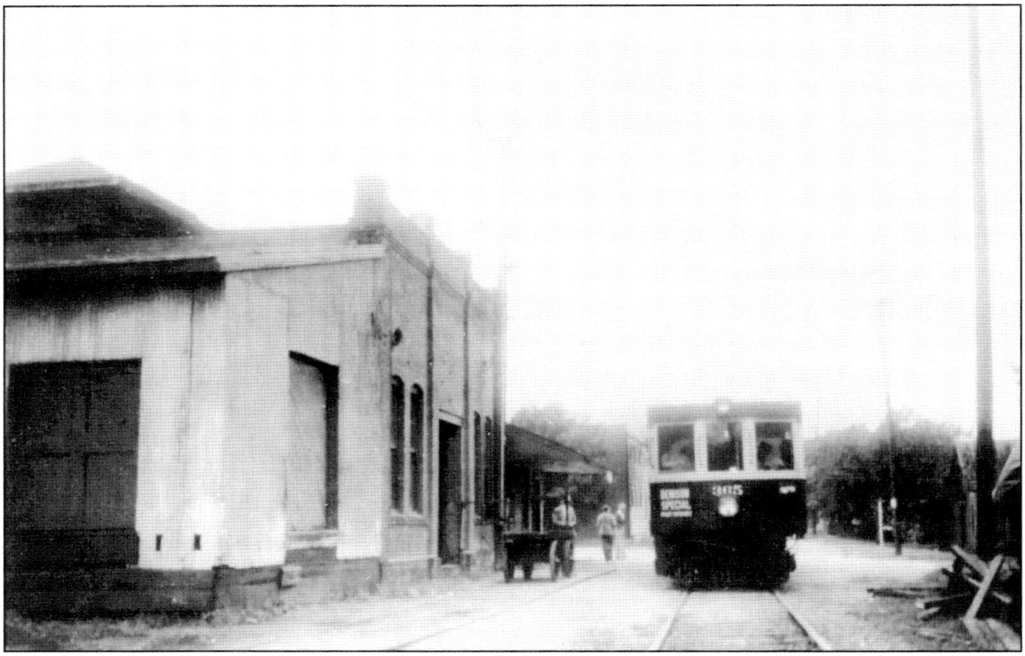

Plano was fortunate to be a primary stop on the Texas Electric Railway when it was built in 1908. The trains linked Dallas and Sherman-Denison with smaller towns on the line. After 1928, the Interurban lines competed successfully with major railroads for both interstate and intrastate freight traffic. The Interurban also enjoyed a large share of passenger traffic, running every hour for years. The frequent service, convenient stops, and lower fares for local passengers made the Interurban Express popular, and, thus, many local passenger trains were abandoned. (Above, courtesy of the City of Plano.)

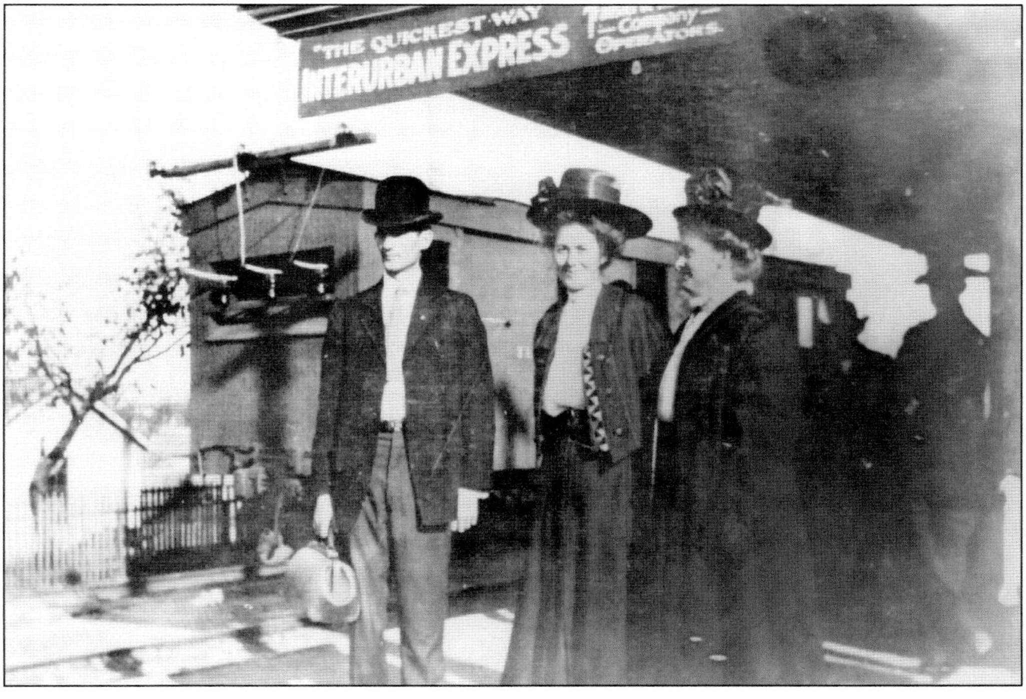

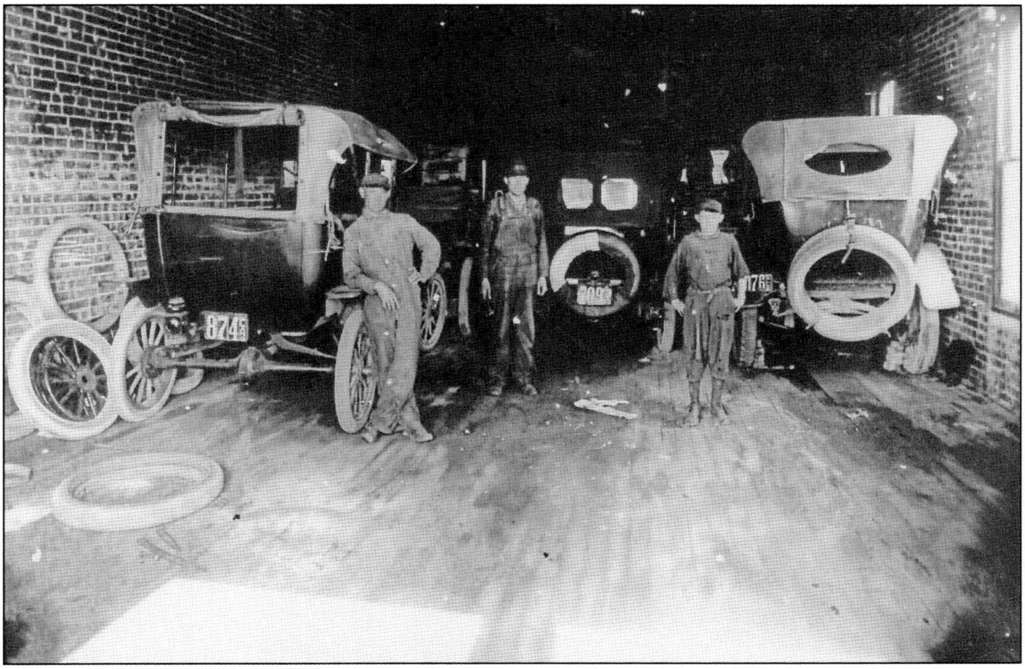

In the mid-1920s, the number of automobiles grew and more auto-oriented businesses surrounded downtown. The blacksmith shop was converted to the Plano Garage, and Harrington Motors, a Ford Dealership, was established. An oil company and service stations, like this Mobil filling station at 909 East Fifteenth Street, answered the growing demand. (Courtesy of the City of Plano.)

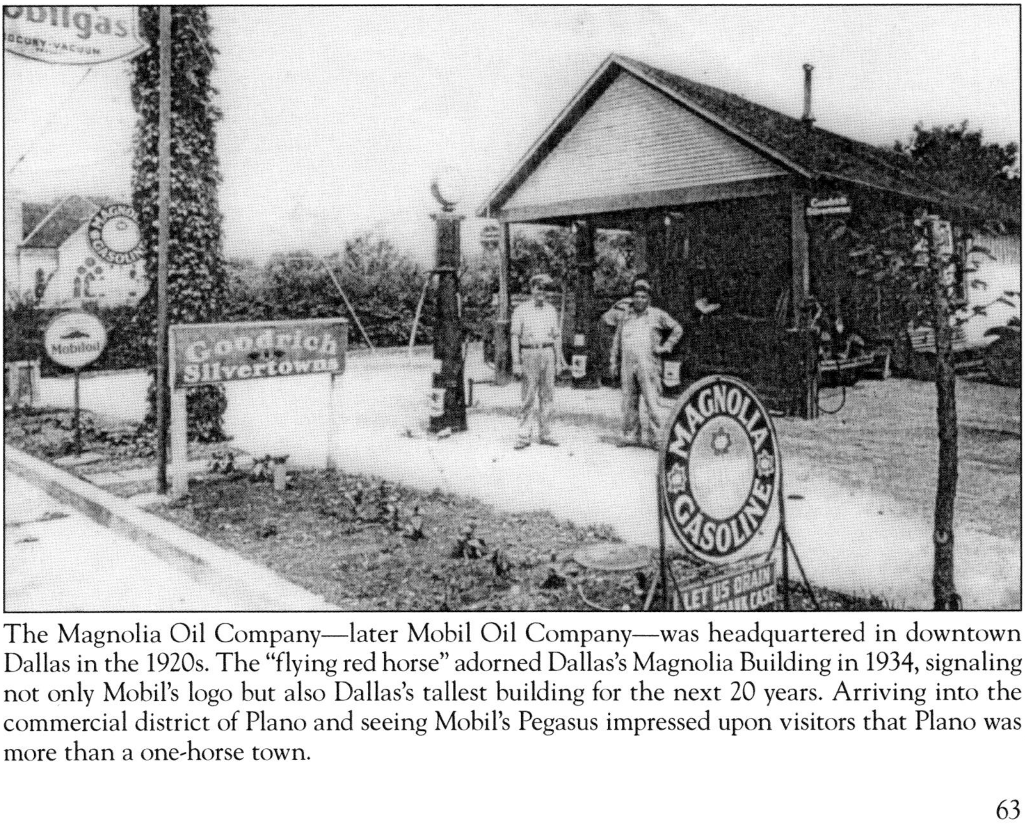

The Magnolia Oil Company—later Mobil Oil Company—was headquartered in downtown Dallas in the 1920s. The "flying red horse" adorned Dallas's Magnolia Building in 1934, signaling not only Mobil's logo but also Dallas's tallest building for the next 20 years. Arriving into the commercial district of Plano and seeing Mobil's Pegasus impressed upon visitors that Plano was more than a one-horse town.

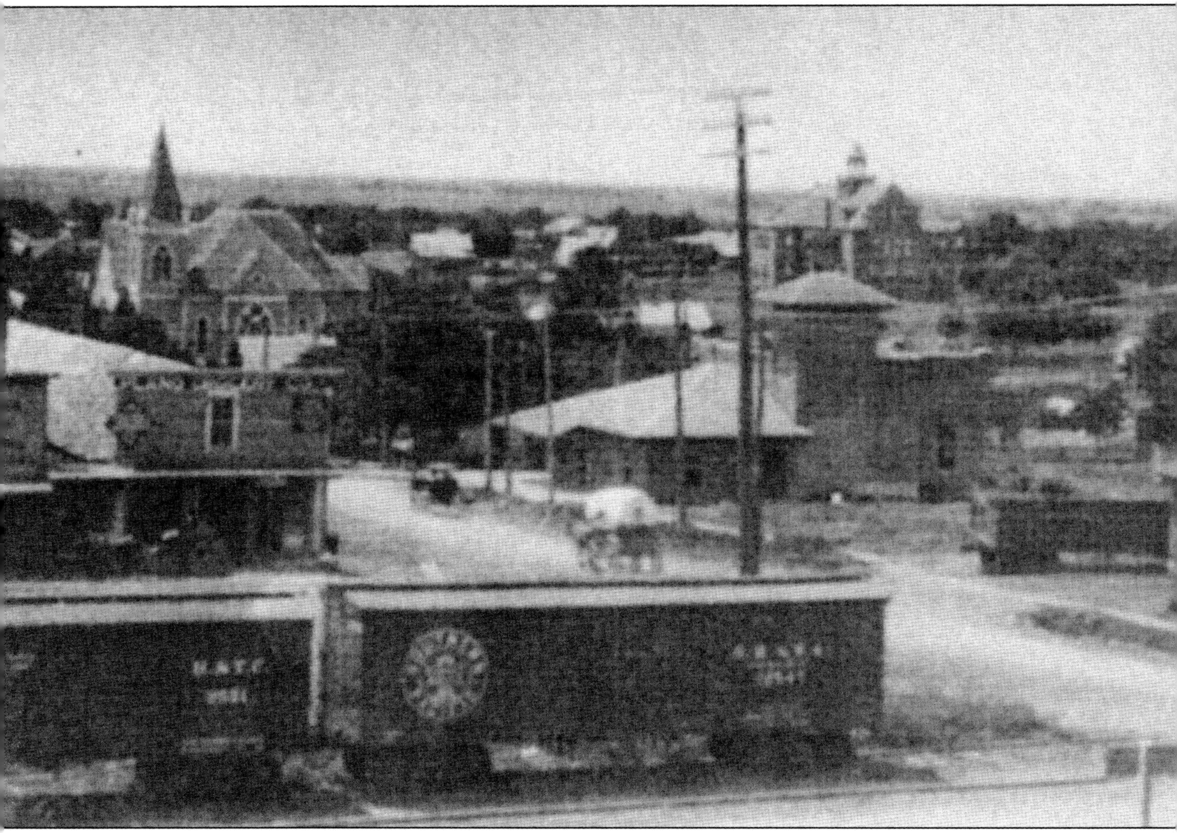

This westward view from the H&TC Railroad in the early 1900s shows the Interurban depot in the center. In the background are the First Christian Church and the adjacent Plano Public School. The neighboring residential area is now known as Haggard Park Heritage District. The view looks northwestward from the railroad to Haggard Park along Mechanic Street (now Fifteenth Street).

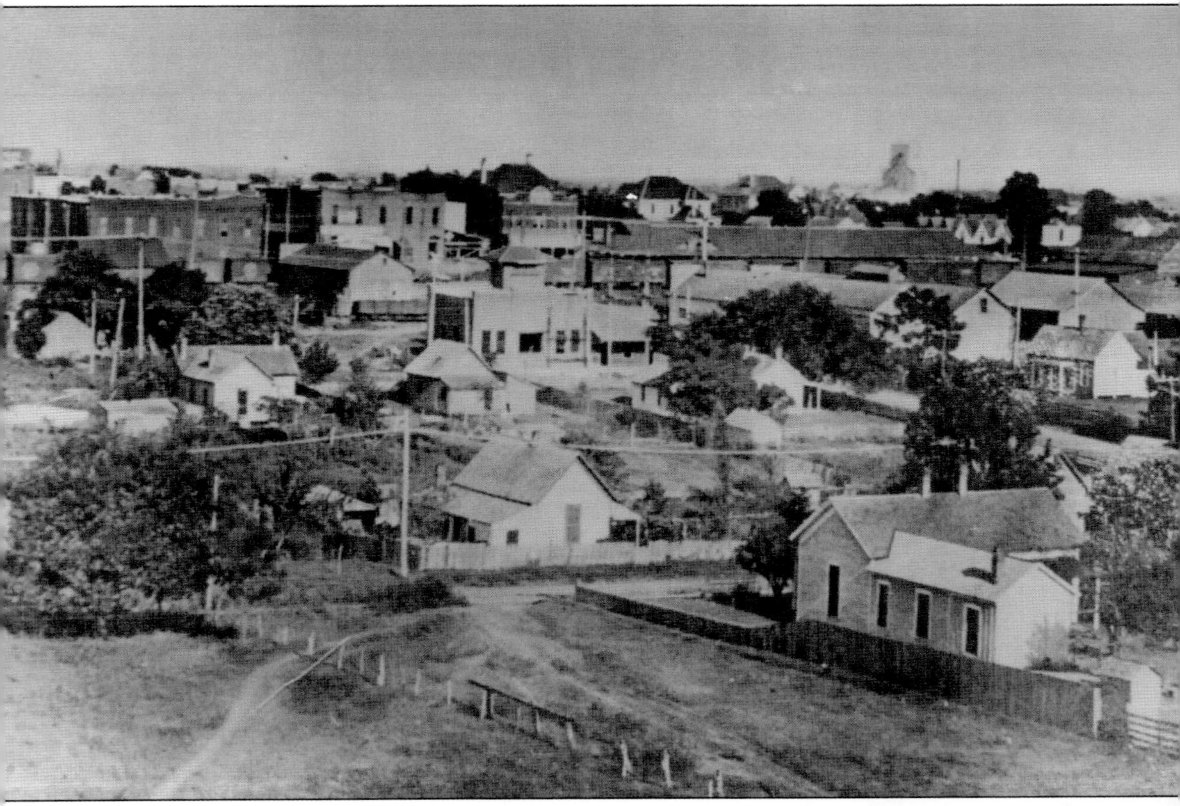

By 1914, Plano was recognized as a suburb of Dallas with fine churches, elegant homes, and hospitable people. This view captures the business district and shows the surrounding houses and buildings that survived or were rebuilt after the devastating fires.

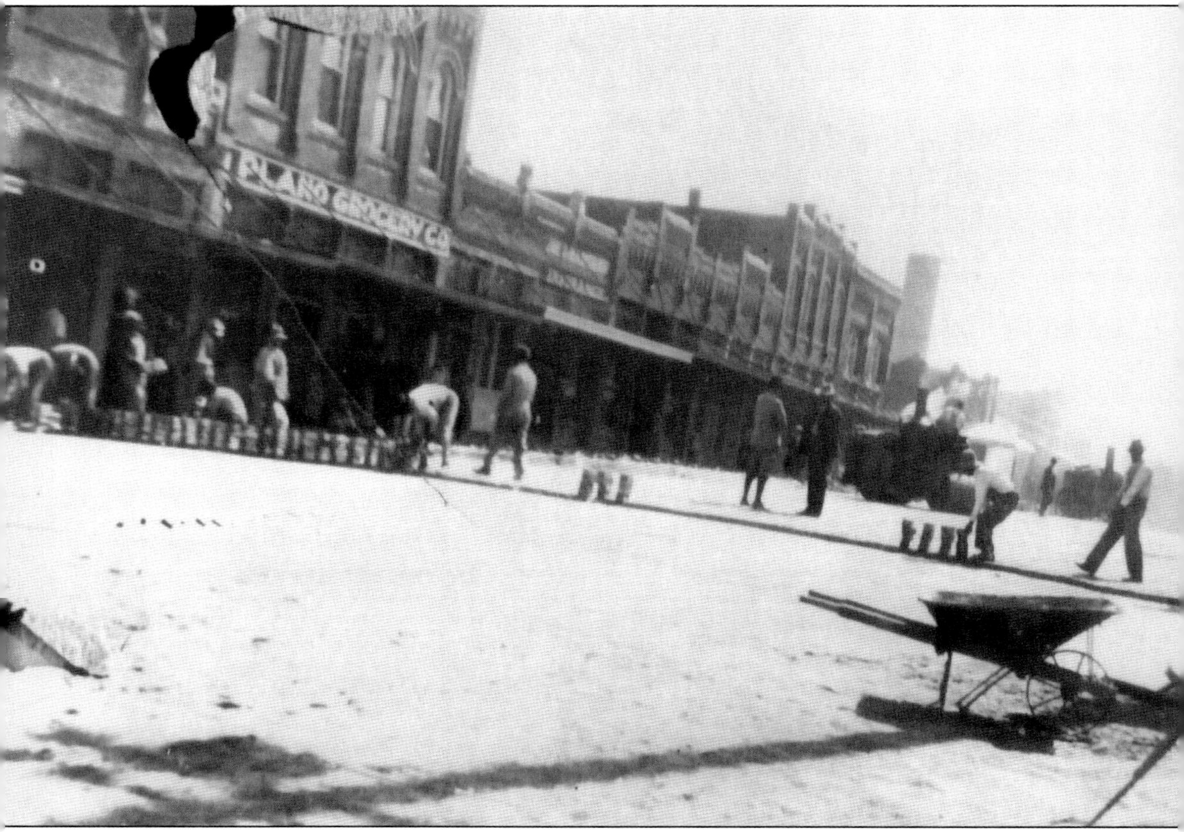

In 1924, Plano became one of the first towns of its size in Texas to pave its streets, the process of which is seen here. In 1947, the streets were given new names, street signs were installed, and addresses were given to the residences and businesses of Plano. Mechanic Street became Fifteenth Street and Main Street changed to K Avenue. Numerical streets ran east–west and lettered streets ran north–south in a grid pattern.

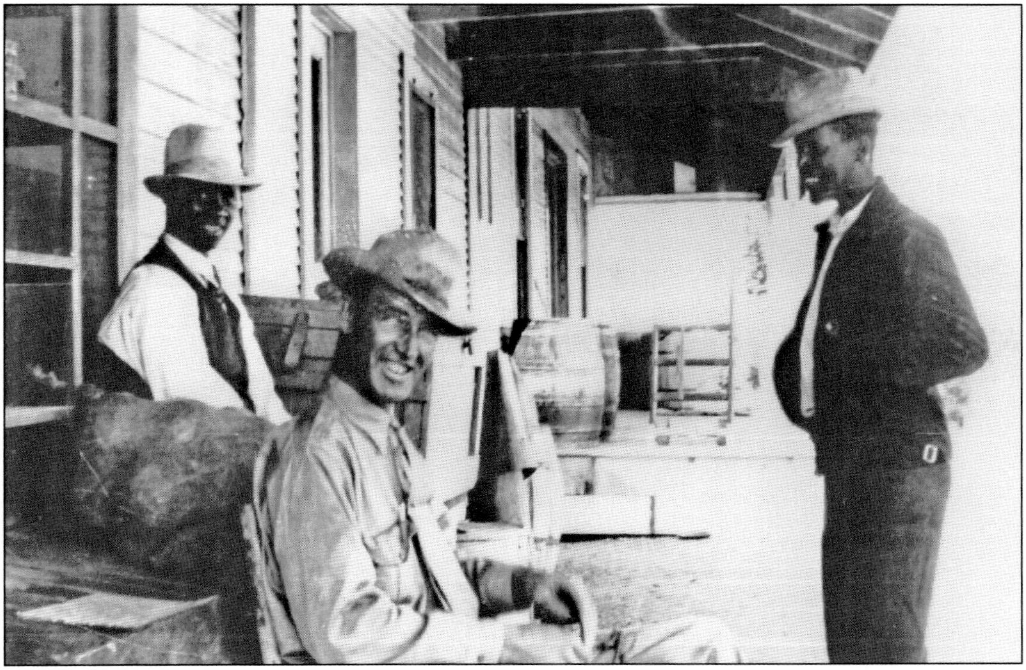

Plano native J. Harold Skaggs was a county agent and distributor for the Northern Oil Company of Fort Worth. In 1931, he bought two acres of land just north of the Plano city limits when the town population was 1,554. The land was part of a farm owned by Merony and Genoa Forman. Skaggs first built a service station and garage to promote his oil business and protect his oil truck and supplies. Later that same year, he built a larger building for a grocery store and meat market and expanded the business to include feed and hardware. His father, H.S. Skaggs, managed the store in the early years, and his younger brothers, Jack and Robert, helped after school. Frank Cothes managed the garage and auto repair shop. (Courtesy of Rodney Haggard.)

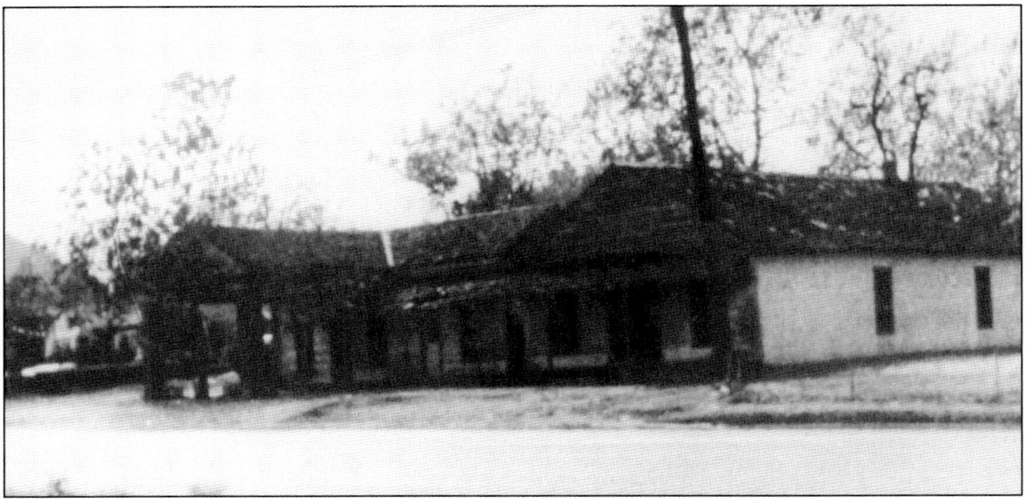

Often in special seasons, watermelons or pumpkins were piled up high on the Skaggs Store porch for quick sales. Skaggs kept a large "police dog" chained to the porch at night to keep pranksters from starting an avalanche of melons or pumpkins onto the parking area. After Skaggs retired in 1986, the land was sold to the city to build Fire Station No. 1 on K Avenue. Later, Rodney Haggard moved the Skaggs Store to Fairview Farms Marketplace and restored it as a general store.

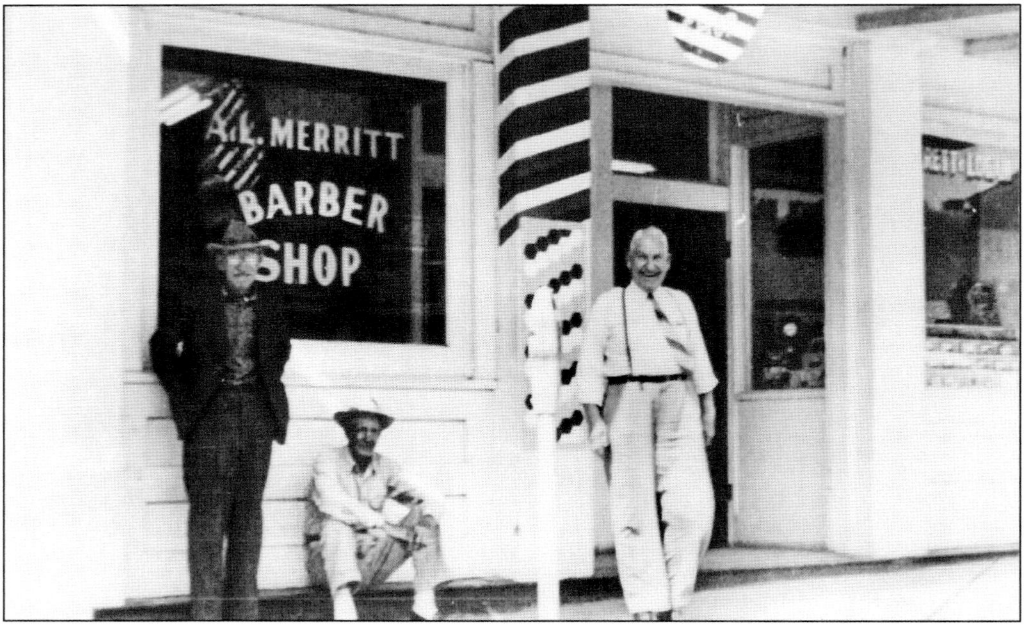

In 1913, A.L. Merritt had a barbershop on Fifteenth Street, hiring Jim Thomas as a "shoe shine boy" and porter. Thomas ran a one-man janitorial service, as well, cleaning nearly all the businesses downtown, including Farmer's State Bank of Plano, The First National Bank of Plano, Moore's Five and Ten, Weatherford's Jewelry, Harrington's Drug Store, Webb's Drug Store, Bradshaw's Insurance Brokerage, Schell's Insurance Brokerage, Dr. Coleman's office, Dr. Harris' office, Thompson's Dry Goods Store, Plano Printing office, the Telephone Company, Attorney Harrington's office, and the Soil Conservation office. He provided the first laundry delivery service for Plano and was the first African American fireman. (Above, courtesy of Rodney Haggard.)

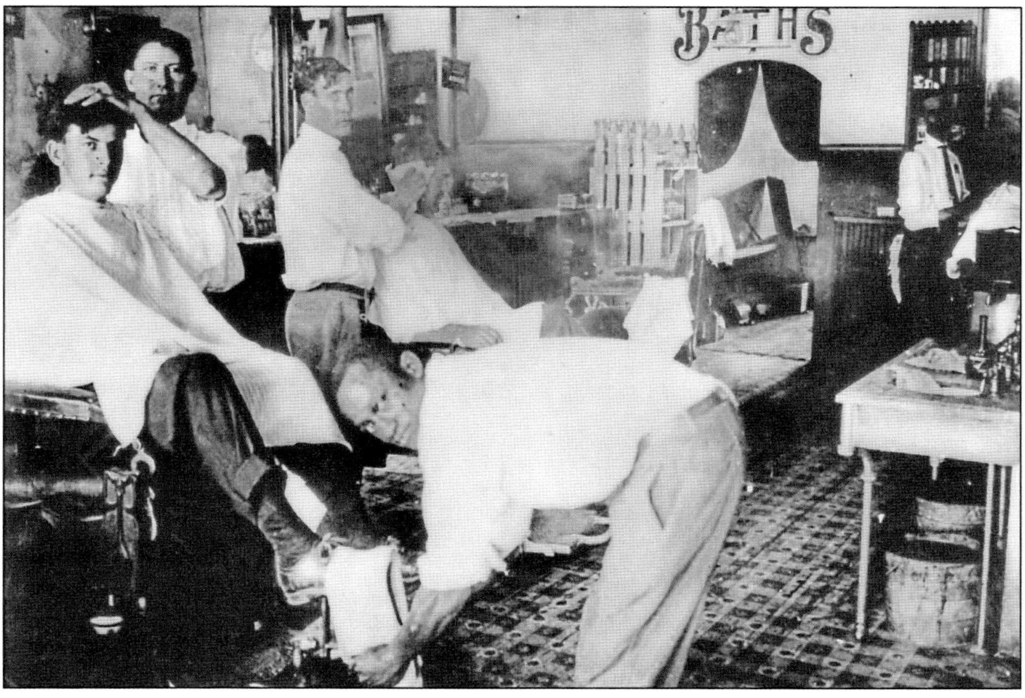

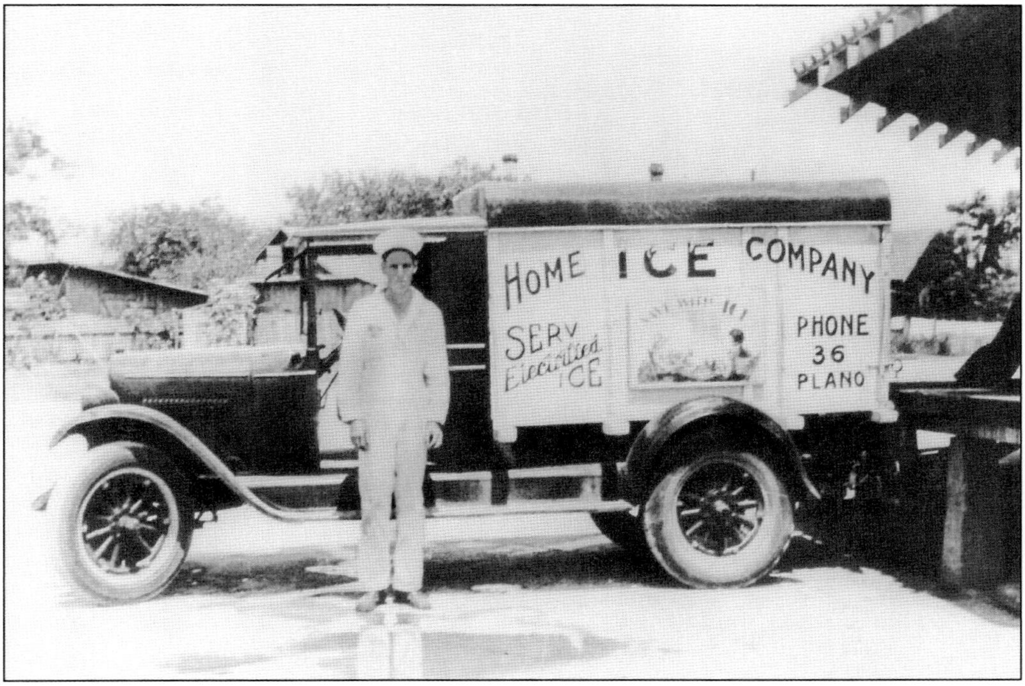

Deliveryman Raymond Dupree, who brought ice for the first iceboxes in town, poses in front of the ice wagon in 1919. Ice was purchased by the pound from a frozen water salesman, similar to the way milkmen delivered milk to homes. When the ice melted into a pan under the icebox, it was time for another ice delivery. The early-1900s storefronts below are still recognizable in Plano. (Below, courtesy of the City of Plano.)

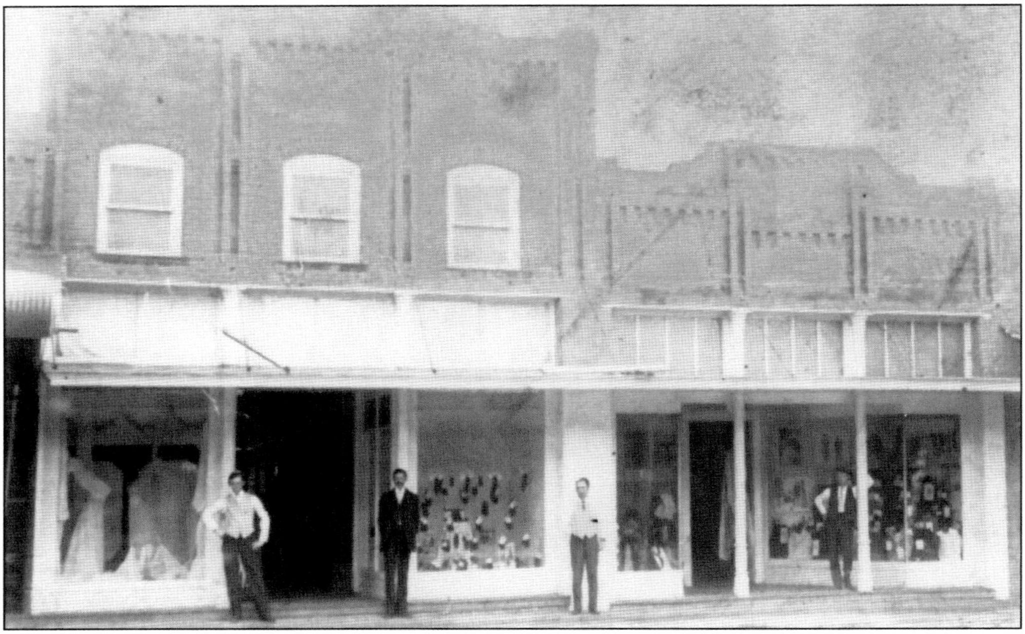

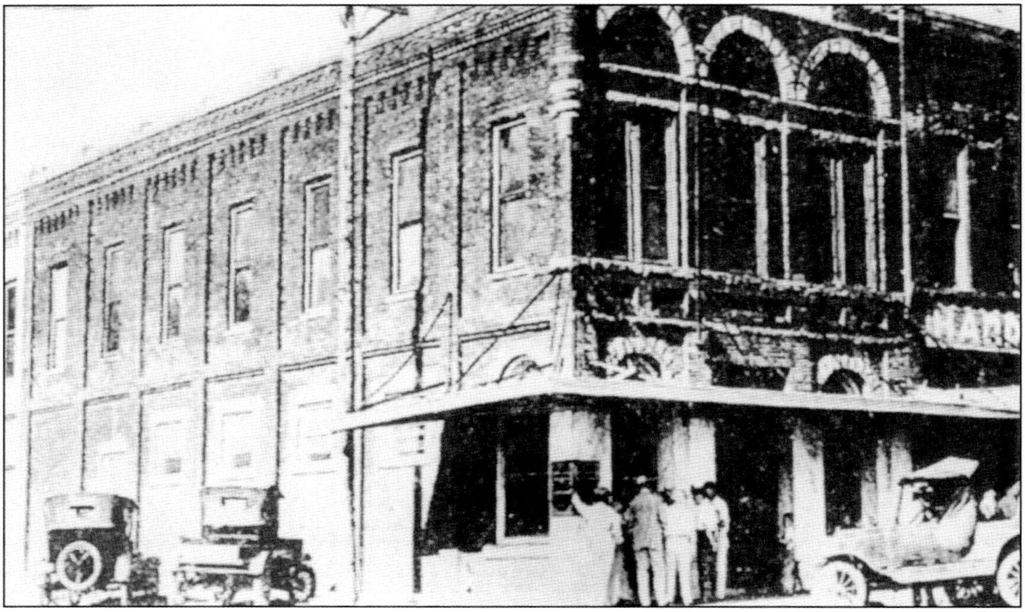

"Bandits Raid Bank at Plano and Get Away," read the *Dallas Morning News* headline on September 16, 1927. The bank was robbed at gunpoint at midday, leaving two innocent bystanders and one of the bandits wounded. Three or four bandits in a getaway car headed toward Dallas, strewing nails and tacks behind them to thwart the Plano men chasing them in cars. In later years, August Lamm, a Plano correspondent for the *Dallas Morning News* since its first issue in 1885, recalled another robbery of the Plano National Bank in 1893 during which $20,000 was taken after the robbers set off a dynamite charge near the safe while a long freight train passed through. The bank was near the H&TC track, so the noise of the train muffled the sound of the explosion. A few days later, T.C. Jasper, the bank cashier, received a package postmarked at Denton containing a small tin savings bank with the attached tag reading, "Keep your money in this."

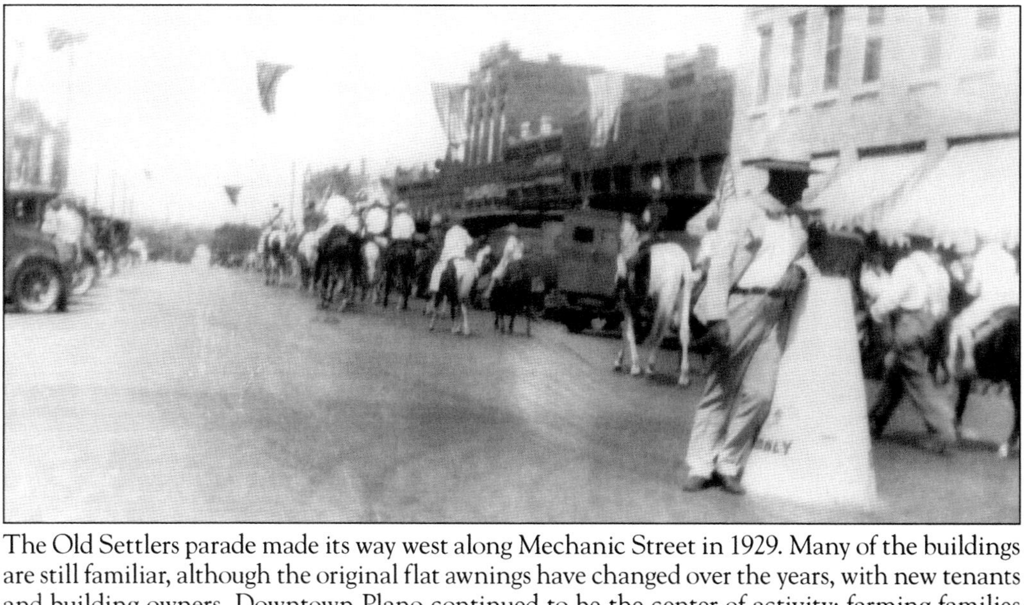

The Old Settlers parade made its way west along Mechanic Street in 1929. Many of the buildings are still familiar, although the original flat awnings have changed over the years, with new tenants and building owners. Downtown Plano continued to be the center of activity; farming families came to town on Saturday nights to catch up with town folks and hear the latest news.

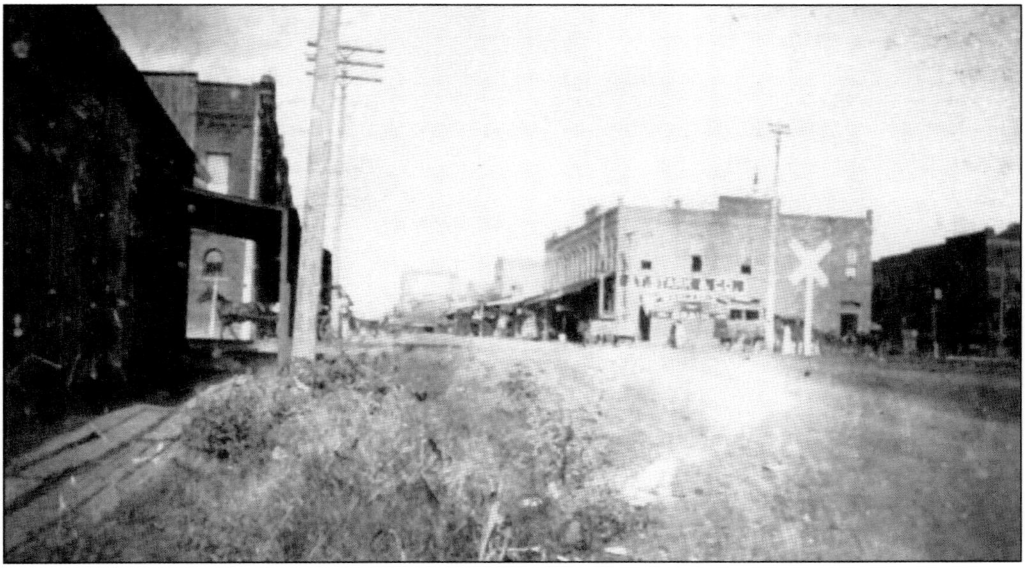

The Great Depression of the 1930s came to Plano just as it did for the rest of the nation, but the strong-knit community remained positive, persevering with its farming roots and industriousness. Gladys Bishop Harrington, born in 1901 in Plano, recalled in an interview with John Wells in the 1990s that she "had one good dress in the summer and one good dress in the winter; the family raised vegetables and farmed with mules, then tractors, and they had their own cows and pigs to provide meat, so there was not much change in the Depression years." They lived on the old Harrington land at Parker and Preston Roads. Most farmers, many of whom were sharecroppers and tenants, were already accustomed to some austerity and therefore did not feel too much more hardship in the Depression than they were already used to. Pictured below are Ray and Lela Skaggs. (Both images courtesy of Rodney Haggard.)

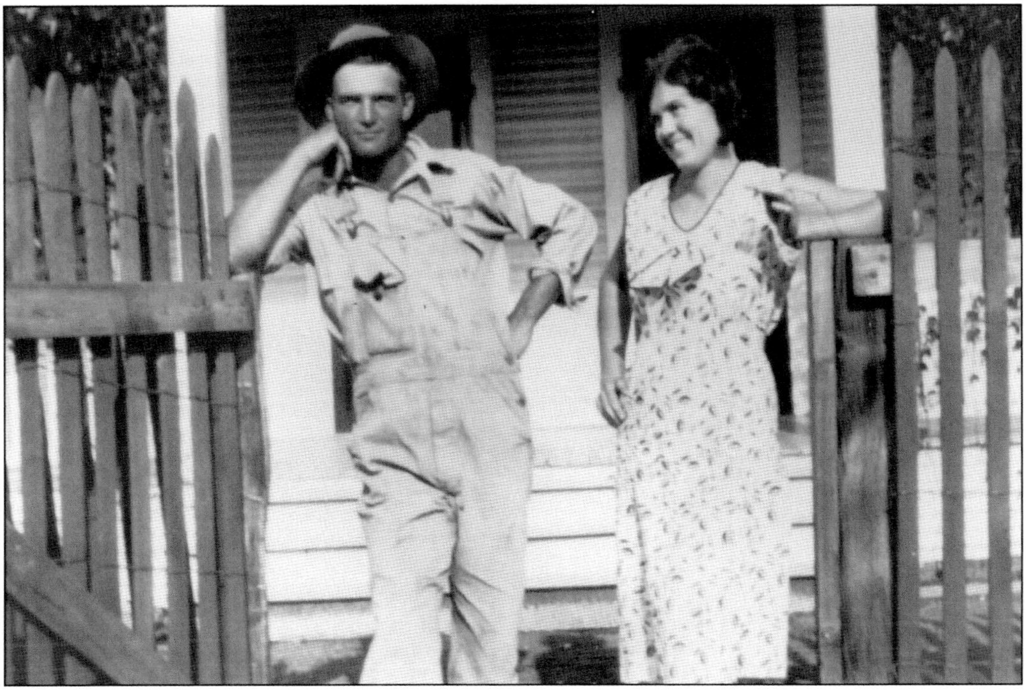

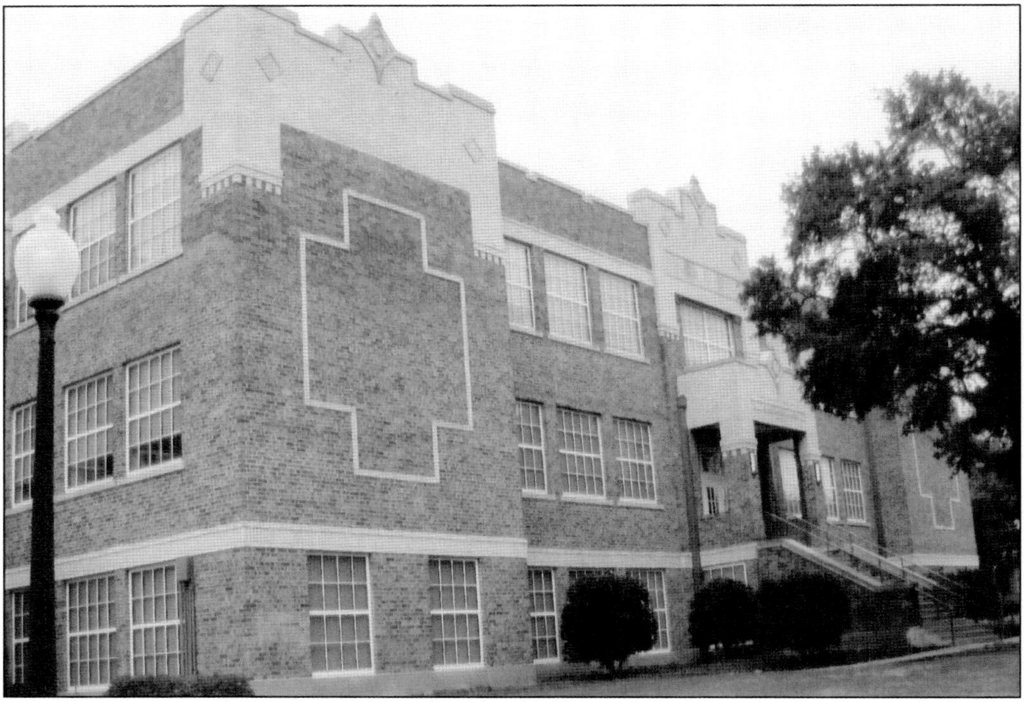

A bright star during the Depression was the school system. Outlying rural schools were challenged by declining attendance, limited funding, and more rigid state standards, so they turned to the larger Plano system, which attracted dedicated teachers. According to the Cox School Museum, Mary Alice "Terry" Skaggs, a beloved 31-year teaching legend and the first to earn a master's degree, said, "Everyone wanted to teach for the Plano School District because of its quality reputation, its new building, and the fact that during the midst of the Depression, teachers were paid in cash and not with vouchers." Consolidation of other districts into Plano's school system increased the student population. In 1935, with funding from the WPA, the Plano Independent School District (PISD) built a gymnasium adjacent to the school on present-day H Avenue across from Haggard Park. The gymnasium has been a significant building in Plano's history and has long exemplified the cultural and social heritage of Plano. Both the school and the gymnasium buildings were designated Texas Historic Landmarks in 2006.

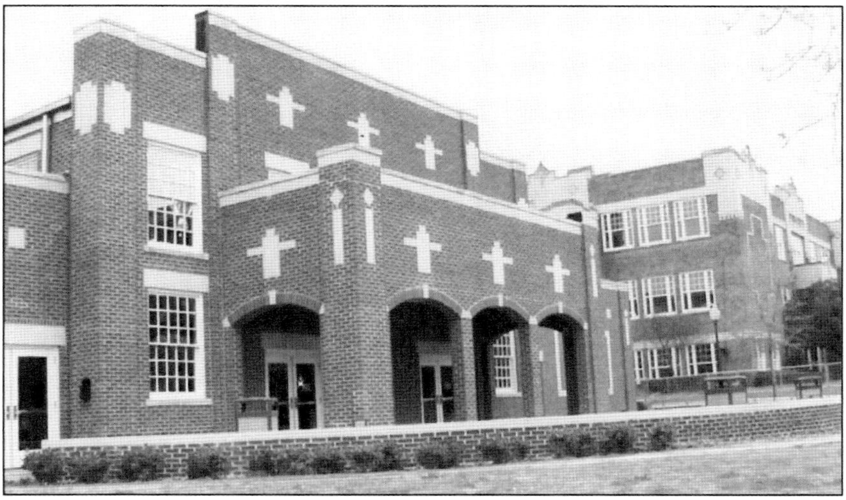

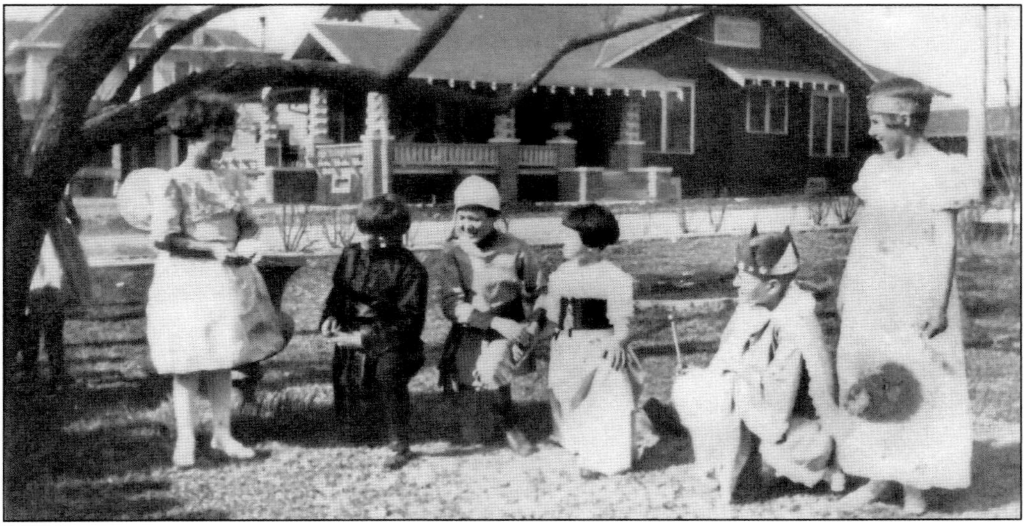

Aspiring actors Sally Harrington, Robert Gee Hudson (in black), Al Weaver Mathis, and others perform an outdoor play in the early 1900s. The distinctive Craftsman-style home in the background is the S.B. Wyatt House. Built around 1910, it is one of the city's historically significant homes, in the Haggard Park Heritage District at 807 Sixteenth Street, across from the old Plano School. (Courtesy of Cynthia Hudson Reed.)

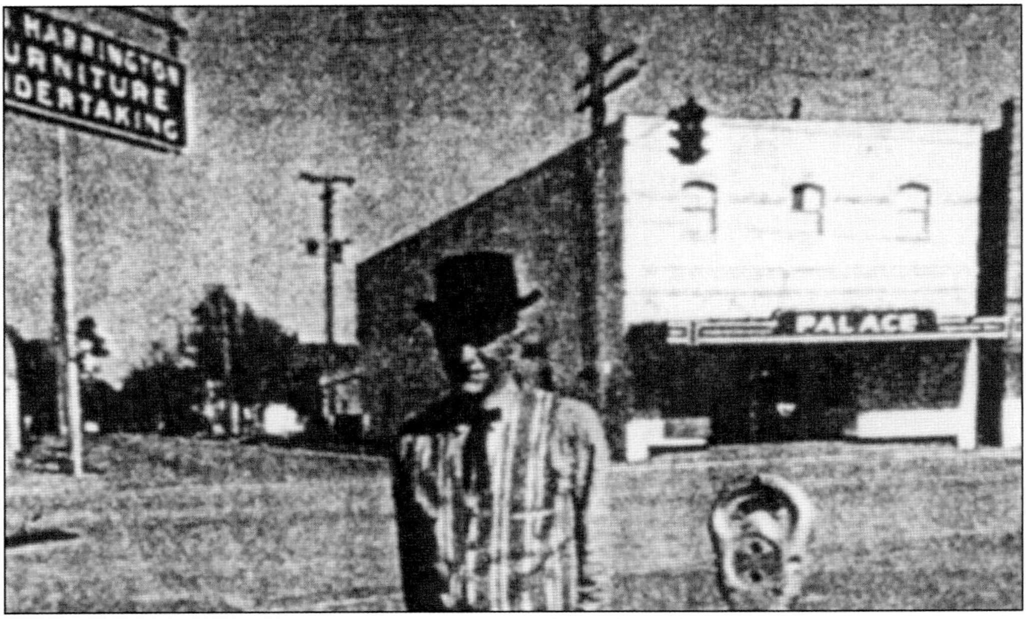

D.L. Wood came to Plano around 1913 and opened the Palace Theater at the southeast corner of Main and Mechanic Streets, where "first class" pictures were shown. The theater was open every night, with a matinee on Saturday. Electric fans cooled the picture show. In the 1940s, Peggy Mitchell recalls that sometimes the film would run faulty, and everyone would clap. African Americans sat in the second-floor balcony. Brenda Kellow, who ran the concession stand at the picture show in the 1950s, sold Royal Crown Colas, peanuts, Moon Pies, popcorn, Butterfinger, Milky Way, Snickers, Chick 'N' Legs, and Milk Duds and saw every movie shown. The picture show was popular with folks from rural Texas who came to town on Saturday nights. Many small Texas towns had a Palace Theater back then. (Courtesy of Peggy Mitchell.)

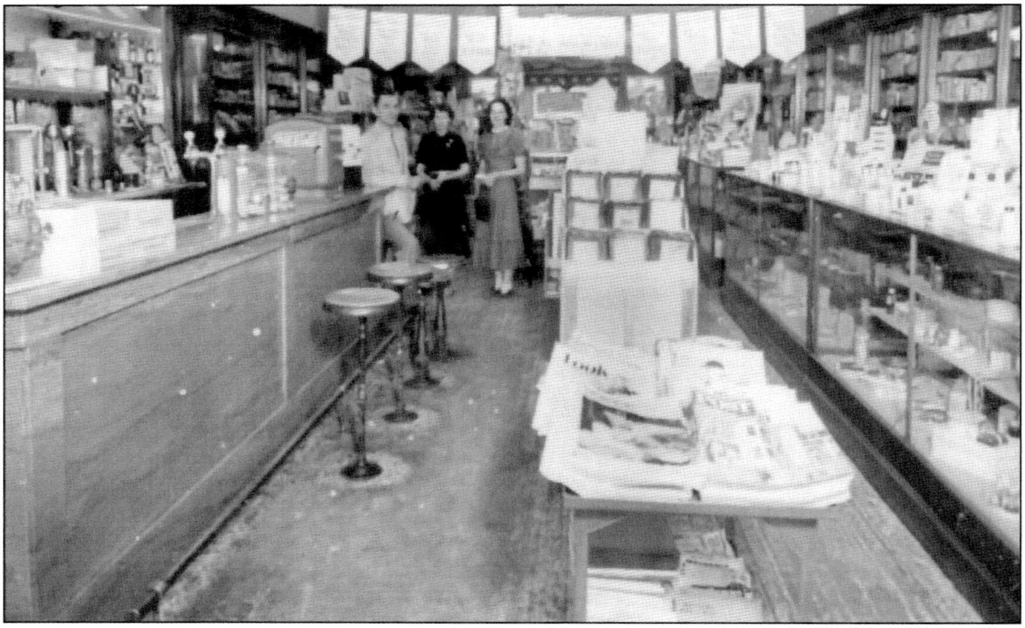

Allen Brothers Drug Store was one of the more popular places for meeting friends after school in the 1940s and 1950s. Downtown businesses like this one continued to be family owned and operated for many years. Here, Jimmy Harrington and Gene Reed (in black) trained a student employee in the business in the 1940s. Peggy Mitchell remembers the old-fashioned soda fountain and the swing-out seats in the drugstore. (Above, courtesy Cynthia Reed; below courtesy of Rodney Haggard.)

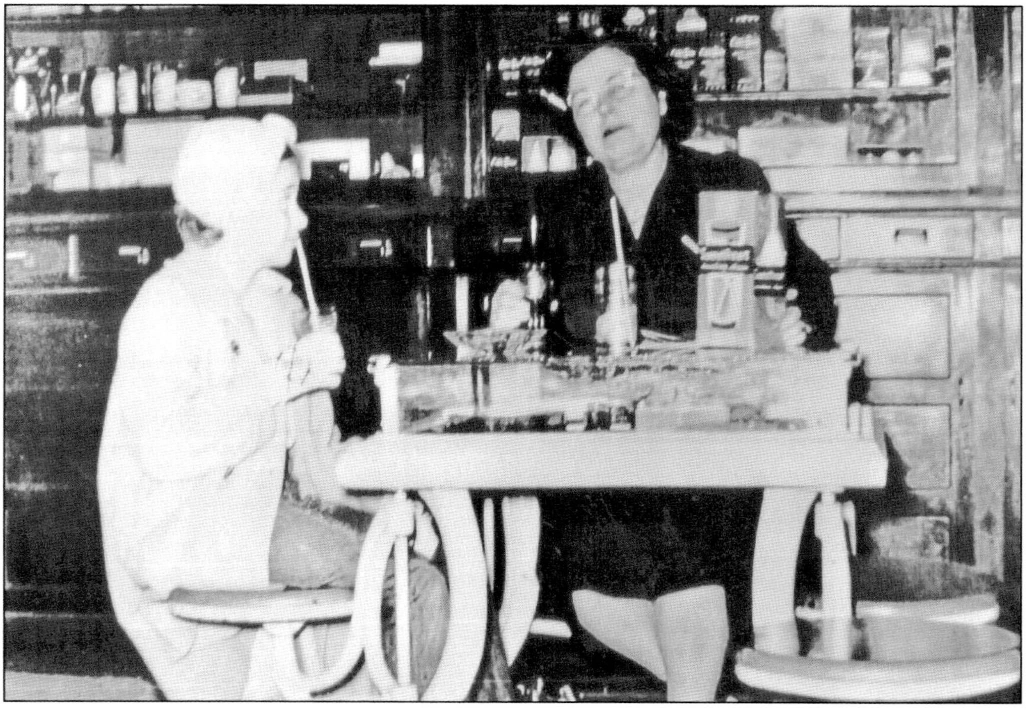

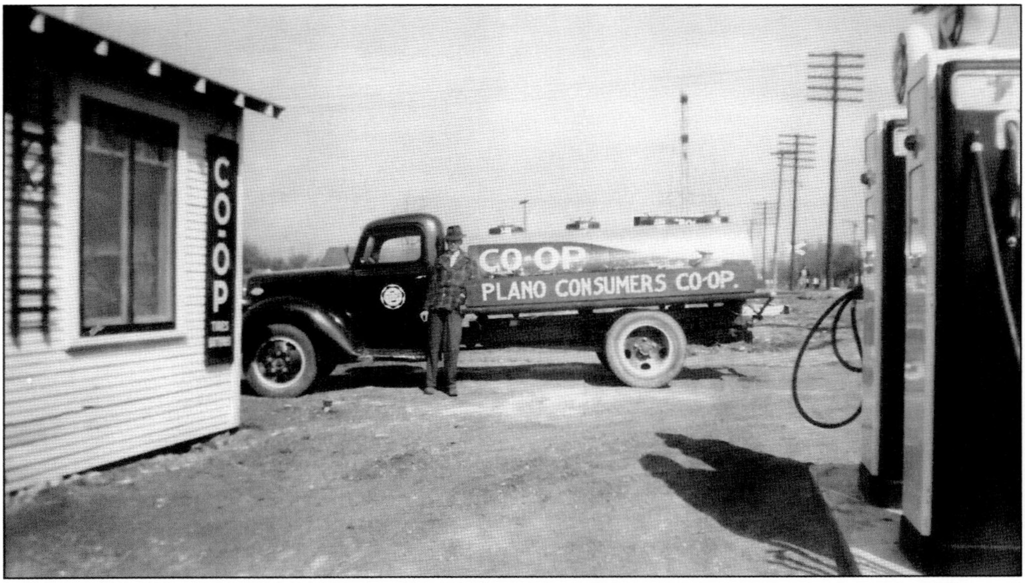

After generations of intensive farming and droughts in the 1850s, 1890s, 1910s, and 1930s, soil erosion became increasingly serious in Plano and throughout Collin County. The dustbowl of the 1930s in West Texas led local farmers to take action. John Dickerson Wells, a seed grower and grain dealer and a descendant of W.H.L Wells, was instrumental in the establishment of the Soil Conservation District to address farming practices and soil conservation in 1946. He also served on the state and national association boards. Among other notable civic involvement, Wells was a founder of the Plano Consumers Coop and the Plano Coop Grocery in downtown Plano. The Plano Consumers Coop tanker truck is seen here around 1940. (Courtesy of Rodney Haggard.)

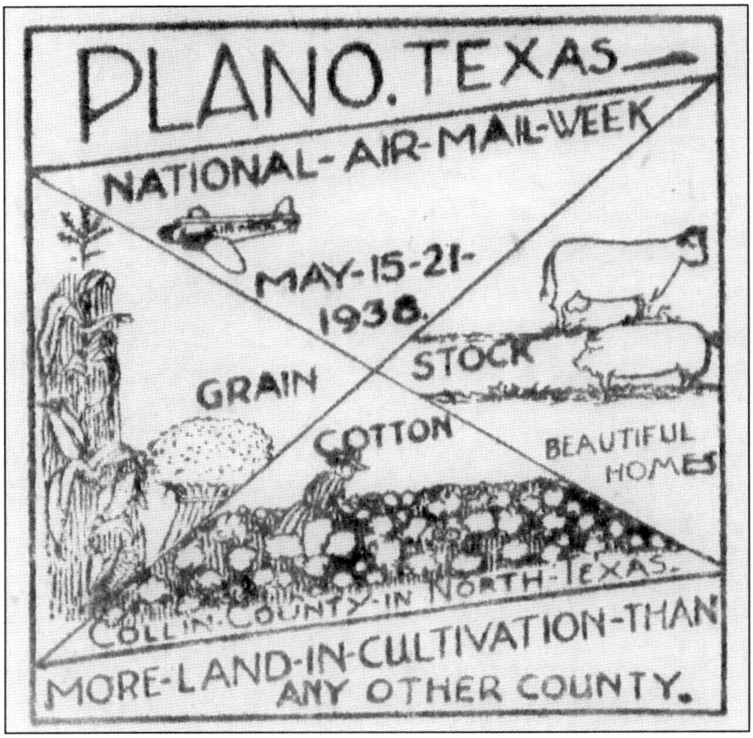

During National Air Mail Week in 1938, a commemorative stamp proclaimed Plano's abundance of livestock, grain, cotton, and beautiful homes and touted Collin County as having more land under cultivation than any other county. (Courtesy of Rodney Haggard.)

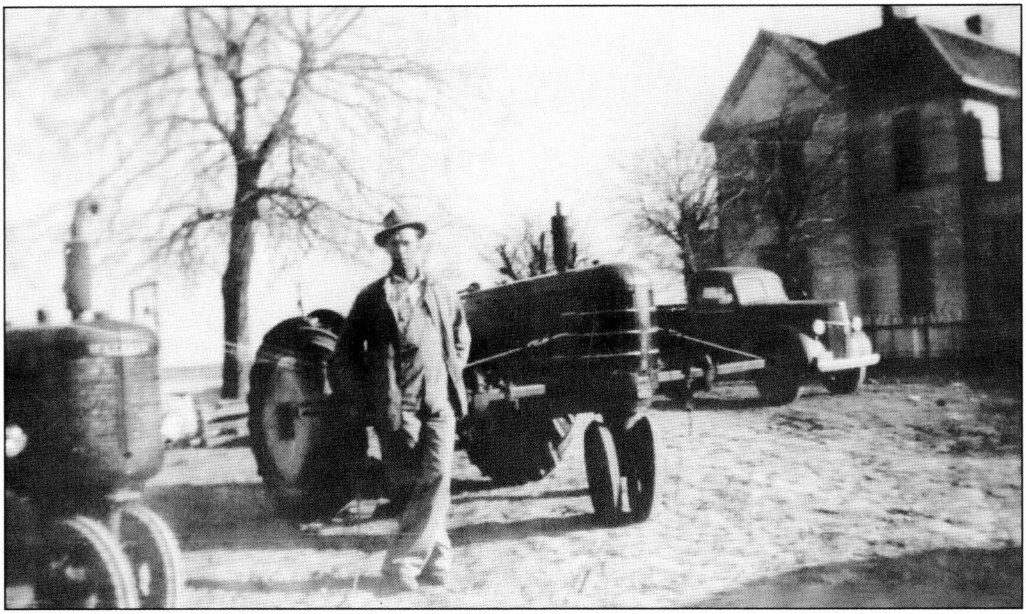

The Wells family has been in Plano since W.H.L. Wells arrived in the 1870s. Wells Brothers Feed Store started in 1959 as Wells Brothers Grain Company, a local grain terminal that bought grain from the farmers in the area. When Plano started growing around that time, their new customers were city folks with no cows to feed or fields to plow. Instead, they had gardens, lawns, and pets, so Wells Brothers started keeping products on hand for the needs of people with smaller acreage and smaller livestock. Today, Wells Brothers Farm Store is still located near the railroad tracks on K Avenue near Spring Creek Parkway. (Courtesy of Rodney Haggard.)

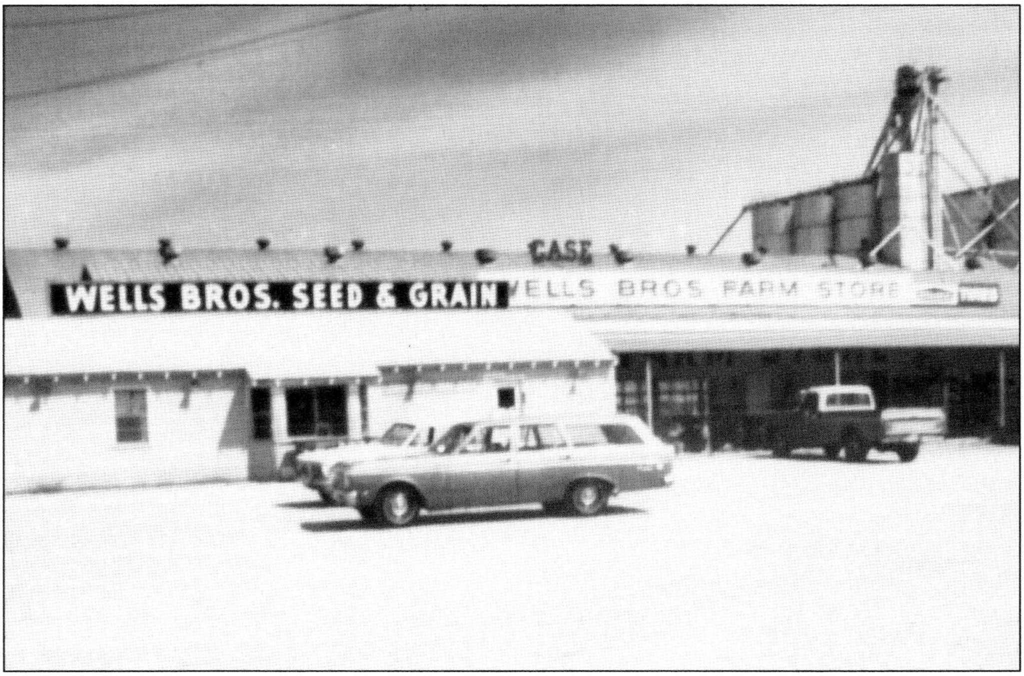

In the 1950s, Ammie Wilson of Plano became the most successful and renowned purebred sheep breeder and show woman in the United States, appearing at livestock shows or at church in the same trademark attire: a tweed jacket, riding boots, gabardine pants, and a diamond brooch. Wilson was one of the first sheep breeders in the United States to cross English and western Hampshires, and she declared this to be the key to her success. Her home was the elaborate Folk Victorian house, which is the centerpiece of the Heritage Farmstead Museum and a middle school is named in her honor. She was president of the Collin County Livestock Association in 1952 and made many other contributions to farming and 4-H Clubs. Below, the Plano Future Farmers of America (FFA) won the Hereford show and won district seven out of eight years in the 1950s. (Below, courtesy of Rodney Haggard.)

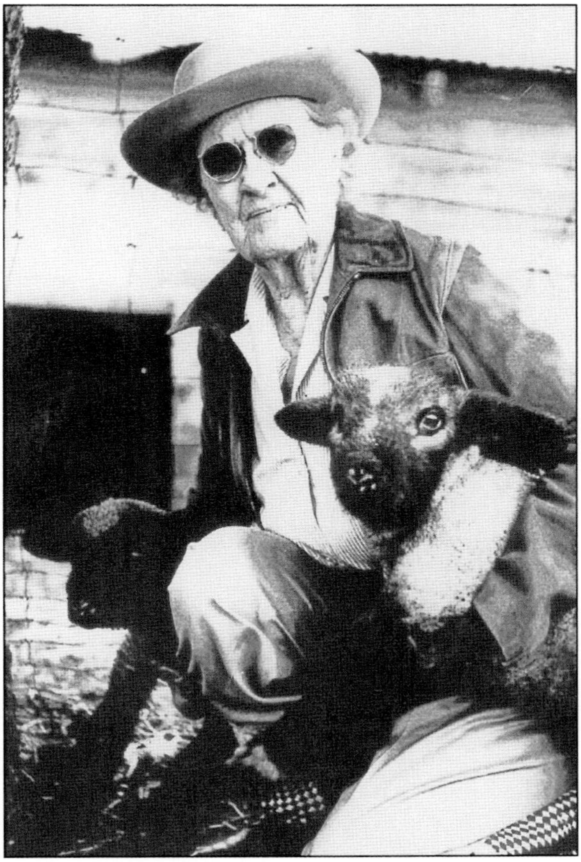

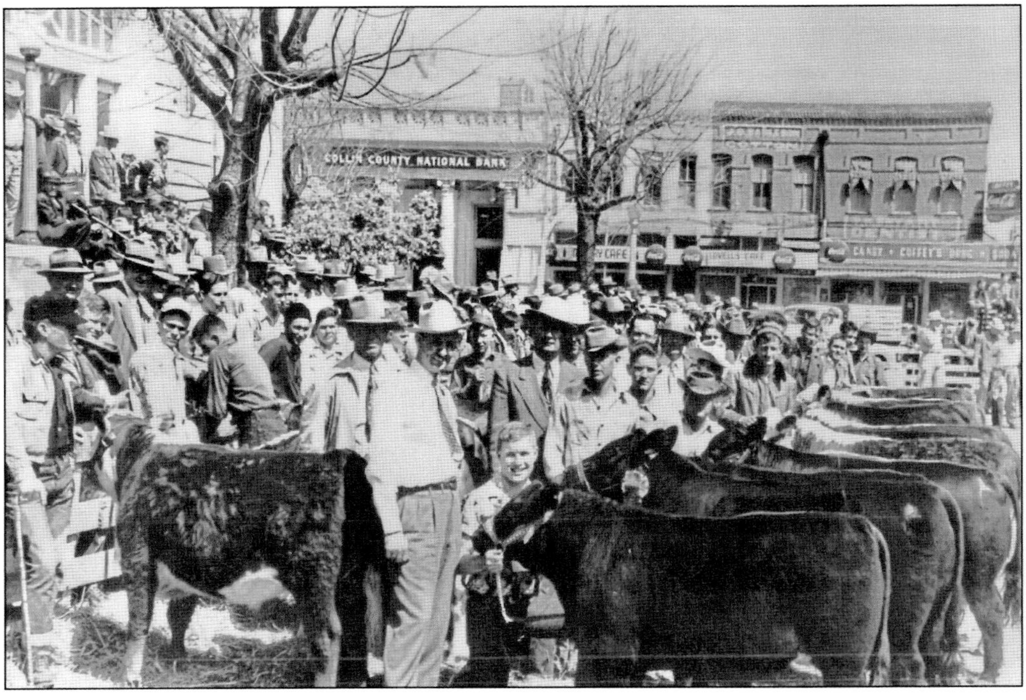

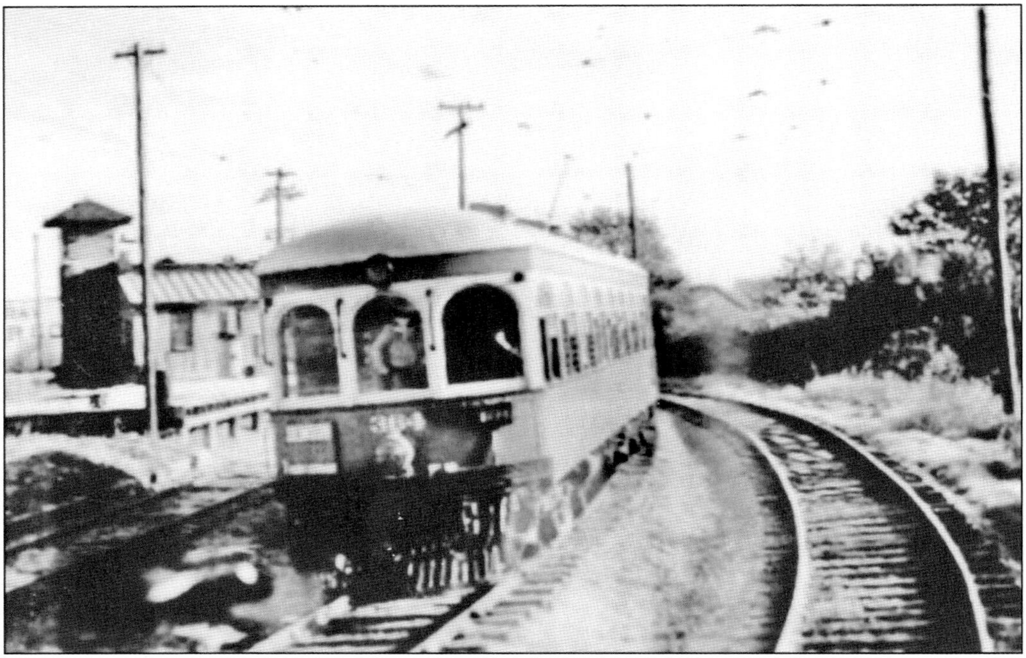

The arrival of the automobile affected the Interurban Railway as much as the Interurban had affected the traditional railroad. As passenger traffic declined and trucking made inroads on freight traffic, the Interurban was abandoned. Gone were the days when Brenda Kellow remembered watching the countryside slide past with large stands of trees signaling a creek crossing. Daily commuters also missed the frequency of trains coming and going to Dallas or a carefree visit to Sherman or Waco. With the growing reliance on automobiles and trucking, the Texas Electric Railway ticket office ceased operations in 1948. (Above, courtesy of the City of Plano.)

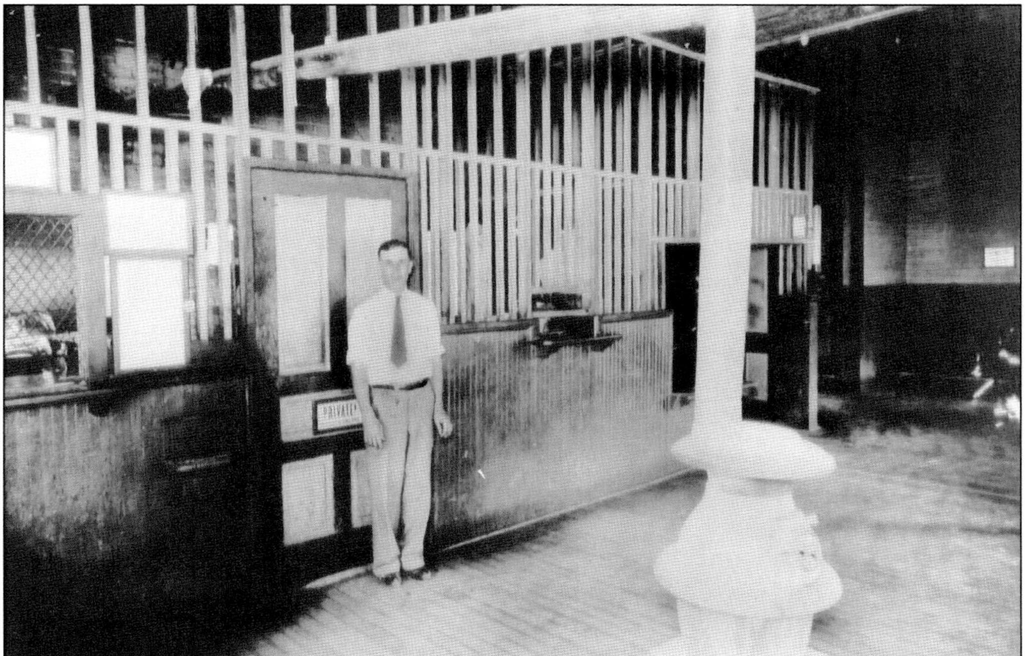

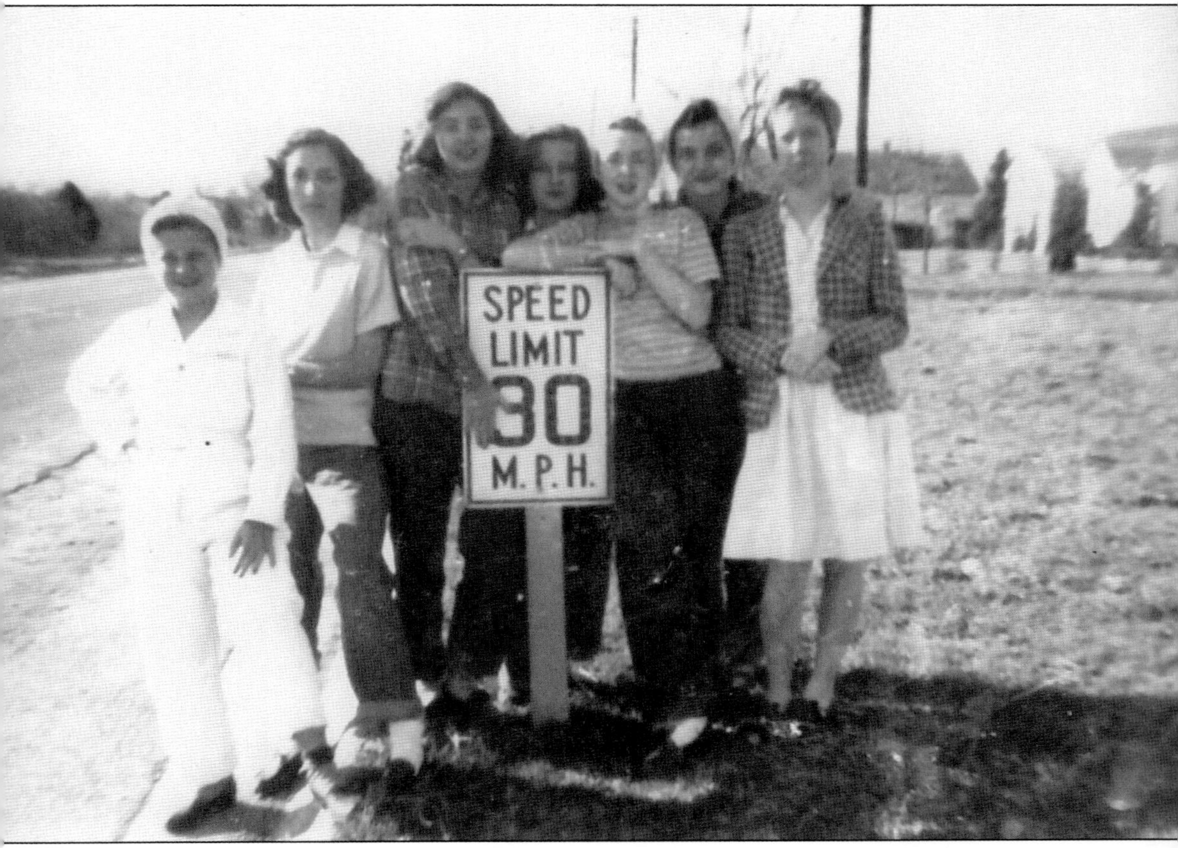

In the early 1900s, the main street running through Plano was a two-lane highway known as Highway 5 (now K Avenue). Starting at the ferry crossing in Galveston and ending at the Canadian border, it was the main road running north and south through Texas. In the mid-1940s, the speed limit was posted at 30 miles per hour through Plano. Peggy Mitchell (far left) remembers this snapshot taken on a slow afternoon with friends. (Courtesy of Peggy Mitchell.)

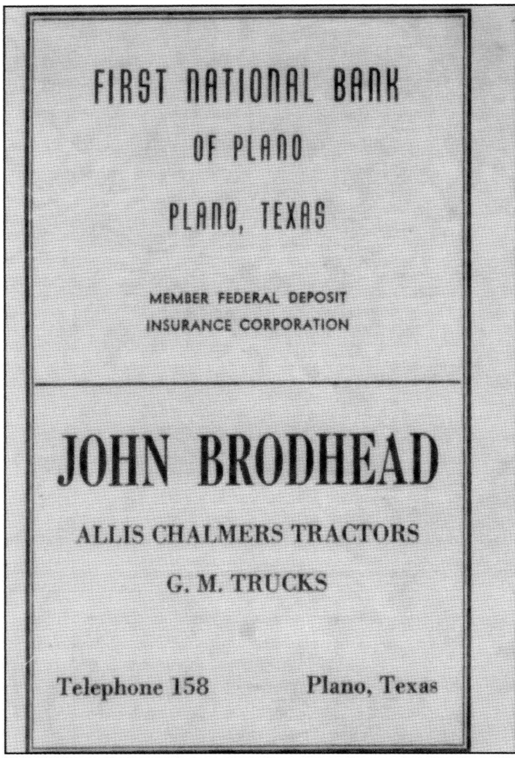

FIRST NATIONAL BANK

OF PLANO

PLANO, TEXAS

MEMBER FEDERAL DEPOSIT
INSURANCE CORPORATION

JOHN BRODHEAD

ALLIS CHALMERS TRACTORS

G. M. TRUCKS

Telephone 158 Plano, Texas

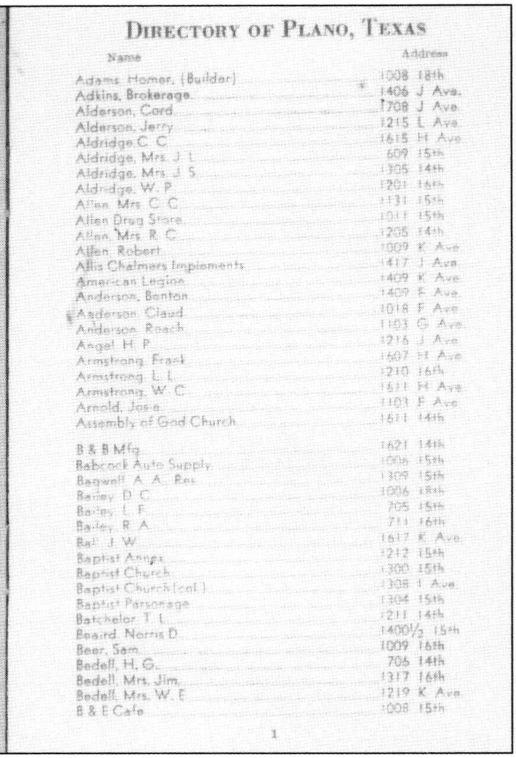

DIRECTORY OF PLANO, TEXAS

Name	Address
Adams Homer, (Builder)	1008 18th
Adkins, Brokerage	1406 J Ave.
Alderson, Cord	1708 J Ave.
Alderson, Jerry	1215 L Ave.
Aldridge C. C.	1615 H Ave.
Aldridge, Mrs. J. L.	609 15th
Aldridge, Mrs. J. S.	1305 14th
Aldridge, W. P.	1201 16th
Allen Mrs. C. C.	1131 15th
Allen Drug Store	1011 15th
Allen Mrs. R. C.	1205 14th
Allen Robert	1009 K Ave.
Allis Chalmers Implements	1417 J Ave.
American Legion	1409 K Ave.
Anderson, Benton	1409 F Ave.
Anderson Claud	1018 F Ave.
Anderson Roach	1103 G Ave.
Angel H. P.	1216 J Ave.
Armstrong Frank	1607 H Ave.
Armstrong L. L.	1210 16th
Armstrong, W. C.	1611 H Ave.
Arnold, Josie	1103 F Ave.
Assembly of God Church	1611 14th
B & B Mfg.	1621 14th
Babcock Auto Supply	1006 15th
Bagwell A. A. Res.	1309 15th
Bailey D. C.	1006 18th
Bailey L. F.	705 15th
Bailey R. A.	711 16th
Ball J. W.	1617 K Ave.
Baptist Annex	1212 15th
Baptist Church	1300 15th
Baptist Church (col.)	1308 I Ave.
Baptist Parsonage	1304 15th
Batchelor T. L.	1211 14th
Beaird Norris D.	1400½ 15th
Beer, Sam	1009 16th
Bedell, H. G.	706 14th
Bedell, Mrs. Jim	1317 16th
Bedell, Mrs. W. E.	1219 K Ave.
B & E Cafe	1008 15th

1

Plano published its first city directory in 1948, listing all the residences and businesses with new street addresses and local phone numbers. Telephone numbers were three digits back then, long before there were area codes. The First National Bank and John Brodhead, among others, helped fund the directory. Brodhead ran Allis Chalmers Tractors and G.M. Trucks, which operated in the abandoned H&TC depot. The Brodheads still own the building on J Place downtown, marked by the 1950s-style "Brodhead Real Estate Loans" sign.

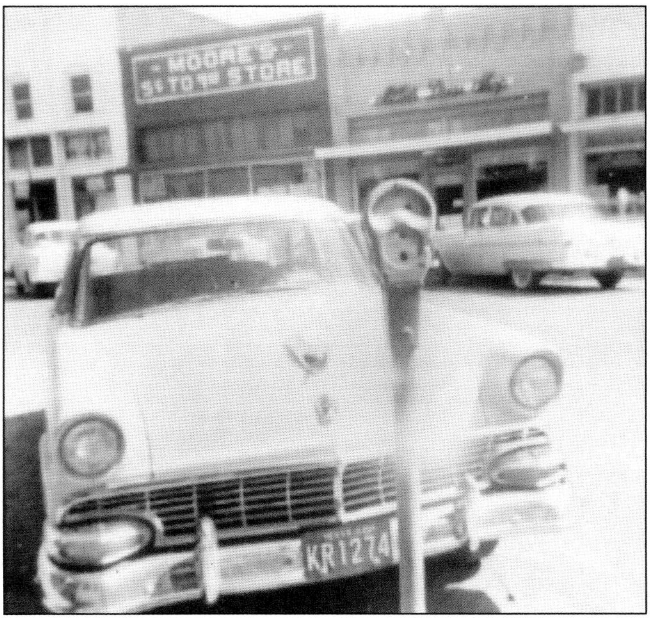

Weatherford Jewelers still served customers in downtown Plano in the mid-1950s. Bedford Moore, Arch Weatherford's son-in-law, purchased a variety store on the south side of Fifteenth Street near the jewelry store, which became Moore's 5¢ to $1 Store and operated in the same location for many years. (Courtesy of Judy Moore.)

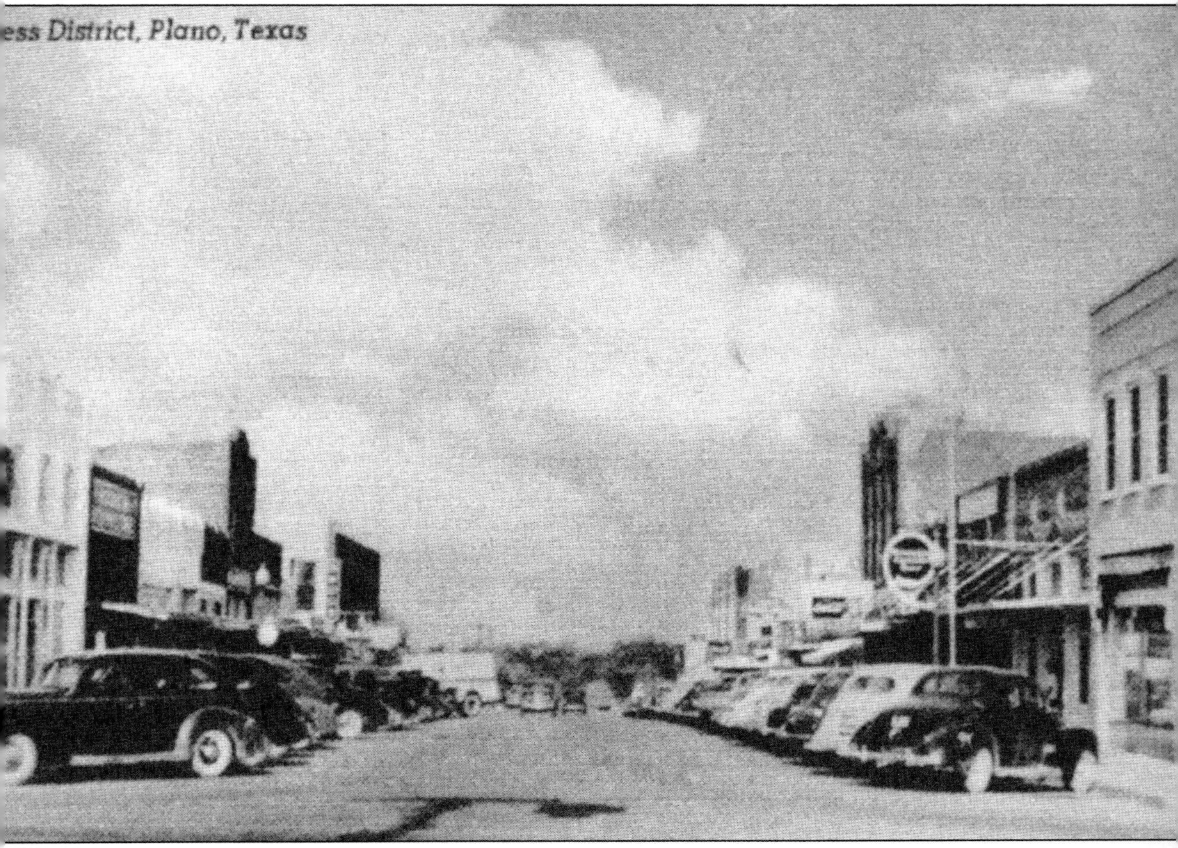

This 1950s postcard shows a robust business district with new automobiles on the scene. The expansion of the greater Dallas metropolitan area and improved access to Richardson and Plano stimulated suburban expansion. Farming was still the lifeblood, but with the automobile and improved roadway system, Plano's city leaders prepared for growth. Advertisements in the Dallas newspapers promoted Plano's good schools and pretty neighborhoods to draw young families from Dallas. (Courtesy of Peggy Mitchell and David Quentin.)

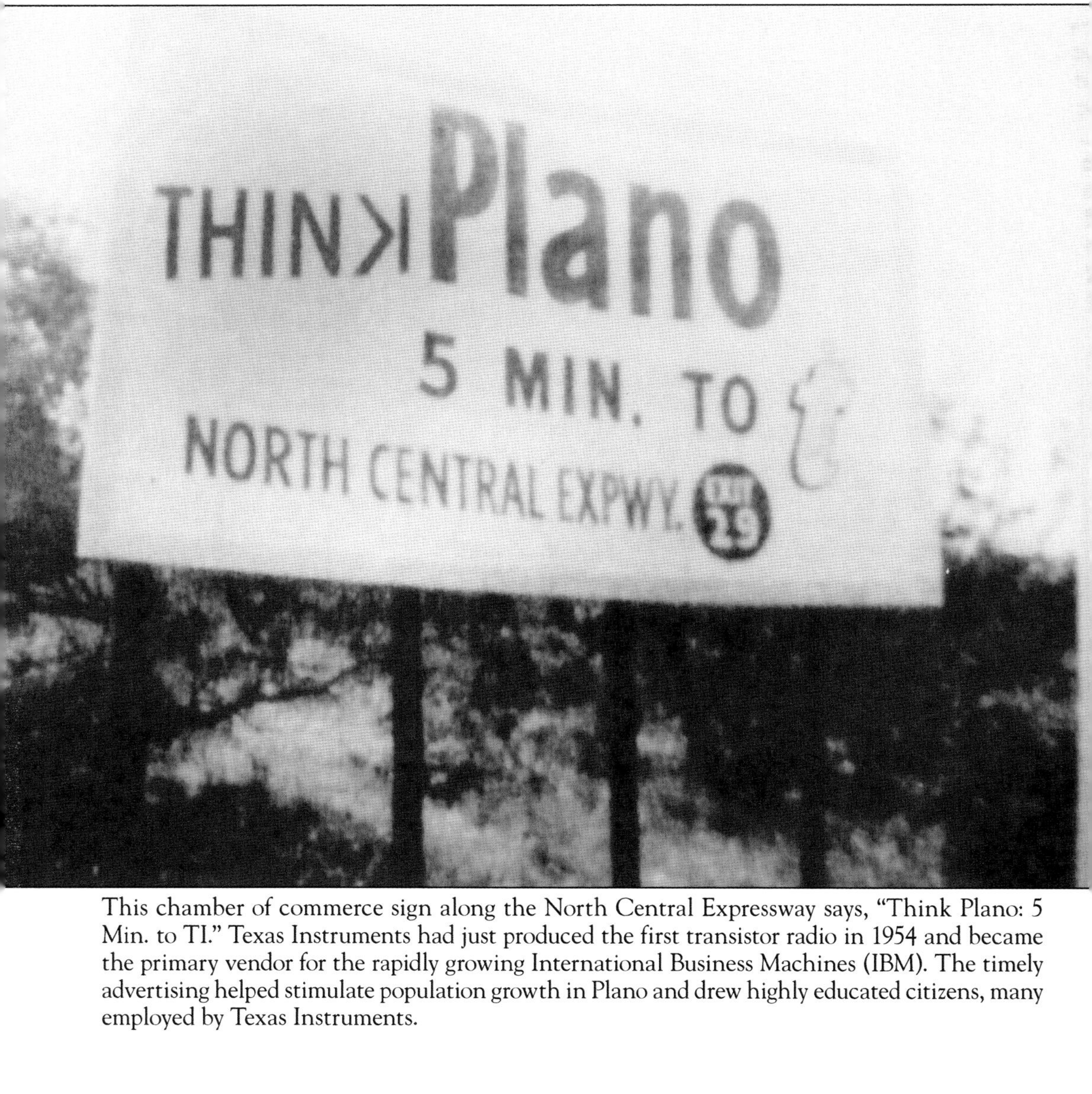

This chamber of commerce sign along the North Central Expressway says, "Think Plano: 5 Min. to TI." Texas Instruments had just produced the first transistor radio in 1954 and became the primary vendor for the rapidly growing International Business Machines (IBM). The timely advertising helped stimulate population growth in Plano and drew highly educated citizens, many employed by Texas Instruments.

Five

MID-CENTURY BOOM LEADS TO PRESERVATION

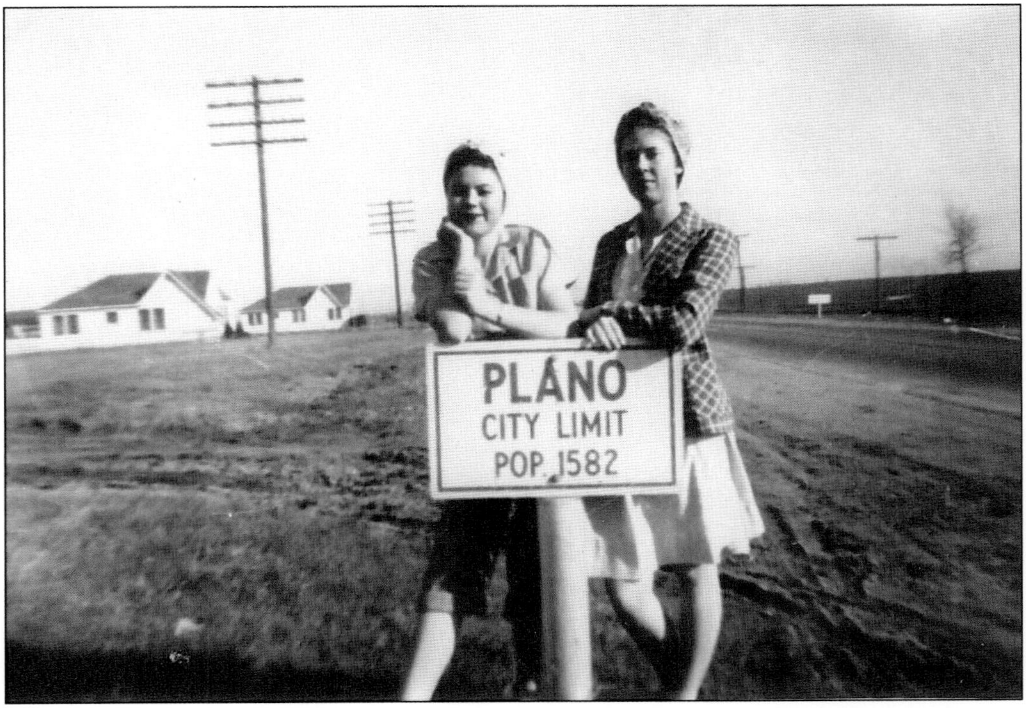

By mid-century, downtown Plano had survived as a relatively viable commercial area with a healthy trade. The same families owned some businesses for several generations. With the improvements to North Central Expressway and the return of soldiers from World War II, the 1940s population of 1,582 was about to explode. The city limits spread from the original crossroads and the streets were renamed. Peggy Mitchell recalls snapping this picture and going "uptown" for ice cream. (Courtesy of Peggy Mitchell.)

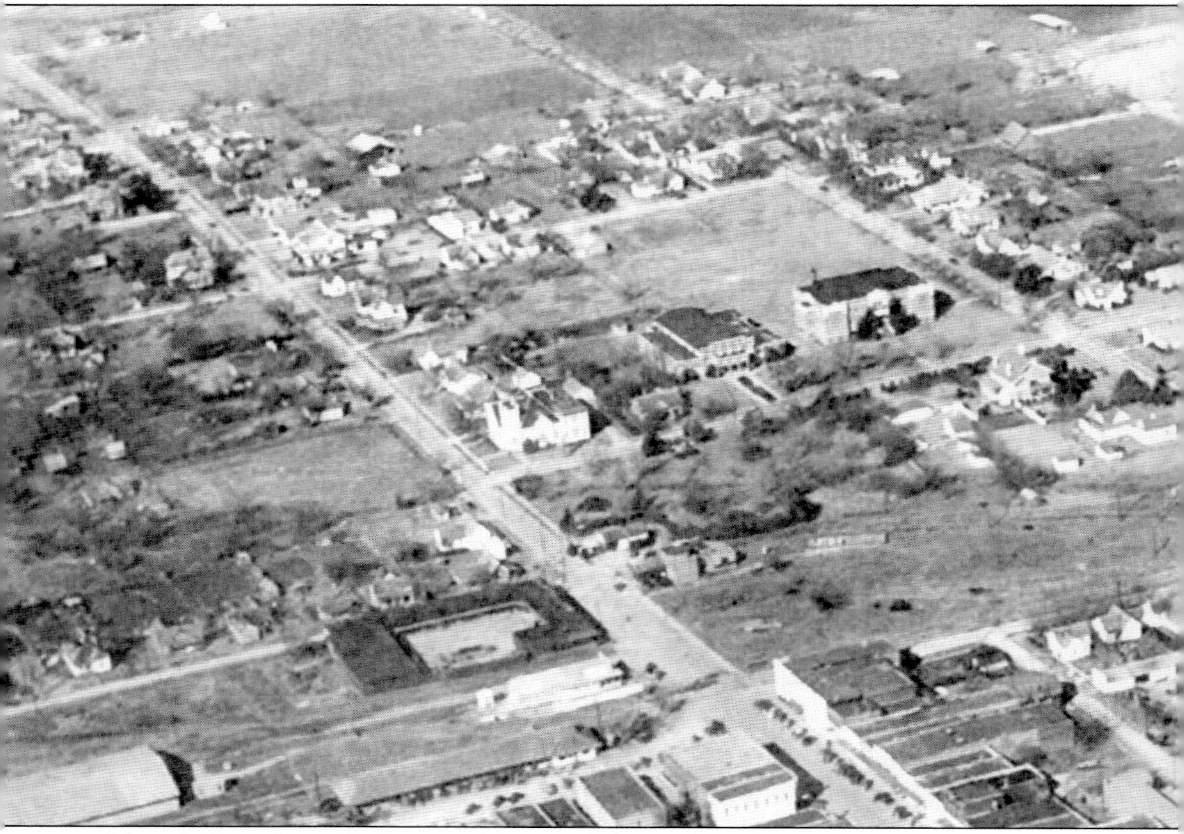

This 1946 aerial view looking northwestward along Fifteenth Street shows a busy downtown in the bottom right, the old H&TC Railway depot—by then an implement store—is in the bottom center, and First Christian Church, the gymnasium, and Plano High School are all on the same present site, with surrounding homes. Haggard Park, in the bottom right, known as the ugliest spot in Plano in 1921, had been a ravine bordering the Interurban tracks. According to the early Lions Club that sought to beautify the eyesore, it had divided the "pretty homes on the commanding eminence of west Plano, from the business section and the pretty homes of the eastern city. It marred an otherwise inviting and attractive town site that everyone passes going from their homes to places of business, worship, entertainment, and school." By 1946, Haggard Park welcomed residents and visitors to Plano's quaint business district. (Courtesy of the City of Plano.)

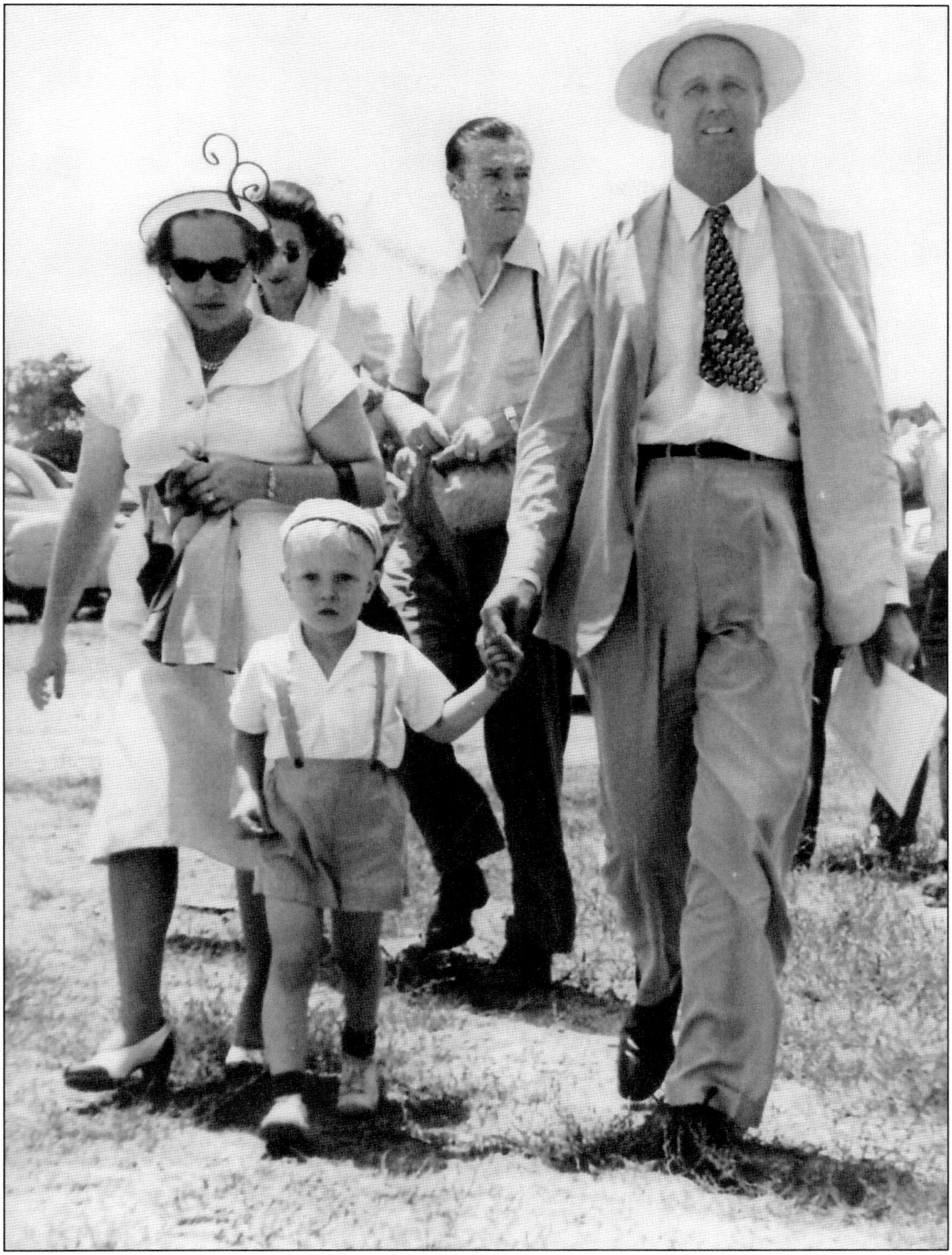

The postwar era brought an influx of young families looking for affordable homes and good schools still close enough to Dallas to drive to work. Reflecting on this childhood picture, Randy Brodhead recalled that his parents were relative newcomers to Plano in the 1950s, but they immediately became active in the community, opening the first after-factory air-conditioning shop for automobiles in downtown Plano. The Brodheads also ran the North Dallas Airport near present-day Legacy Drive and Custer Parkway as Randy grew up in the family home on K Avenue near downtown. (Courtesy of Randy Brodhead.)

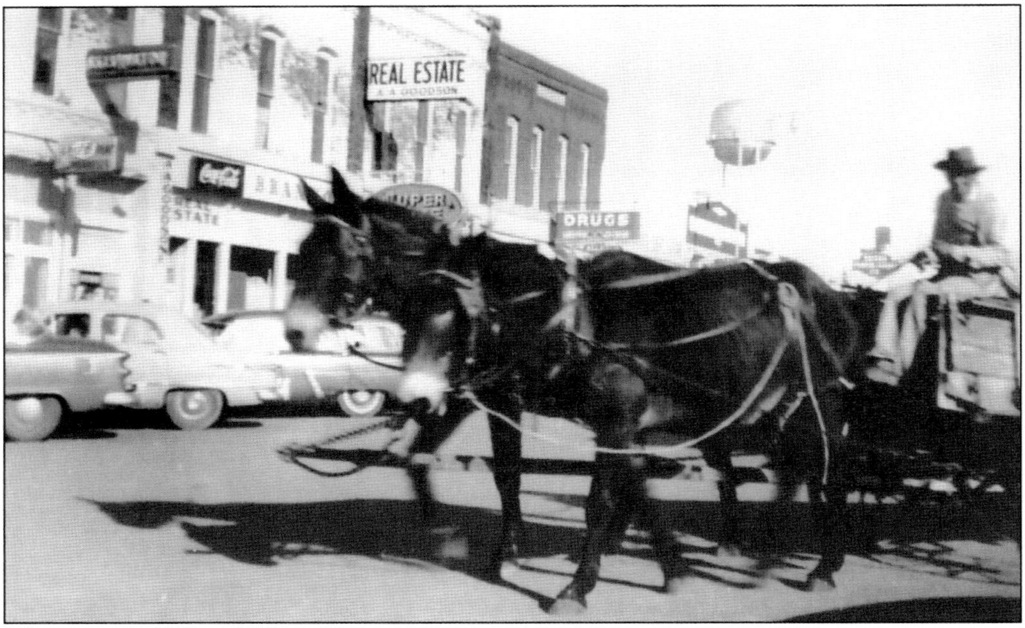

Old Settlers' Day parades still took place downtown in the 1950s. Peggy Mitchell snapped the photograph above as the mule team followed the parade leaders through town. Everyone gathered in the park to reunite and share picnic lunches. The community still had the close-knit feeling of a farming community. The Old Settlers continue to reunite today at the Haggard Party Barn. Efforts to revive heritage days downtown are being led by C.S. Haggard's descendants and other volunteers. Below, another snapshot in the 1960s is from the same vantage point, showing that not much changed downtown for decades, except for the names of the businesses, the introduction of cars, and colorful floats. (Above, courtesy of Peggy Mitchell; below, courtesy of Rodney Haggard.)

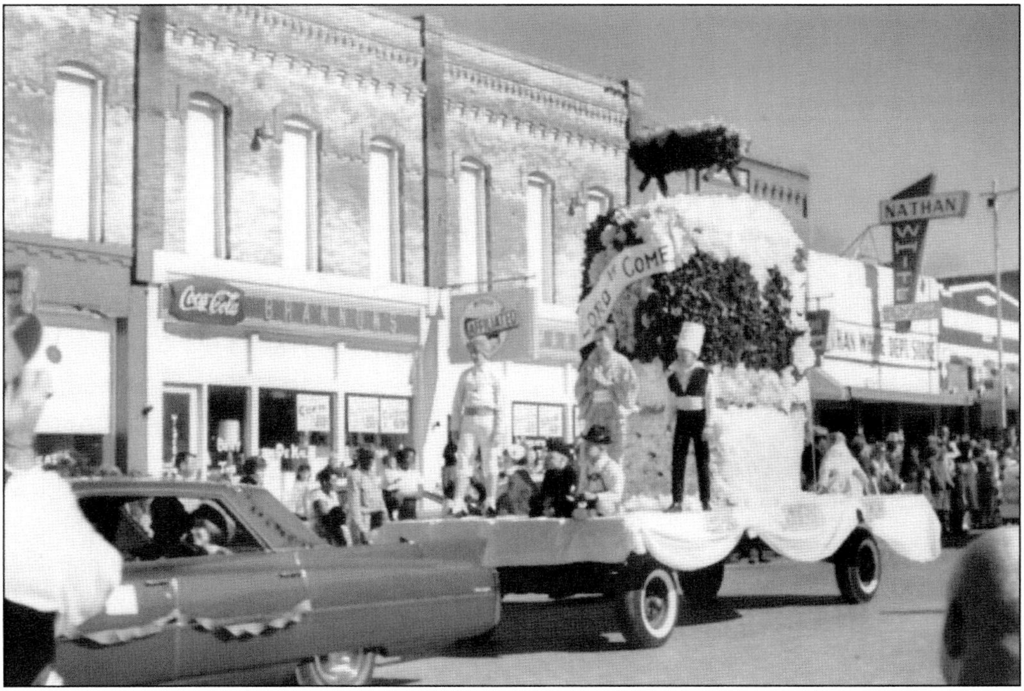

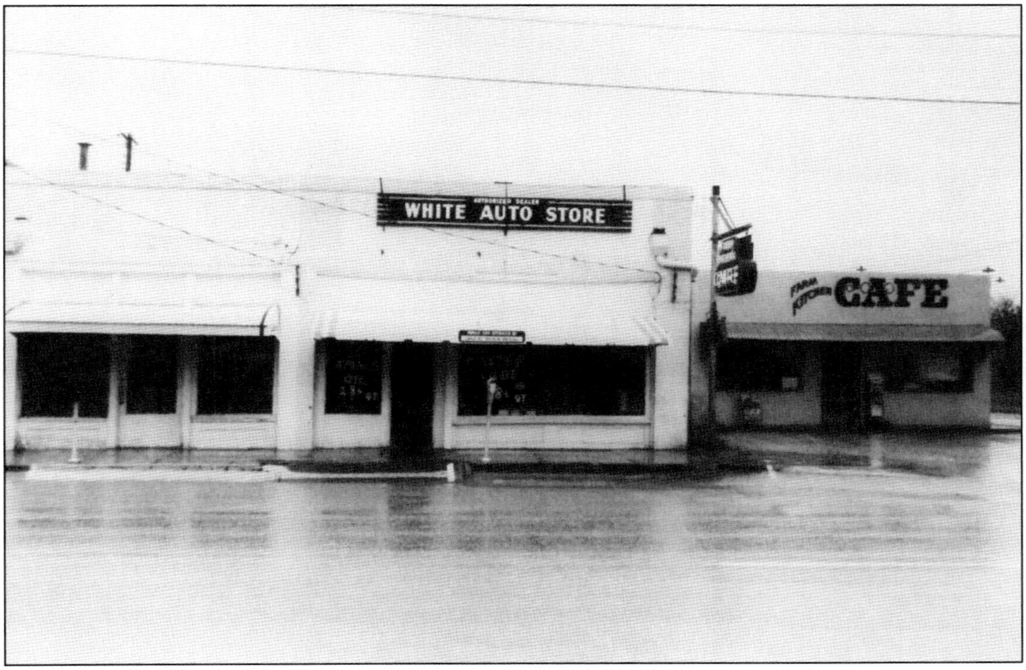

There were several grocery stores in the area well into the 20th century, and locally owned mom-and-pop stores still occupied most of the buildings. With the advent of the automobile, more auto-related businesses sprang up around downtown and stores offering auto supplies and repair services became popular. This automobile is parked between two tractors at Christie's on the northwest corner of K Avenue and Fifteenth Place downtown in the 1960s. (Below, courtesy of Rodney Haggard.)

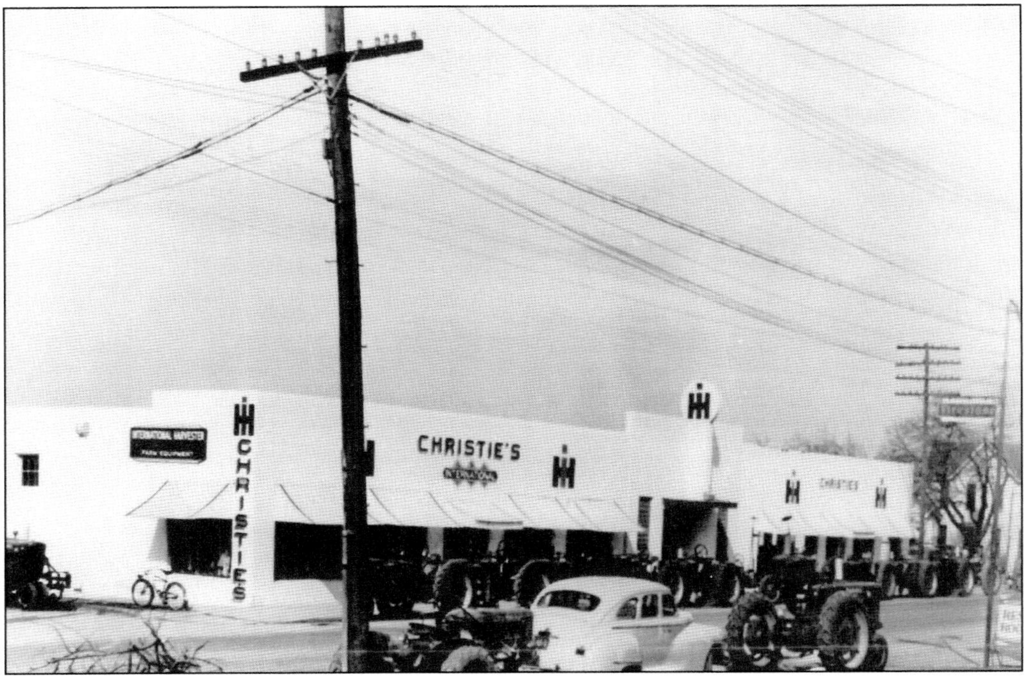

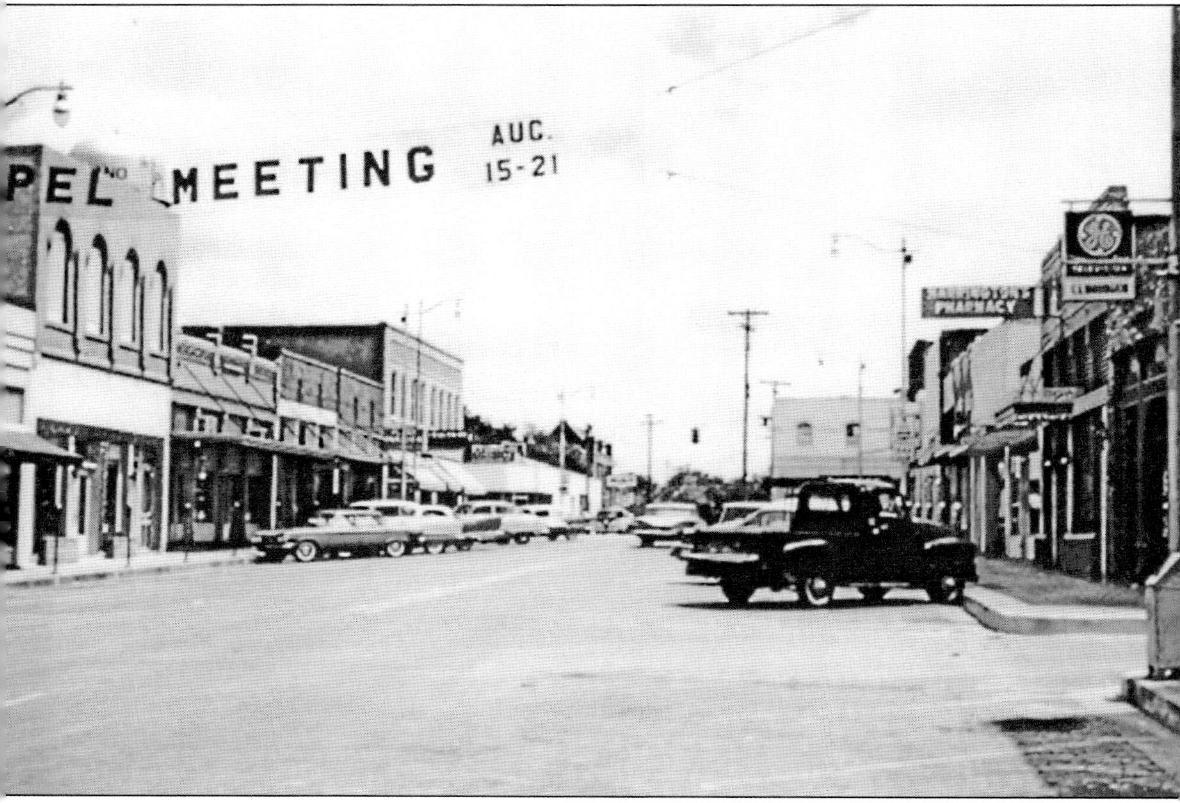

In this 1960 view, the building facades remained virtually as they had been for over half a century after the last destructive fires. But by the late 1960s, Plano, which had been a small town surrounded by rich farmland, was being altered by development from the south. The population grew from 1,582 in the 1940s to 3,695 in 1960. In 1968, the Plano North Shopping Center opened just a few blocks north of downtown on K Avenue, bringing grocery, drug, and variety stores—downtown's first real competition. The downtown grocery store went out of business and Fifteenth Street went through vacancies and turmoil. It was no longer the place to shop, but it was still home to parades, holiday events, and the city's 1973 centennial celebration. Hayden Mitchell recalled that at age 14 he heeded the city's call for town kids to clean the old brick street for the big celebration. Flooded with $600 in coins and soap detergent, the kids got in with scrub brushes to clean the streets and pocket all the coins they could find. The city worked diligently to retain its historical flavor while keeping up with the growth before its adoption of the Historic Landmark Preservation Ordinance in 1979. (Photograph by Don Lair.)

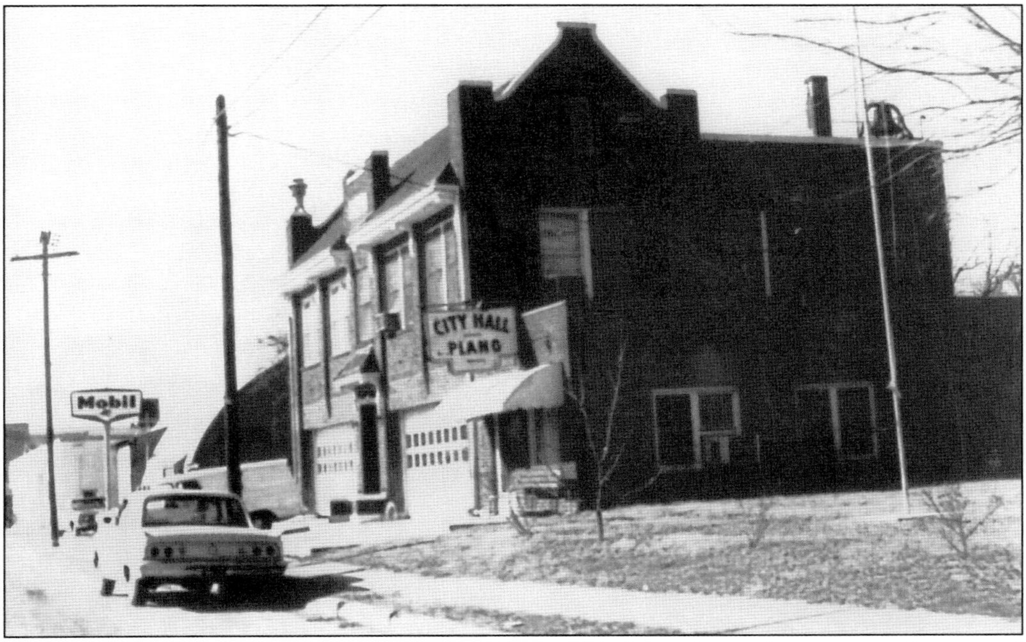

From the time the Plano was incorporated in 1873 until 1957, the law enforcement staff consisted of one city marshal appointed by the mayor and city council and one night watchman. The Plano Police Department was organized in 1957. The mayor received a portion of the fines imposed for traffic violations and misdemeanor cases until 1959, when Mayor David McCall Jr. secured an ordinance creating the first judge who was paid on a salary basis. In 1961, Plano voters adopted a home-rule city charter with greater freedom to govern its activities. In 1965, the police and fire stations were housed in the same building on Fifteenth Street east of K Avenue. (Below, courtesy of Rodney Haggard.)

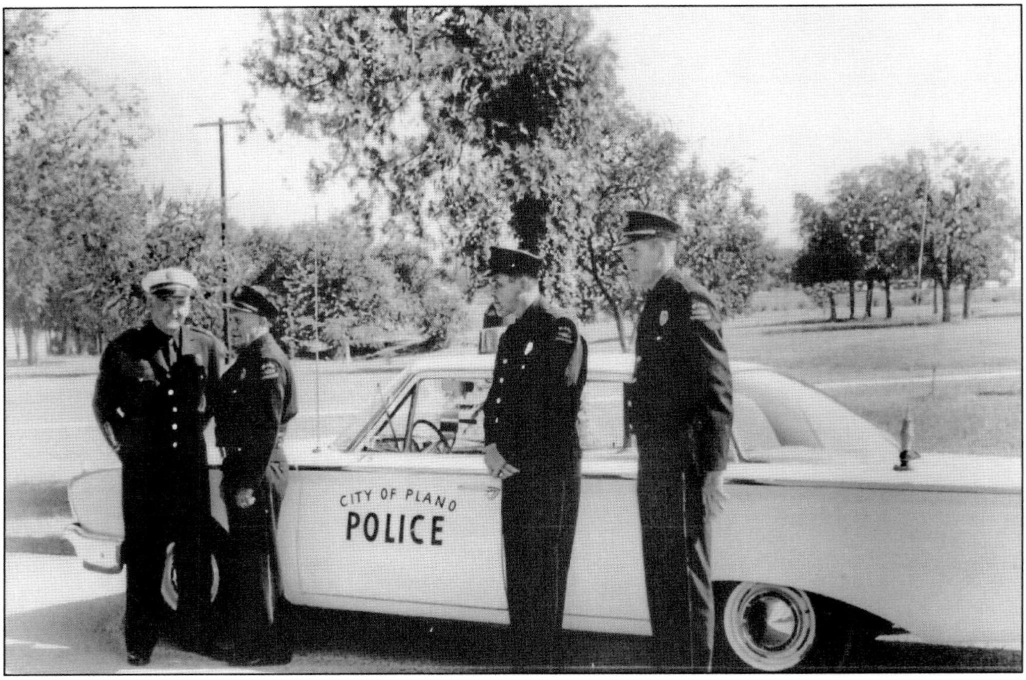

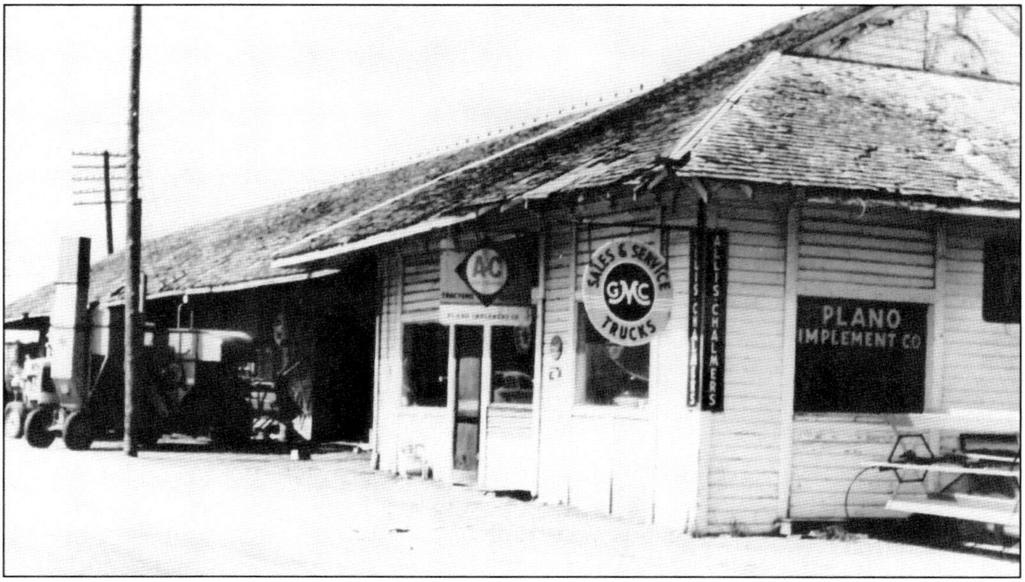

Throughout the early years, Plano lost a great deal of its architectural and historical legacy because of deterioration. The defunct railroads left buildings adapted into implement stores and lawnmower repair shops, but demolition of two railroad depots robbed Plano of important history, which had enabled the town's survival. Failed efforts to save these and other major landmarks led the city council to appoint a seven-member Historical Landmark Committee to safeguard Plano's historic and cultural landmarks. The city sought to enhance the attractions to visitors in order to stimulate business and strengthen the economy. (Courtesy of Rodney Haggard.)

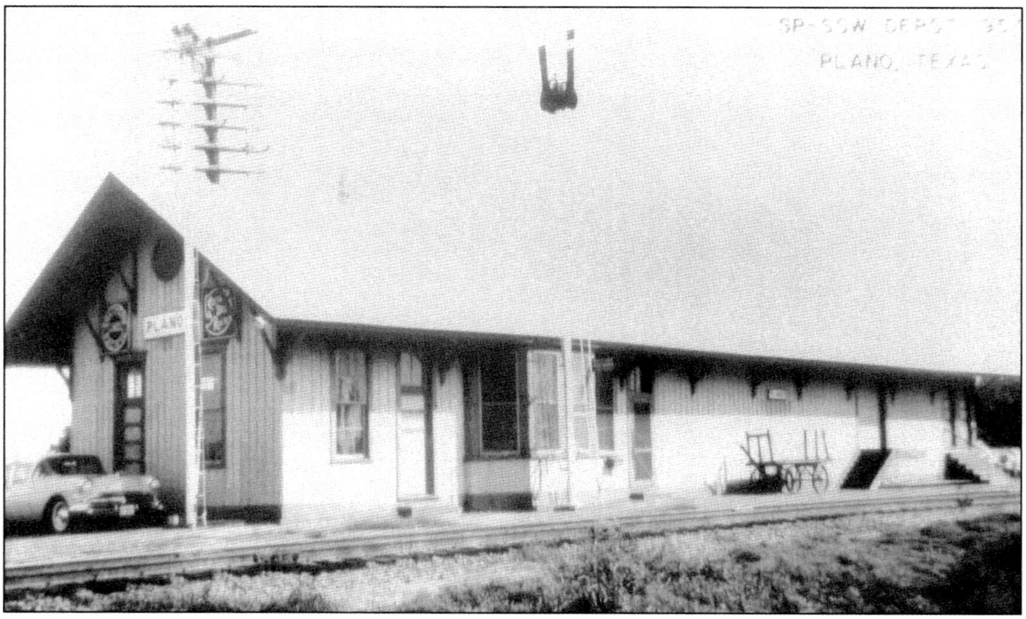

The old Cotton Belt depot located south of town and the H&TC Railroad depot on J Place shown here were landmarks lost in the path of progress. Other historic structures were threatened by road construction, high property values, and dilapidation. Several owners offered to donate threatened structures to a designated site; however, these offers were refused because of the lack of funding for restoration and maintenance.

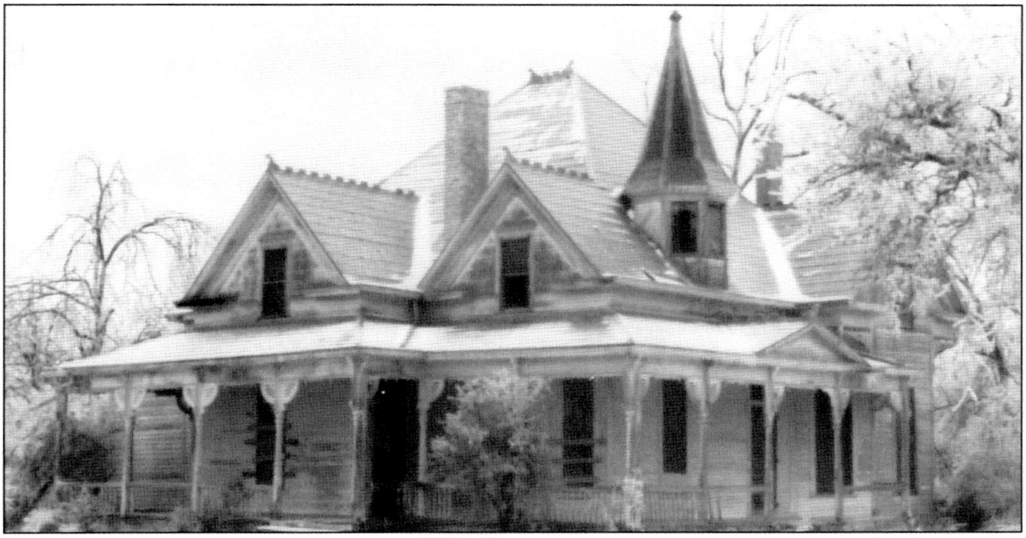

The George House, built in Plano in 1900 by D.C. George as a wedding present for his wife, had fallen into disrepair and was threatened with demolition when the city built the new Municipal Center in the 1980s. Efforts to save the old house resulted in its move to Old City Park in Dallas. The Queen Anne–style house, featuring bay windows, a turret, and jigsaw trim, was popular in both middle-class and upper-class 1900-era homes. Innovations such as electric light fixtures, linoleum floors, a cast-iron cook stove, and a metal roof indicate the new level of comfort available in Plano homes in the early 1900s. Below, the Wetsel house was another structure in the path of progress when the municipal center was built. It was moved to Mitchell property on Sixteenth Street to avoid demolition. In 2010, preservation efforts led by Clint Haggard again saved the 100-year-old building. Pictured from left to right are Doy Ballard, Richard Lack (Eco Roofing), Janice Cline, Peggy Mitchell, Clint Haggard, and Dorothy Mitchell Johnston.

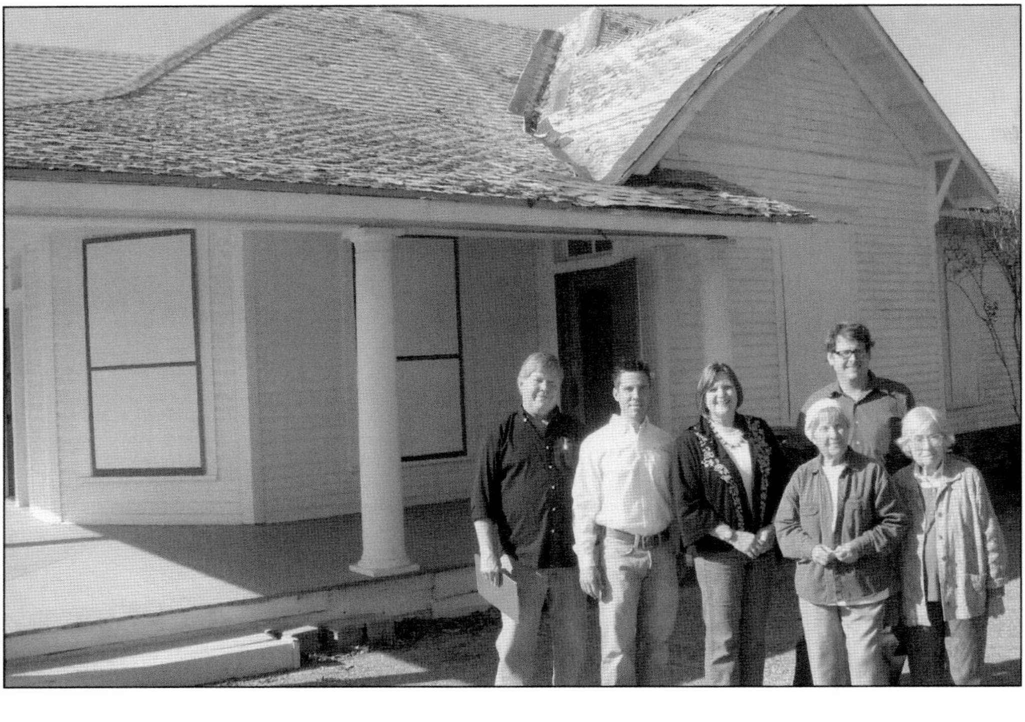

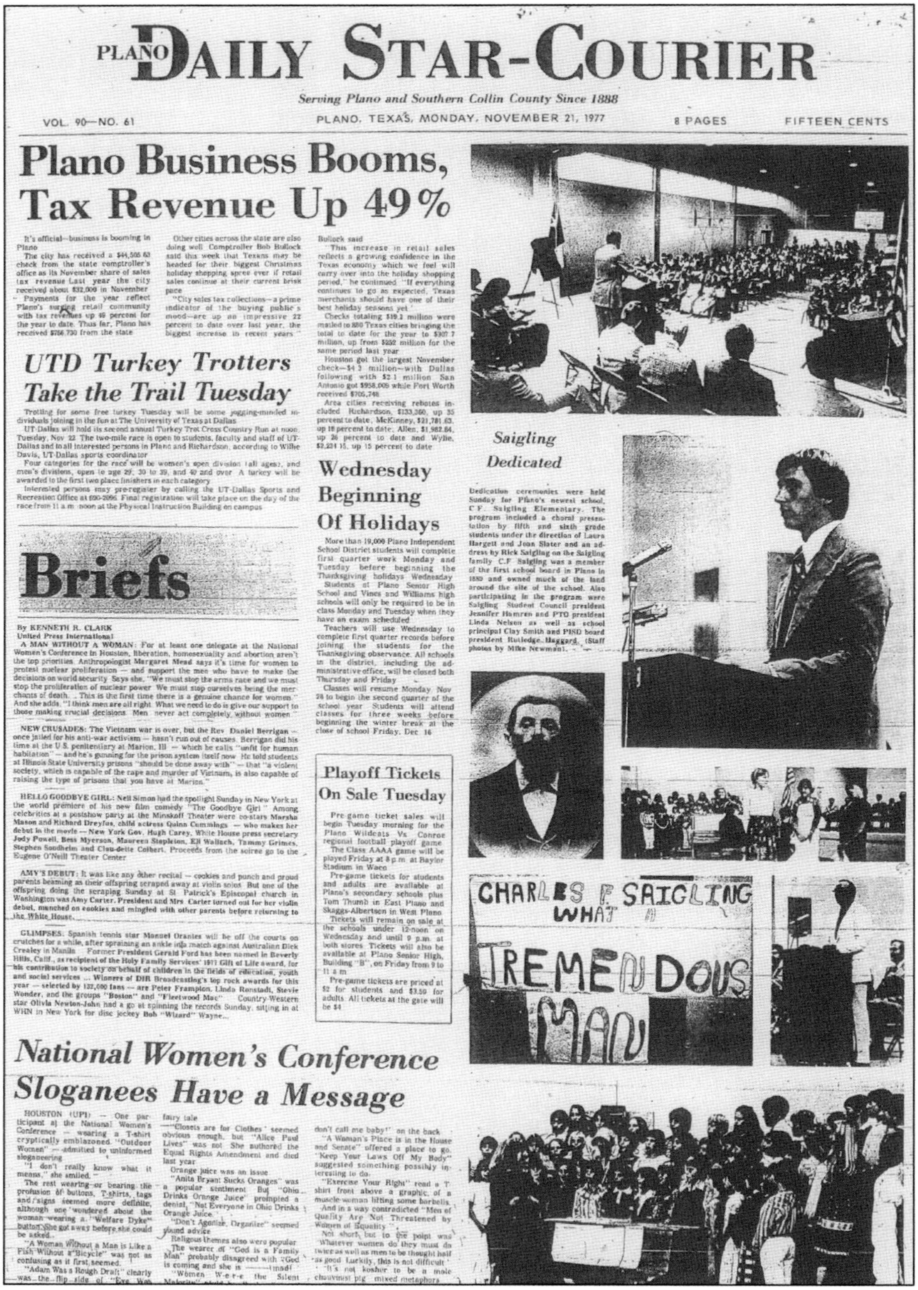

PLANO DAILY STAR-COURIER

Serving Plano and Southern Collin County Since 1888

VOL. 90—NO. 61 | PLANO, TEXAS, MONDAY, NOVEMBER 21, 1977 | 8 PAGES | FIFTEEN CENTS

Plano Business Booms, Tax Revenue Up 49%

It's official—business is booming in Plano

The city has received a $44,505.63 check from the state comptroller's office as its November share of sales tax revenue Last year the city received about $32,000 in November

Payments for the year reflect Plano's surging retail community with tax revenues up 49 percent for the year to date. Thus far, Plano has received $766,730 from the state

Other cities across the state are also doing well Comptroller Bob Bullock said this week that Texans may be headed for their biggest Christmas holiday shopping spree ever if retail sales continue at their current brisk pace

"City sales tax collections—a prime indicator of the buying public's mood—are up an impressive 22 percent to date over last year, the biggest increase in recent years" Bullock said

"This increase in retail sales reflects a growing confidence in the Texas economy which we feel will carry over into the holiday shopping period," he continued "If everything continues to go as expected, Texas merchants should have one of their best holiday seasons yet"

Checks totaling $19.1 million were mailed to 880 Texas cities bringing the total to date for the year to $307.7 million, up from $252 million for the same period last year

Houston got the largest November check—$4.3 million—with Dallas following with $2.1 million San Antonio got $958,009 while Fort Worth received $705,748

Area cities receiving rebates included Richardson, $133,360, up 35 percent to date, McKinney, $21,781.63, up 18 percent to date, Allen, $1,982.84, up 26 percent to date and Wylie, $2,234.15, up 15 percent to date

UTD Turkey Trotters Take the Trail Tuesday

Trotting for some free turkey Tuesday will be some jogging-minded individuals joining in the fun at The University of Texas at Dallas

UT-Dallas will hold its second annual Turkey Trot Cross Country Run at noon Tuesday, Nov 22 The two-mile race is open to students, faculty and staff of UT-Dallas and to all interested persons in Plano and Richardson, according to Willie Davis, UT-Dallas sports coordinator

Four categories for the race will be women's open division (all ages), and men's divisions, open to age 29, 30 to 39, and 40 and over A turkey will be awarded to the first two place finishers in each category

Interested persons may pre-register by calling the UT-Dallas Sports and Recreation Office at 690-2096 Final registration will take place on the day of the race from 11 a.m.-noon at the Physical Instruction Building on campus

Wednesday Beginning Of Holidays

More than 19,000 Plano Independent School District students will complete first quarter work Monday and Tuesday before beginning the Thanksgiving holidays Wednesday

Students at Plano Senior High School and Vines and Williams high schools will only be required to be in class Monday and Tuesday when they have an exam scheduled

Teachers will use Wednesday to complete first quarter records before joining the students for the Thanksgiving observance. All schools in the district, including the administrative office, will be closed both Thursday and Friday

Classes will resume Monday Nov 28 to begin the second quarter of the school year Students will attend classes for three weeks before beginning the winter break at the close of school Friday, Dec 16

Saigling Dedicated

Dedication ceremonies were held Sunday for Plano's newest school, C.F. Saigling Elementary. The program included a choral presentation by fifth and sixth grade students under the direction of Laura Hargett and Joan Slater and an address by Rick Saigling on the Saigling family C.F Saigling was a member of the first school board in Plano in 1880 and owned much of the land around the site of the school. Also participating in the program were Saigling Student Council president Jennifer Hamren and PTO president Linda Nelson as well as school principal Clay Smith and PISD board president Rutledge Haggard. (Staff photos by Mike Newman).

Briefs

By KENNETH R. CLARK
United Press International

A MAN WITHOUT A WOMAN: For at least one delegate at the National Women's Conference in Houston, liberation, homosexuality and abortion aren't the top priorities Anthropologist Margaret Mead says it's time for women to protest nuclear proliferation — and support the men who have to make the decisions on world security Says she, "We must stop the arms race and we must stop the proliferation of nuclear power We must stop ourselves being the merchants of death. .. This is the first time there is a genuine chance for women." And she adds, "I think men are all right What we need to do is give our support to those making crucial decisions Men never act completely without women"

NEW CRUSADES: The Vietnam war is over, but the Rev Daniel Berrigan — once jailed for his anti-war activism — hasn't run out of causes Berrigan did his time at the U.S. penitentiary at Marion, Ill — which he calls "unfit for human habitation" — and he's gunning for the prison system itself now He told students at Illinois State University prisons "should be done away with" — that "a violent society, which is capable of the rape and murder of Vietnam, is also capable of raising the type of prisons that you have at Marion."

HELLO GOODBYE GIRL: Neil Simon had the spotlight Sunday in New York at the world premiere of his new film comedy "The Goodbye Girl" Among celebrities at a postshow party at the Minskoff Theater were co-stars Marsha Mason and Richard Dreyfus, child actress Quinn Cummings — who makes her debut in the movie — New York Gov. Hugh Carey, White House press secretary Jody Powell, Bess Myerson, Maureen Stapleton, Eli Wallach, Tammy Grimes, Stephen Sondheim and Clau-dette Colbert. Proceeds from the soiree go to the Eugene O'Neill Theater Center

AMY'S DEBUT: It was like any other recital — cookies and punch and proud parents beaming as their offspring scraped away at violin solos But one of the offspring doing the scraping Sunday at St Patrick's Episcopal church in Washington was Amy Carter. President and Mrs Carter turned out for her violin debut, munched on cookies and mingled with other parents before returning to the White House.

GLIMPSES: Spanish tennis star Manuel Orantes will be off the courts on crutches for a while, after spraining an ankle in a match against Australian Dick Crealey in Manila Former President Gerald Ford has been named in Beverly Hills, Calif., as recipient of the Holy Family Services' 1977 Gift of Life award, for his contribution to society on behalf of children in the fields of education, youth and social services ... Winners of DIR Broadcasting's top rock awards for this year — selected by 132,000 fans — are Peter Frampton, Linda Ronstadt, Stevie Wonder, and the groups "Boston" and "Fleetwood Mac" Country-Western star Olivia Newton-John had a go at spinning the records Sunday, sitting in at WHN in New York for disc jockey Bob "Wizard" Wayne...

Playoff Tickets On Sale Tuesday

Pre-game ticket sales will begin Tuesday morning for the Plano Wildcats Vs Conroe regional football playoff game

The Class AAAA game will be played Friday at 8 p.m. at Baylor Stadium in Waco

Pre-game tickets for students and adults are available at Plano's secondary schools plus Tom Thumb in East Plano and Skaggs-Albertson in West Plano

Tickets will remain on sale at the schools under 12-noon on Wednesday and until 9 p.m. at both stores Tickets will also be available at Plano Senior High, Building "B", on Friday from 9 to 11 a.m

Pre-game tickets are priced at $2 for students and $3.50 for adults All tickets at the gate will be $4

National Women's Conference Sloganees Have a Message

HOUSTON (UPI) — One participant at the National Women's Conference — wearing a T-shirt cryptically emblazoned "Outdoor Women" — admitted to uninformed sloganeering

"I don't really know what it means," she smiled.

The rest wearing or bearing the profusion of buttons, T-shirts, tags and signs seemed more definite, although one wondered about the woman wearing a "Welfare Dyke" button. She got away before she could be asked.

"A Woman Without a Man is Like a Fish Without a Bicycle" was not as confusing as it first seemed.

"Adam Was a Rough Draft" clearly was the flip side of "Eve Was ... fairy tale

—"Closets are for Clothes" seemed obvious enough, but "Alice Paul Lives" was not She authored the Equal Rights Amendment and died last year

Orange juice was an issue

"Anita Bryant Sucks Oranges" was a popular sentiment But "Ohio Drinks Orange Juice" prompted a denial, "Not Everyone in Ohio Drinks Orange Juice."

"Don't Agonize, Organize" seemed sound advice

Religous themes also were popular

The wearer of "God is a Family Man" probably disagreed with "God is coming and she is ——— mad!"

"Women W-e-r-e the Silent Majority" ... don't call me baby!" on the back

"A Woman's Place is in the House and Senate" offered a place to go. "Keep Your Laws Off My Body" suggested something possibly interesting to do.

"Exercise Your Right" read a T-shirt front above a graphic of a muscle-woman lifting some barbells.

And in a way contradicted "Men of Quality Are Not Threatened by Women of Equality".

Not short, but to the point was "Whatever women do they must do twice as well as men to be thought half as good Luckily, this is not difficult"

"It's not kosher to be a male chauvinist pig" mixed metaphors ...

In 1977, the *Plano Daily Star-Courier* front page proclaimed, "Plano Business Boom, Tax Revenue up 49%." A 1970s brochure touted Plano's beautiful homes, modern schools, adequate fire protection, and progressive industries. City fathers were doing yeoman's work, approving new school buildings and preparing the infrastructure for the boom that was underway. Plano was growing by leaps and bounds due in large part to marketing efforts touting the abundance of available land for homes, a desirable school district, and a favorable business climate for corporations to relocate. But most of the growth was on the west side of town, where a new hospital—later Plano Medical Center—was built. Downtown Plano was still a small-town strip of mom-and-pop shops centered on Fifteenth Street and K Avenue. (Courtesy of the City of Plano.)

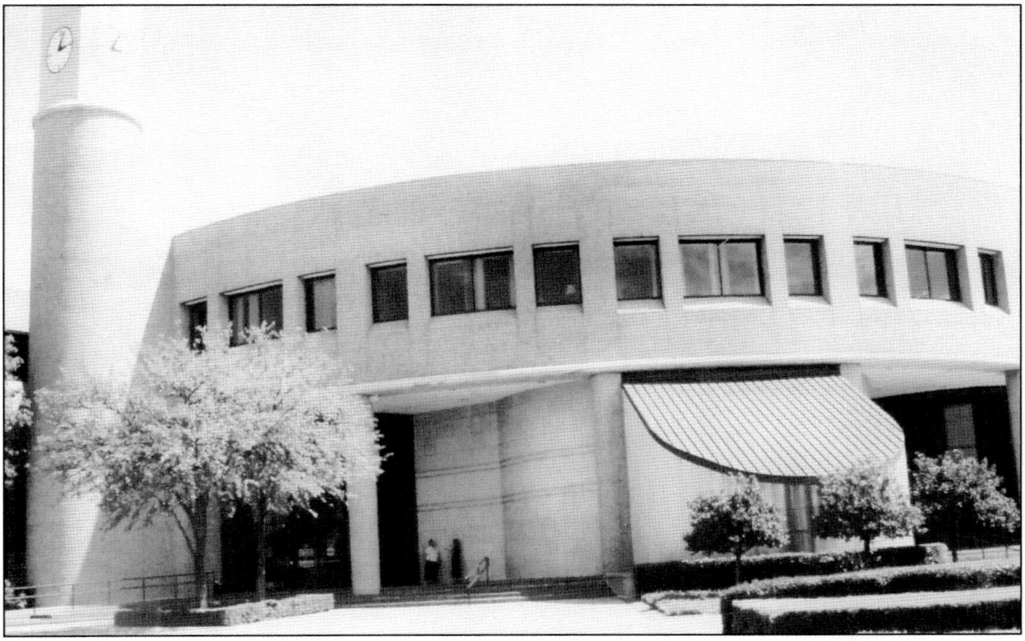

Plano's growth necessitated a new government services buildings. Around 1980, houses were moved and streets were reconfigured to make way for the new municipal center that sits on a high point uptown on K Avenue and Municipal. The new clock tower could be seen for miles. A police station and municipal court building were constructed on Fifteenth Street to keep pace with population growth, punctuating the city's commitment to old Plano's viability as a government and business center. There was growing concern that the downtown area could not maintain its level of activity with shopping centers being developed on the west side of Central Expressway. (Courtesy of the City of Plano.)

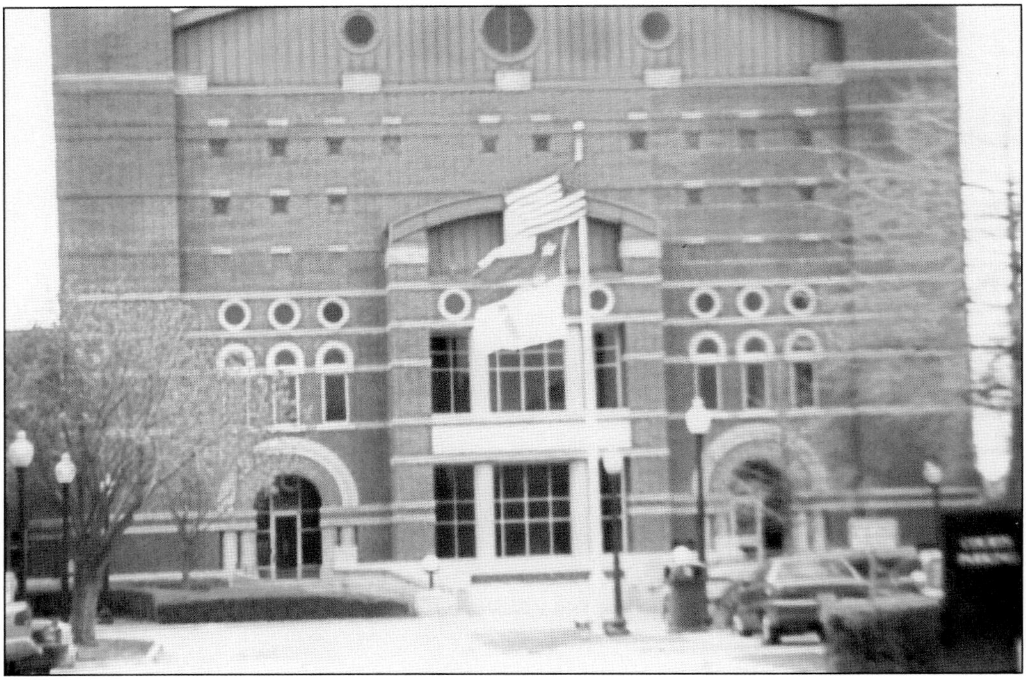

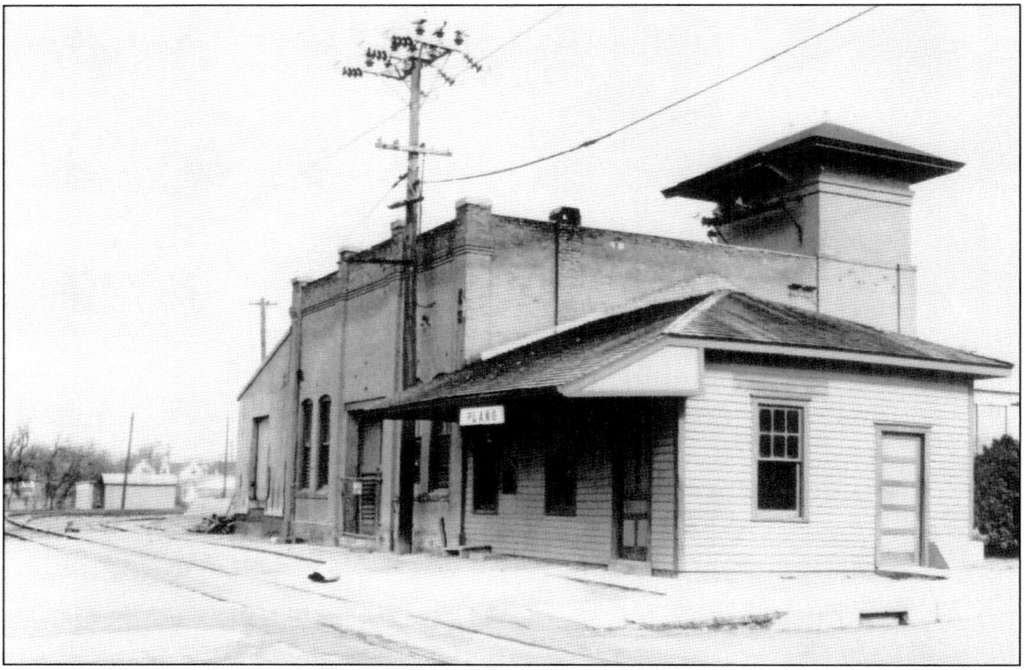

The Interurban Station was restored as the Interurban Electric Railway Museum in the 1990s. The nonprofit Plano Conservancy for Historic Preservation, Inc. runs the museum, which is funded in part by the City of Plano. Haggard Park was expanded to almost five acres to provide needed open space and remove unsightly businesses from downtown and this gazebo was constructed during 1986. (Courtesy of the City of Plano.)

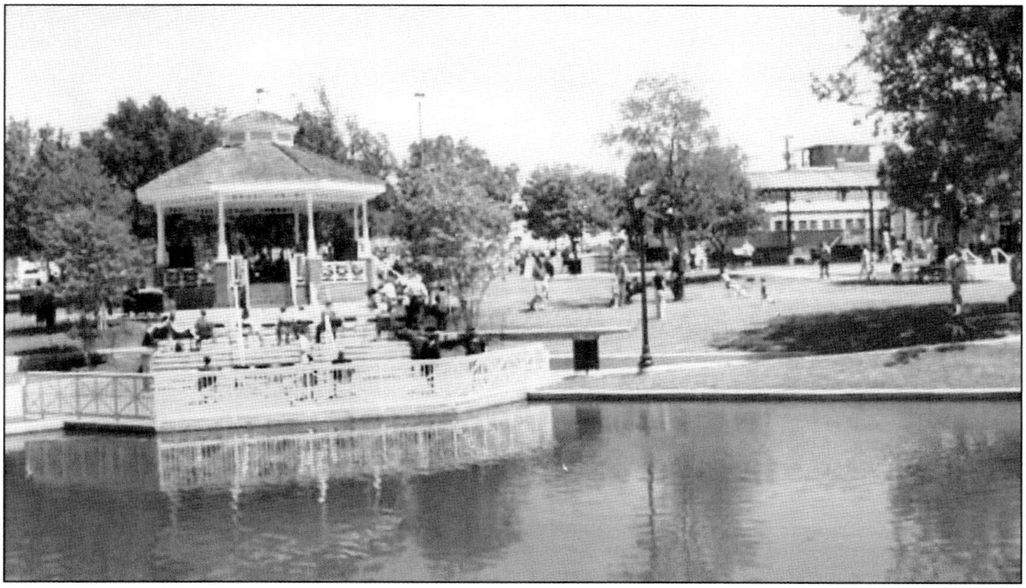

Haggard Park's design complements the historical character of downtown and its surrounding neighborhoods. Once an eyesore, the park has been transformed over the years and is now used for family outings, weddings, and concerts, and is the center of festivals and other community events. Haggard Park integrates downtown with the adjacent neighborhoods into a community and is the city's ceremonial heart.

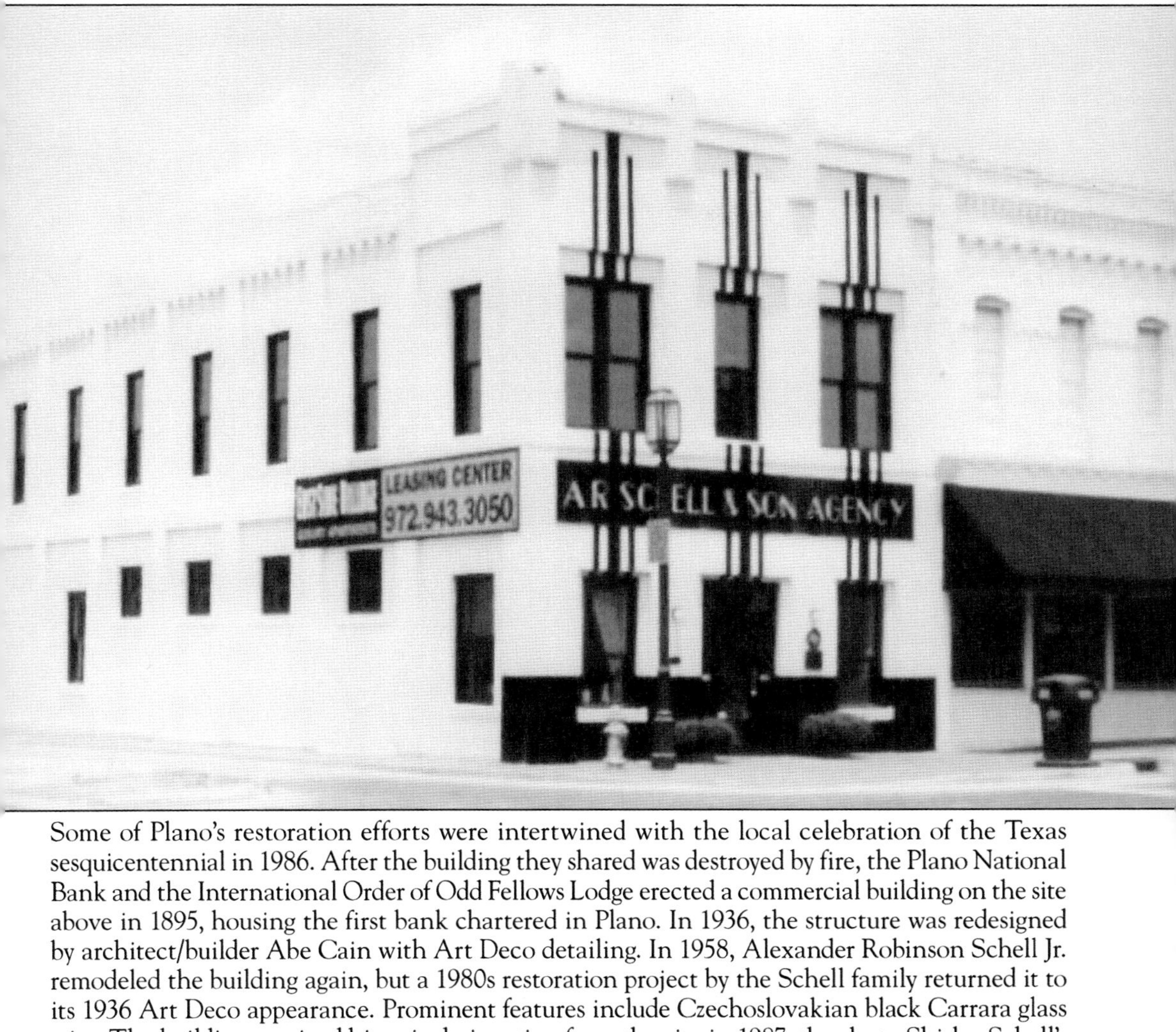

Some of Plano's restoration efforts were intertwined with the local celebration of the Texas sesquicentennial in 1986. After the building they shared was destroyed by fire, the Plano National Bank and the International Order of Odd Fellows Lodge erected a commercial building on the site above in 1895, housing the first bank chartered in Plano. In 1936, the structure was redesigned by architect/builder Abe Cain with Art Deco detailing. In 1958, Alexander Robinson Schell Jr. remodeled the building again, but a 1980s restoration project by the Schell family returned it to its 1936 Art Deco appearance. Prominent features include Czechoslovakian black Carrara glass trim. The building received historic designation from the city in 1987, thanks to Shirley Schell's splendid documentation of not only the building, but of Plano and the Schell and Schimelpfenig families who have served Plano for more than 100 years. The author interviewed A.R. Schell III in the bank vault turned conference room shortly before Schell's death in January 2010.

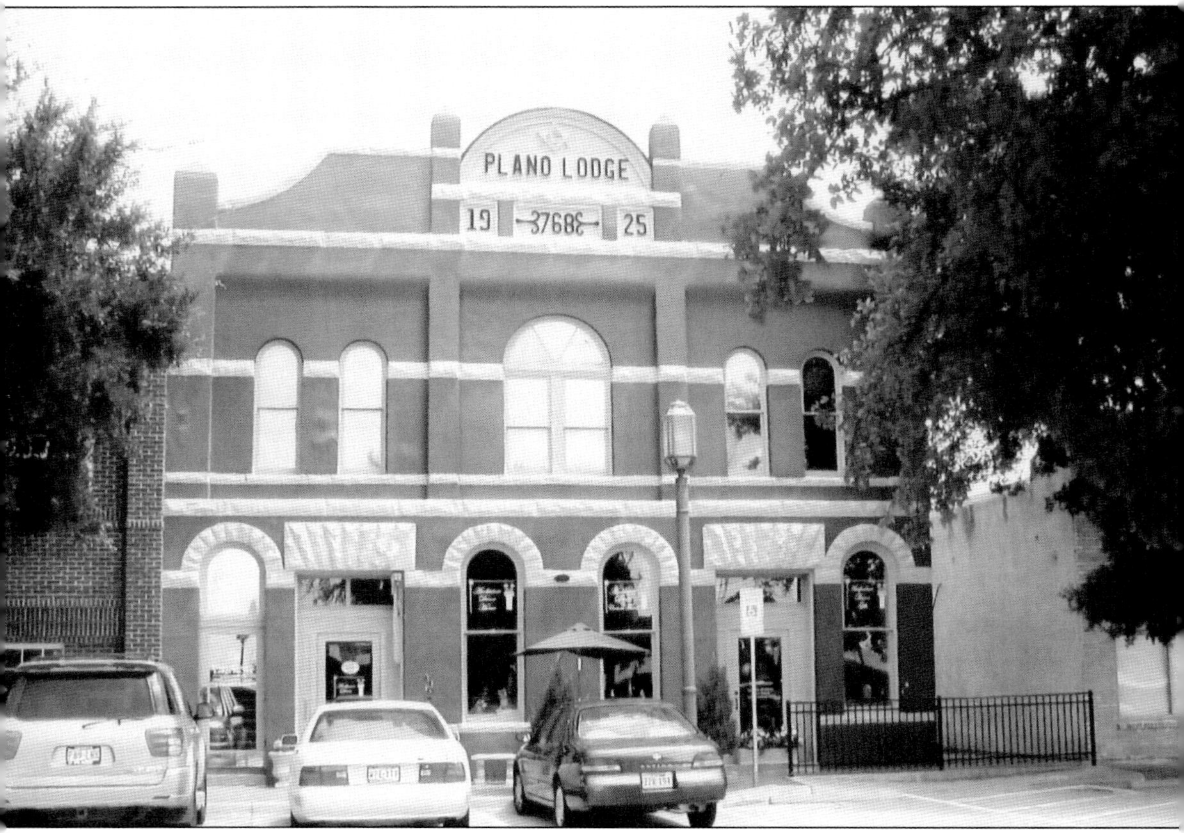

Plano Lodge No. 768 was also designated as a historic landmark in 1987 by the city. The two-story structure built in 1898 was altered with stucco covering in 1925 and has been used by the Masons ever since. It was originally built as the Moore House, a hotel catering to railroad travelers. In the 1986 Preservation Plan Update, a survey was completed of all pre-1945 buildings and sites for consideration as designated city historic landmarks. Criteria for local designation include a well-documented history of at least 40 years, and architectural integrity of its period. This building is an example of early 1900s renovation that has endured.

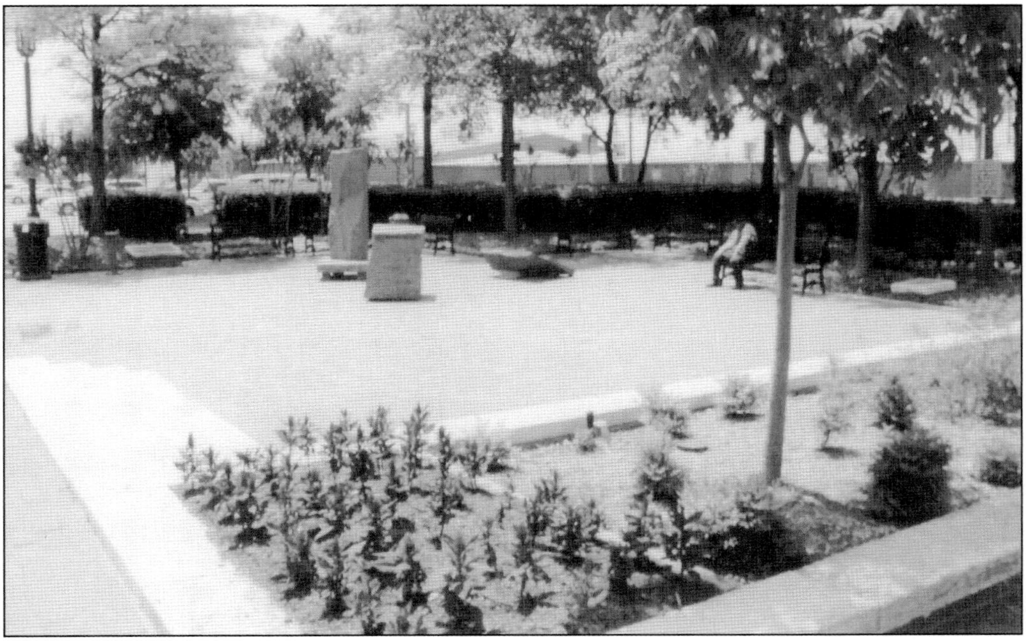

In preparation for the Texas sesquicentennial celebration in 1986, the city restored its original brick streets, installed brick sidewalks, and added ornamental streetlights and benches to enhance the historical charm of downtown. A plaza also created a peaceful retreat at the west end of downtown next to the railroad crossing at Fifteenth Street. The plaza was the centerpiece of Plano's celebration of the sesquicentennial, featuring an ornamental clock, a cascading water fountain to mask street noise, and landscaping and art sculptures to increase the attractiveness of downtown. The plaza was later named McCall Plaza in memory of David B. McCall Jr., Plano mayor, PISD principal, and civic leader.

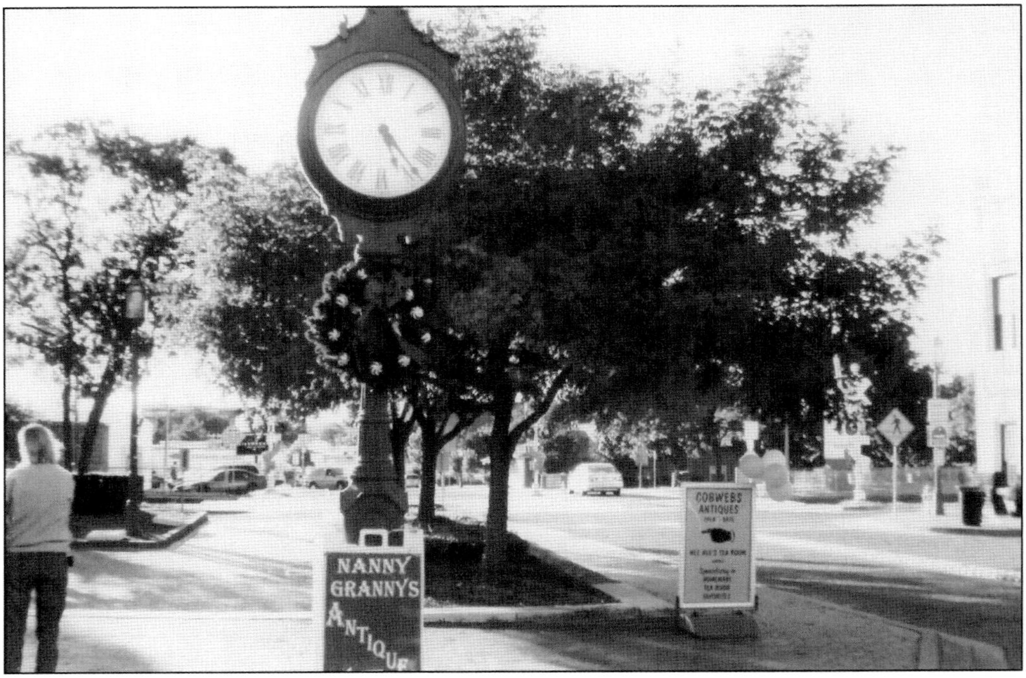

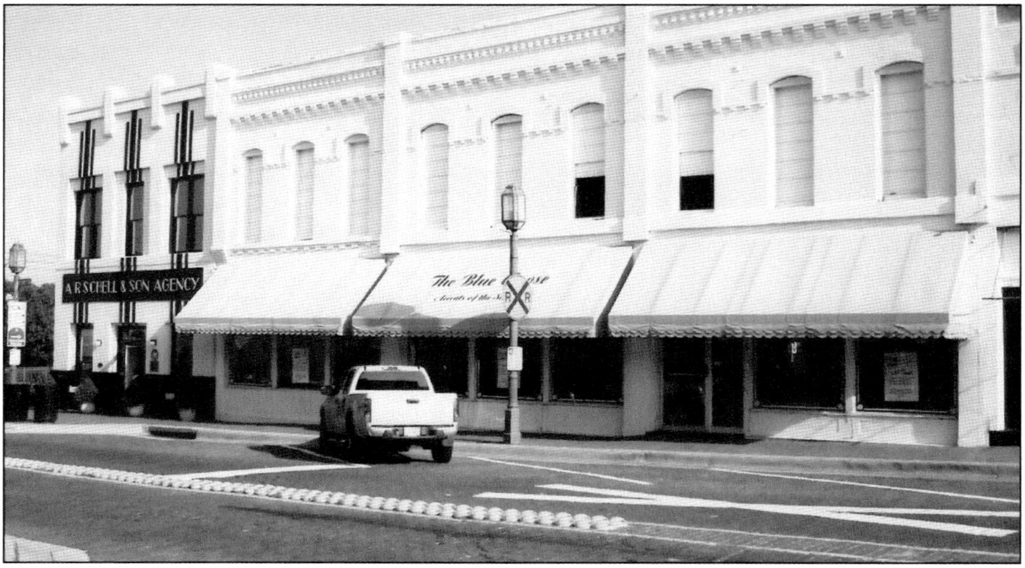

The original business district retained its historical flavor while attracting a unique mix of shops as more buildings were restored in the 1990s. An example is the Spillman Building, built in 1898, which had been completely destroyed in the fire of 1895. D.C. George Hardware, Brannon's Grocery, and the Market Sampler were located here over the years and Beverly and Jim Hiegel's Blue Goose Market opened here in 1996.

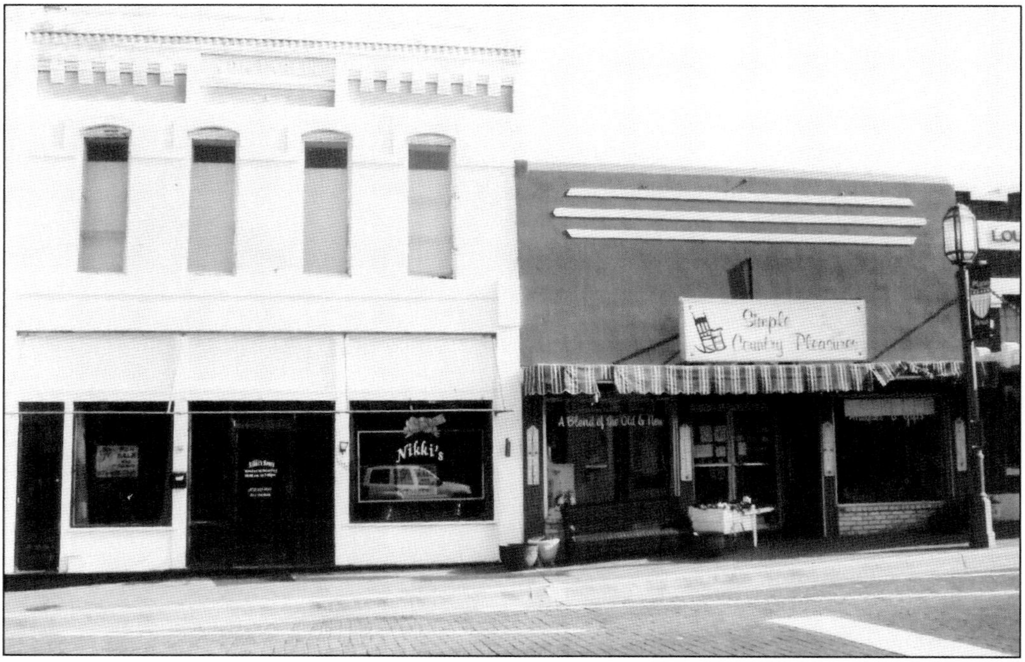

East of the Spillman Building is the two-story W.D.M. McFarlin building, which housed a grocery store as early as 1885. This building was also home to Carpenter Drugstore and later the Allen Brothers Drug Store for many years. Next-door, the Mathews Department Store occupied the building at 1013 Fifteenth Street for 52 years; followed by Federated Stores and Nathan White's Department Store in the mid-1900s. Later, Simple Country Pleasures sold antiques until Sharon Lloyd purchased the building in 2008 and began operating Teacup Antiques.

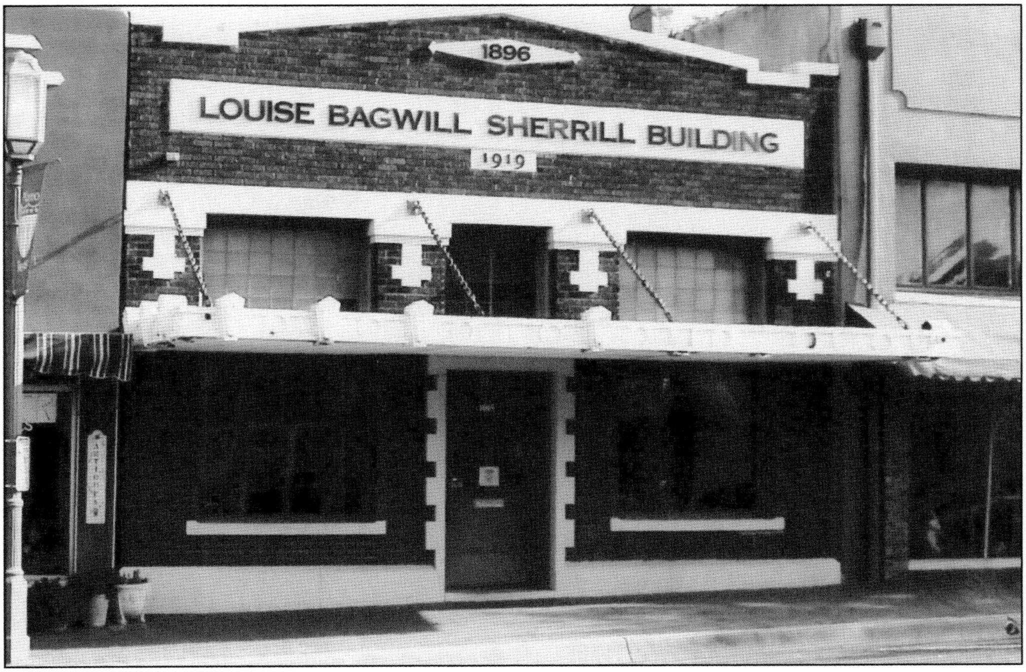

Former mayor Jeran Akers once owned the Louise Bagwill Sherrill Building, named for the family that ran the *Plano Star-Courier* for three generations. Edna Houston, the daughter of Plano's Olney Davis and widow of Sam Houston's grandson, Harry H. Houston, owned this former bank building in the late 1930s. The site was originally the Farmers and Merchants Bank, and then the First National Bank of Plano. It is an excellent example of early 20th century commercial architecture restored to its original grandeur.

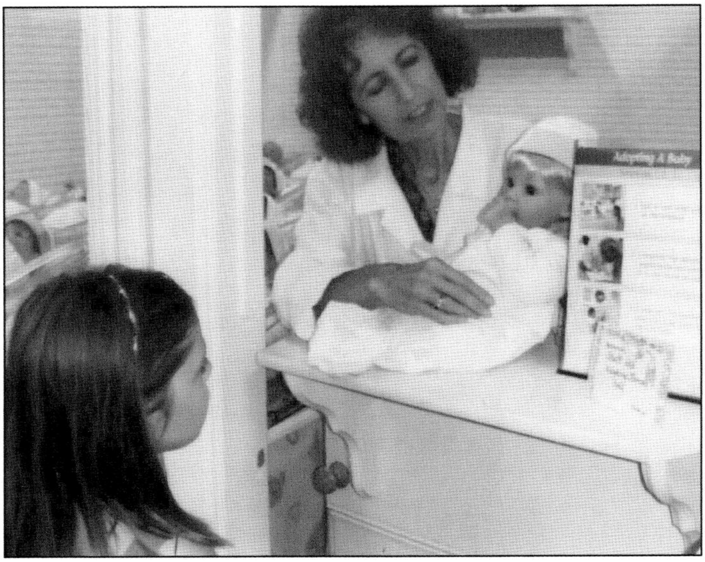

This old-timey dry goods store was home to Fred Schimelpfeing's store, Bestway Sportswear, and Lorch Manufacturing in the mid-1900s. It is one of the largest stores in old Plano, with its 5,600 square feet now filled with Nooks N Krannies gifts and collectibles. In the back, Into My Garden Tearoom offers luncheon specials. The shop features a lifelike doll nursery where, in 2008, Mary Jo Montgomery brought new life to Skylar Belloni's Heritage Day in grand old Plano.

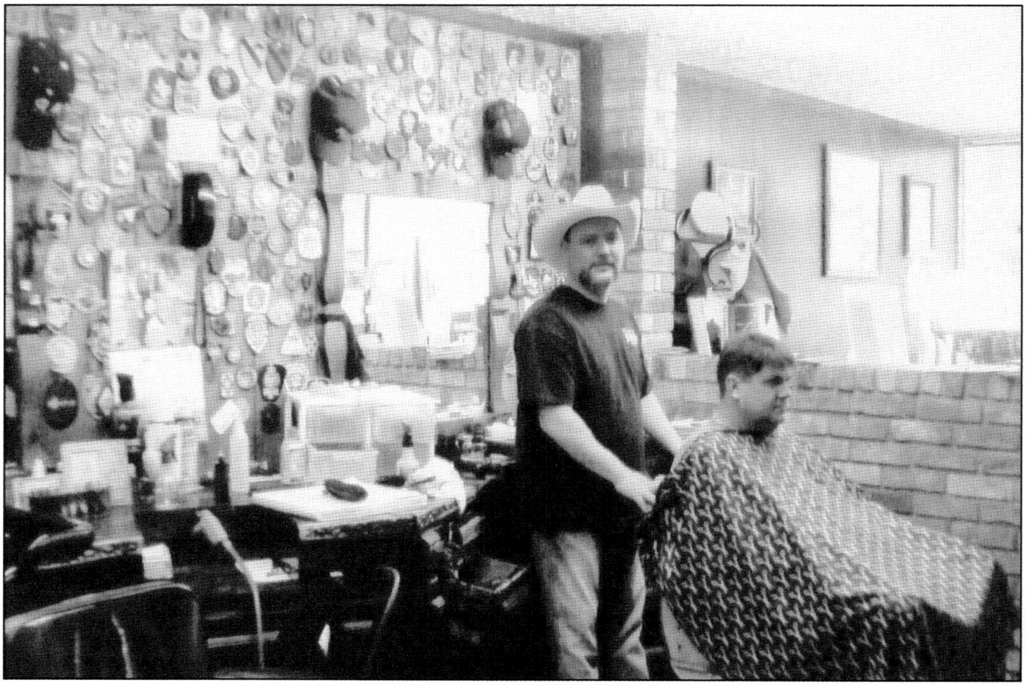

The barber pole on Fifteenth Street harkens back to the old days when one could walk in and get a shave, a haircut, and a bath. Plano Barbers has been a longtime establishment downtown and continues to serve loyal customers in a casual atmosphere. Described as "cowboy poets with shears," the proprietors are never short of news and sports talk. James Russell and his brother Randy wear cowboy hats as they serve patrons like the family has for over 40 years—the old-fashioned barber way.

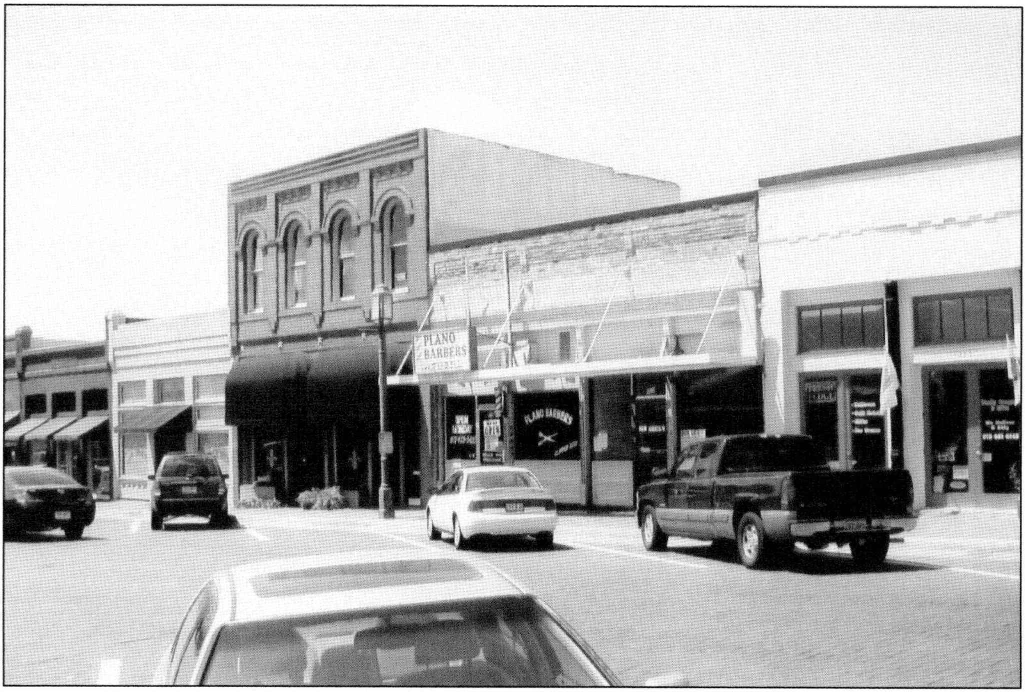

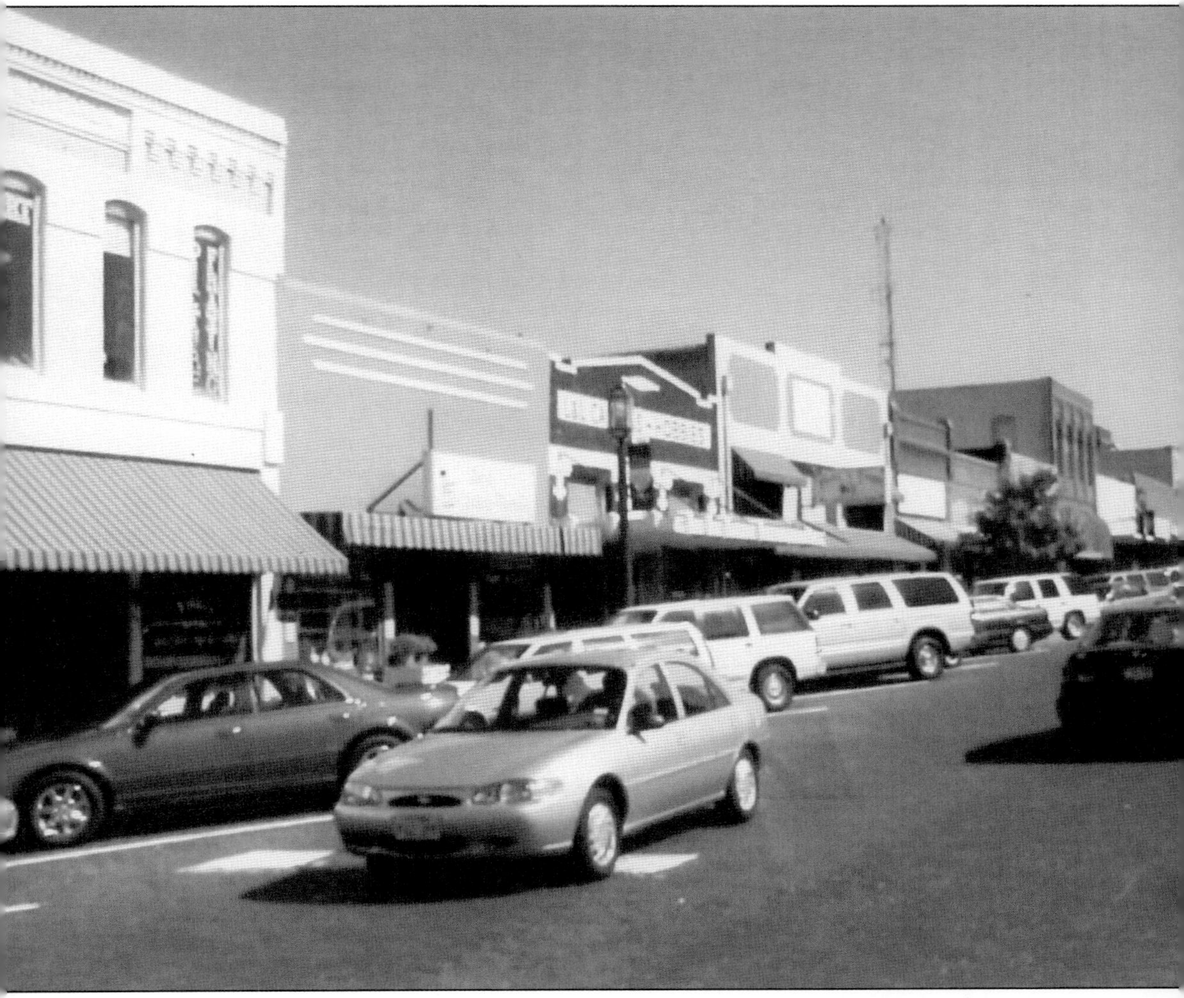

Heading east along the north side of Fifteenth Street toward K Avenue is a mixture of one-story and two-story buildings, some of which bear the names of early owners, merchants, or businessmen. In the middle of the block is the Merritt Building, built after the last devastating fire of 1915. The Chandler Store next-door supplied groceries and hardware from 1882 until 1897, was the site of Griffin's Men's Store in the mid-1900s, and is now home to a law office.

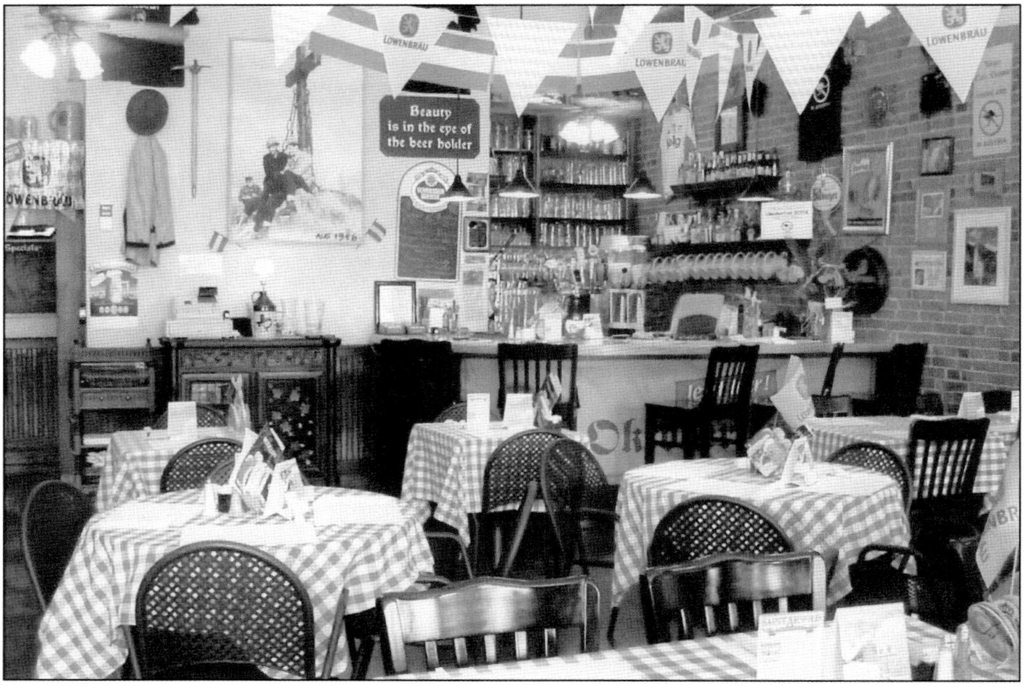

Jorg's Café Vienna, featuring authentic Austrian cuisine, opened in 2002. Jorg Fercher was one of the early investors in Plano's revitalization efforts, restoring and improving on the one-story building that once served as a post office near the original crossroads. Named one of the best neighborhood restaurants by *D Magazine* in 2008, Café Vienna enjoys a niche in the market extending beyond downtown Plano. The "biergarten" is a favorite gathering spot.

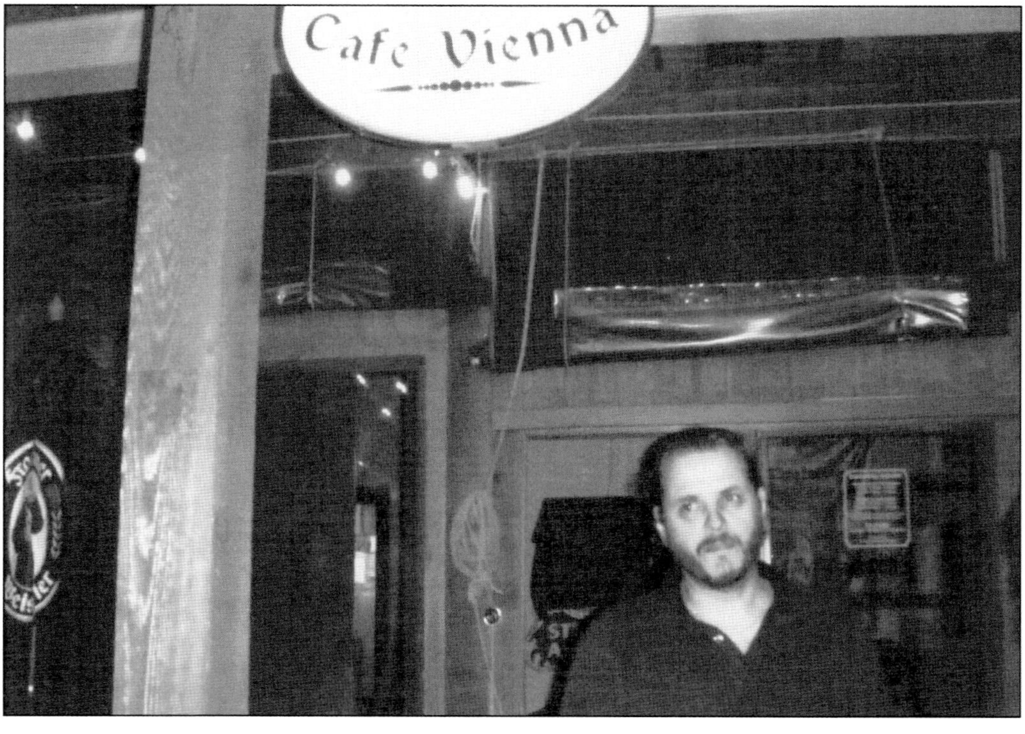

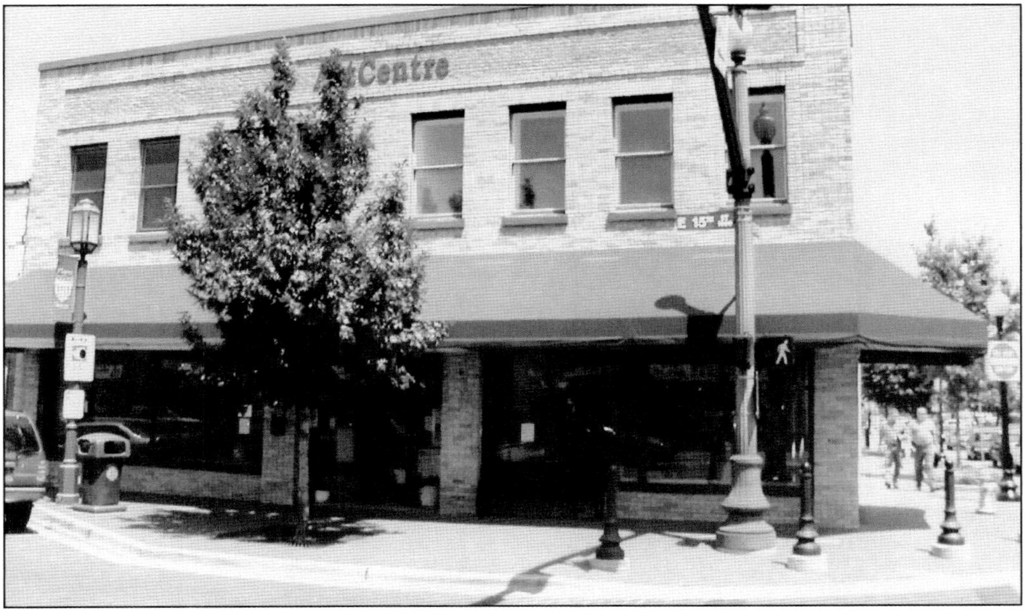

The Art Centre of Plano, formerly the Cultural Arts Council of Plano, purchased the Harrington Furniture building on the northwest corner of Fifteenth Street and K Avenue in order to expand its programming in 1991. After work was completed to restore and stabilize the building, the rebuilt Art Centre featured art galleries and instructional space for 10 years. The building has housed a saloon hall and musical instruments over the years, but spent a century as Harrington Furniture. Conversion of a separate warehouse building into a theater occurred in 1992. The Art Centre Theater featured live performances. The Art Centre complex was the center for local arts and cultural activities here until 2010, when it relocated to the Olney Davis House, another historical building on Eighteenth Street adapted for commercial use.

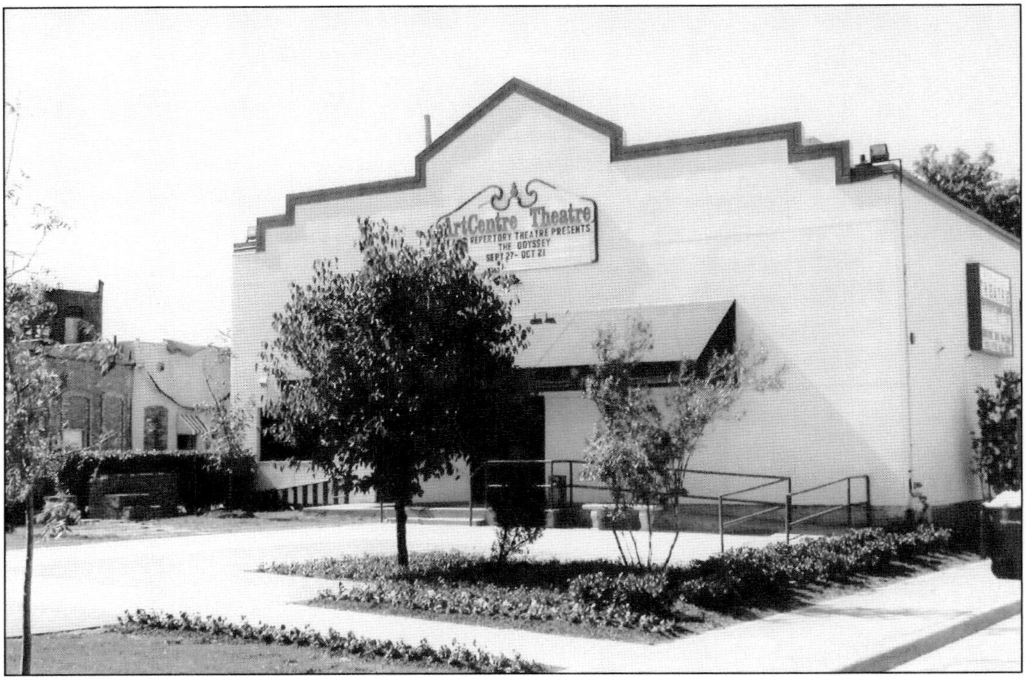

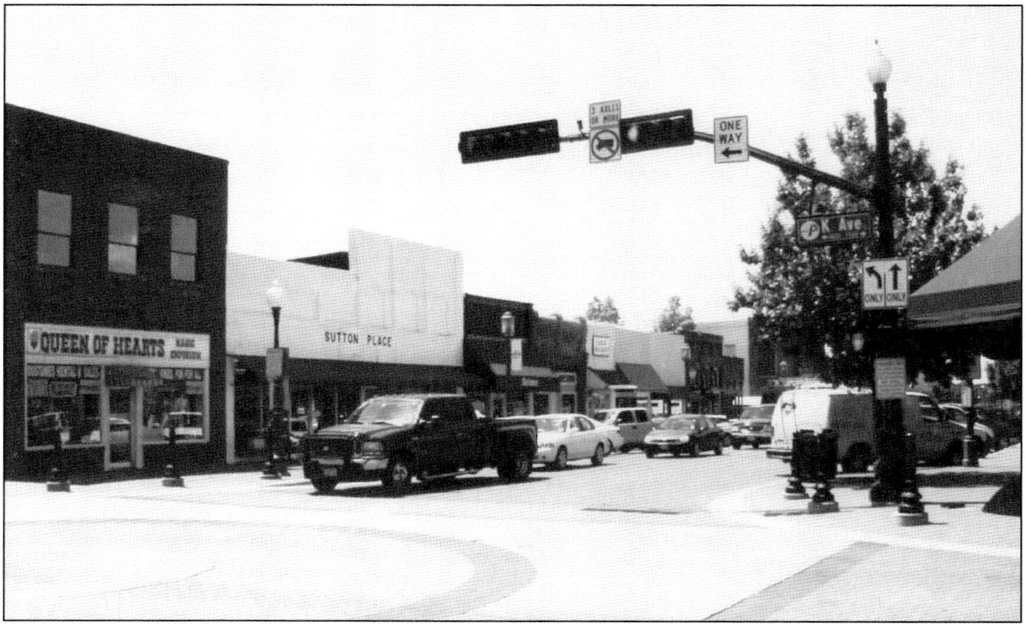

For more than 20 years, the Chaddick Building (far left) housed the Queen of Hearts costume shop on the southwest corner until closing in early 2011. Built in 1890, the Chaddick Building has anchored the south side of the street with a myriad of uses including a grocery, a drugstore, a restaurant, and a cinema. This building is one of the first developed at the original intersection of Main and Mechanic Streets on the early stagecoach route.

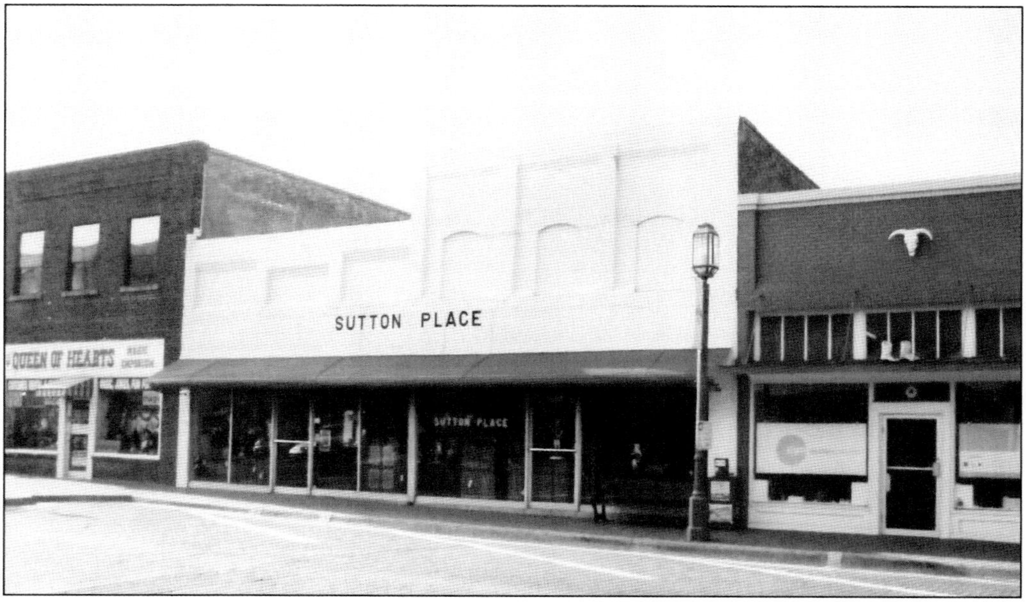

Next-door to the Chaddick Building is Sutton Place. Richard Sutton, who, with the help of his son Kevin, has invested time and money into historic preservation, finally purchased the building he has occupied for many years. This 2009 view shows the painted stucco covering the second-story windows. The furniture and antique store is in the midst of an extensive restoration and remodeling project in 2012. Over the past century, the buildings have been used for clothing, dry goods, a harness shop, a hardware store, and an automobile repair shop.

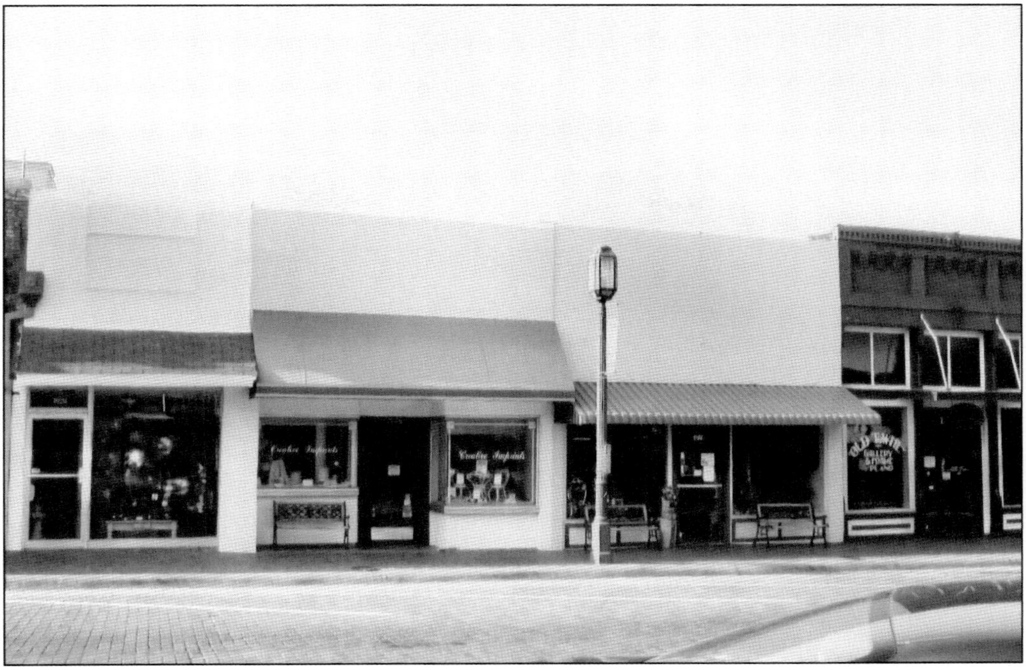

Some buildings have existed for over 100 years in downtown Plano and have been painted and changed over the years to match the tenant's needs. Below, the former Harrington Pharmacy Building is left of the alley on the south side of Fifteenth Street. These 2008 photographs reflect a mix of carefully preserved exteriors and some that barely resemble the original structures.

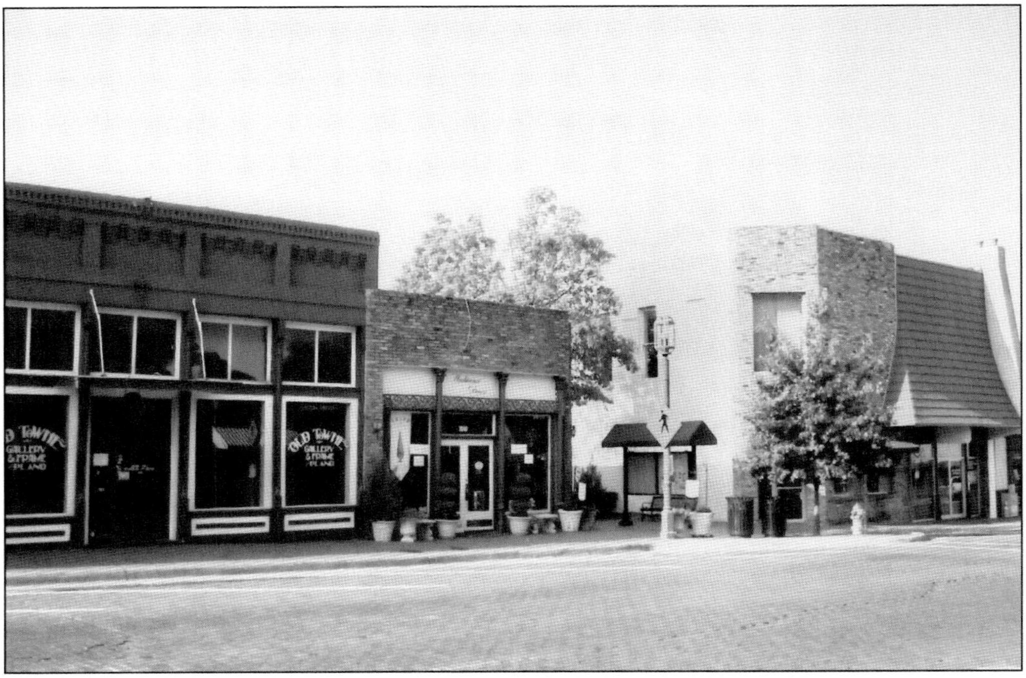

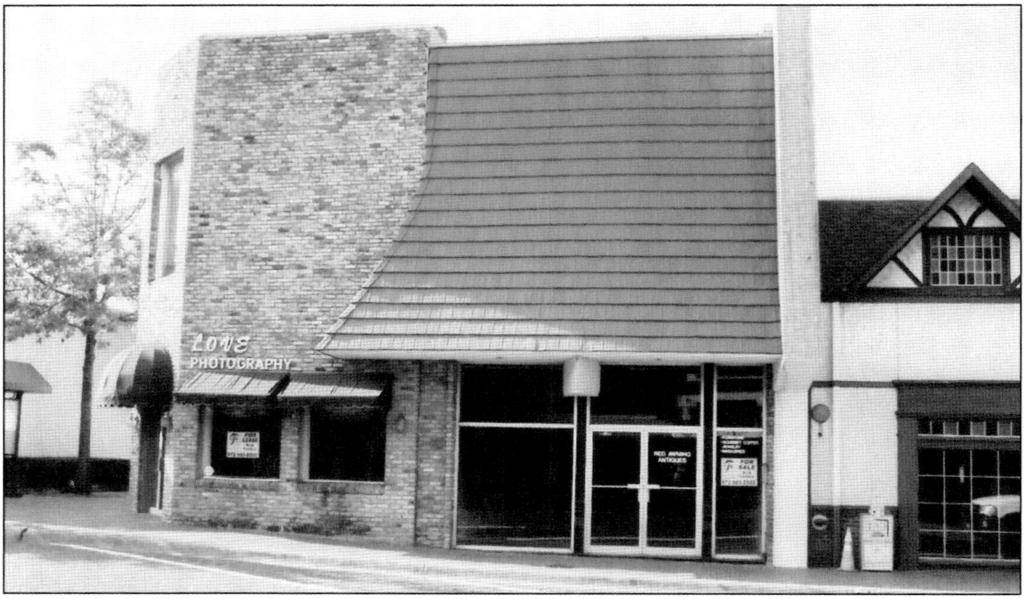

The Sanborn Fire Insurance map of 1901 shows a saloon in the building on the left next to the extant alley. The cover image of this book was taken in the interior of this building in the early 1900s. Restaurants occupied this space for over half a century. Love Photography Studio occupied this two-story building for 30 years when new brick covered the second-story windows. Next-door, the George Building (above, middle), originally a harness shop, is really a two-story building, but the upper floor has been covered by a mansard roof for many years.

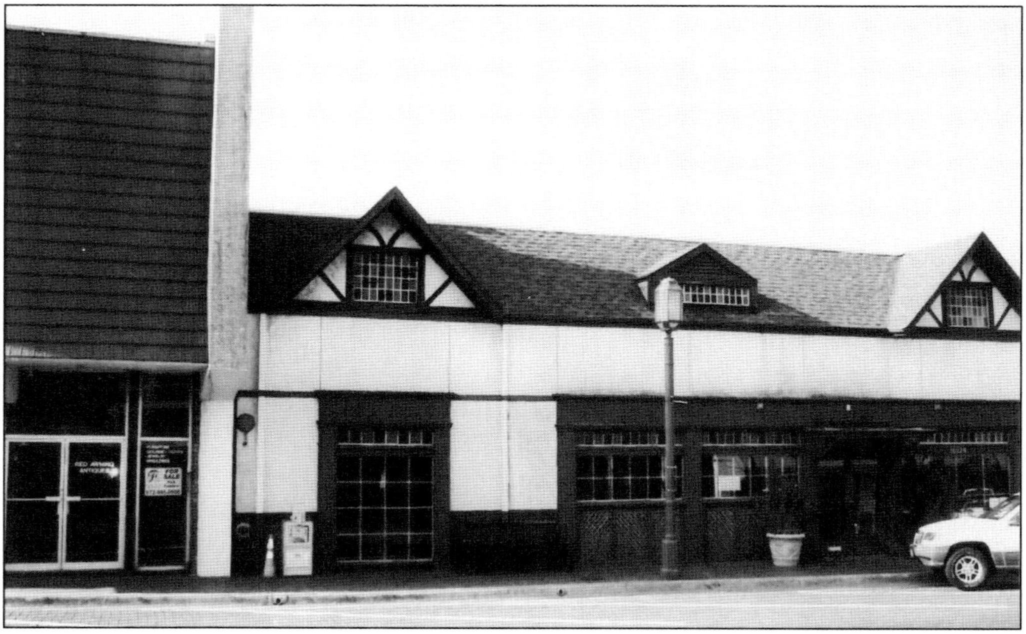

This Tudor-style building is a relatively new style for the business district. Harrington Pharmacy was located here for a time during the mid-1900s. The original commercial building was destroyed by fire in the 1970s. Prior to the fire, the site housed a photography store, a hardware store, offices, a grocery, an agricultural implements store, and a cold storage vault since it first appeared on the 1885 Sanborn Fire Insurance map.

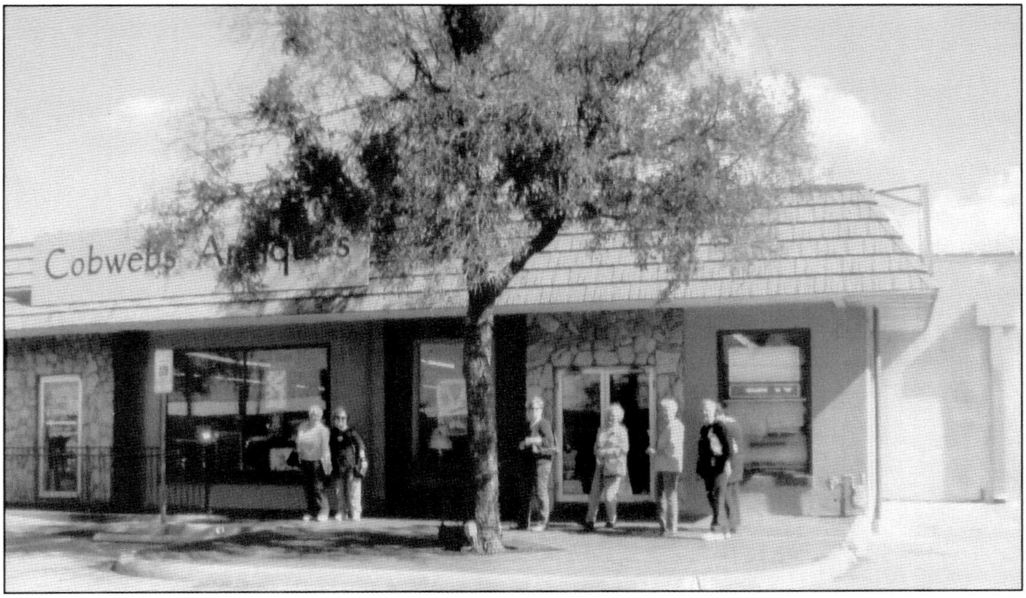

J Avenue is home to Cobwebs Antiques and Nanny Granny's Antiques. When Collin Creek Mall opened in 1980, many of the shopkeepers worried that downtown businesses would suffer as the brand-name stores and giant supercenters sprang up west of Central Expressway. But the old-town feel is still evident along this popular strip of shops, which sit on the historic site of J.W. Shepard's Livery Stable.

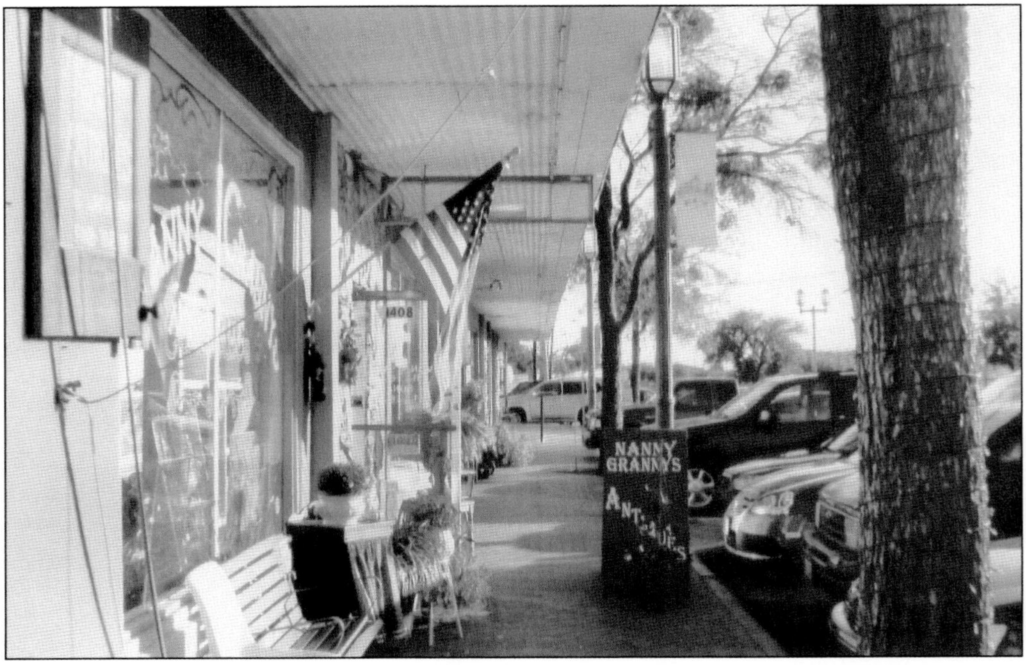

As Plano's population boomed, reaching 100,000 in the early 1990s, the downtown area began to attract the attention of the city leaders. A renaissance began as gift boutiques, offices, and specialty shops were well stocked to attract a share of the commerce. At the city's urging, the Downtown Merchants Association was formed to promote the area and the city hired two employees to work on historic preservation.

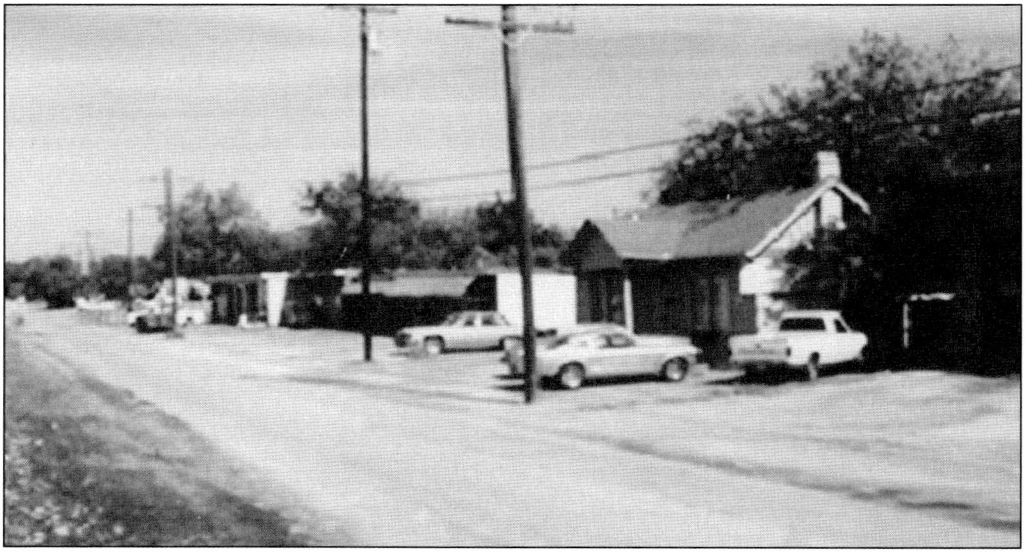

The 1990s photograph above shows a typical mixture of houses and businesses along the old railroad north of Fifteenth Street at the intersection with Fifteenth Place. In 1991, at a time when downtown Plano was challenged by its eroding economic position, absentee landlords, physical deterioration, and lack of reinvestment, the city adopted the Downtown Development Plan. Focusing on downtown as a center for government and the arts, with a nod to the emerging new urbanism movement, the plan addressed the potential for residential development in downtown as an important component to future development. In 1999, the city council adopted Downtown Plano: A Vision and Strategy for Creating a Transit Village, with the DART light rail as a catalyst for downtown's transformation. The vision became reality in this same view after development of DART's new Downtown Station (below). (Courtesy of the City of Plano.)

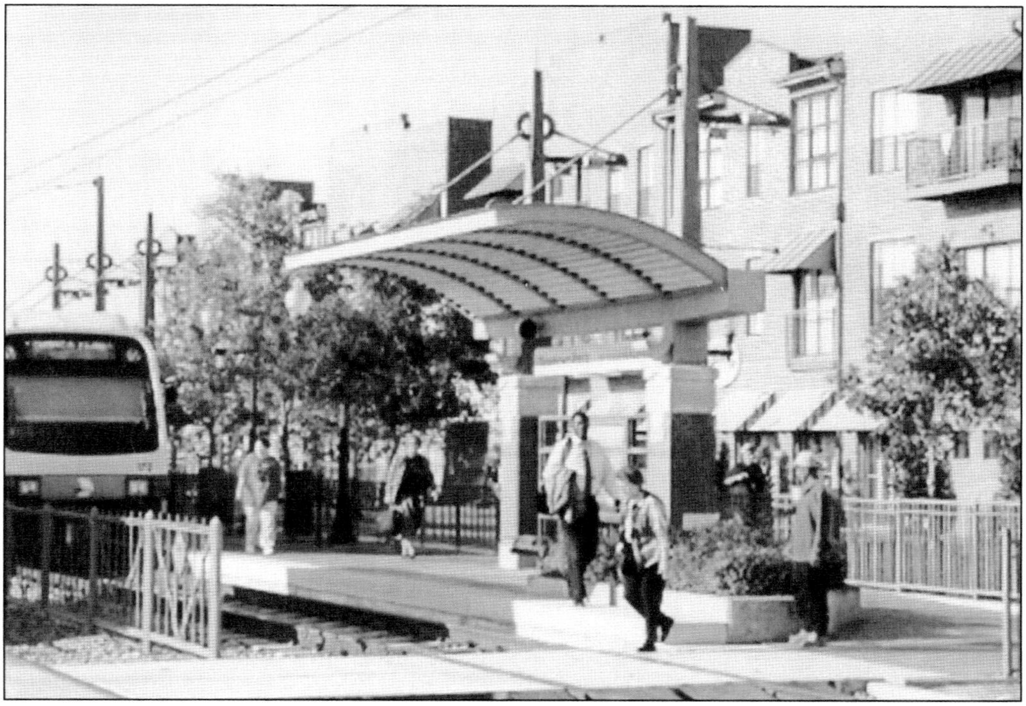

Six

Revitalization and Redevelopment

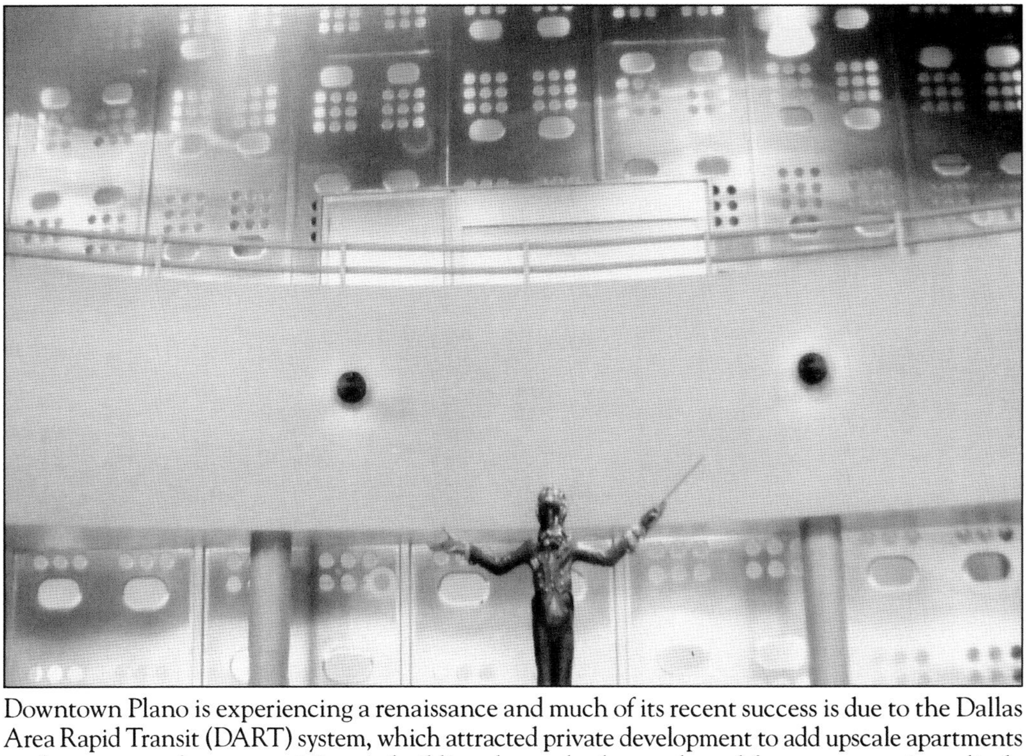

Downtown Plano is experiencing a renaissance and much of its recent success is due to the Dallas Area Rapid Transit (DART) system, which attracted private development to add upscale apartments to the compact downtown. Historic buildings have also been adapted for reuse, creating a lively town center. (Courtesy of the City of Plano.)

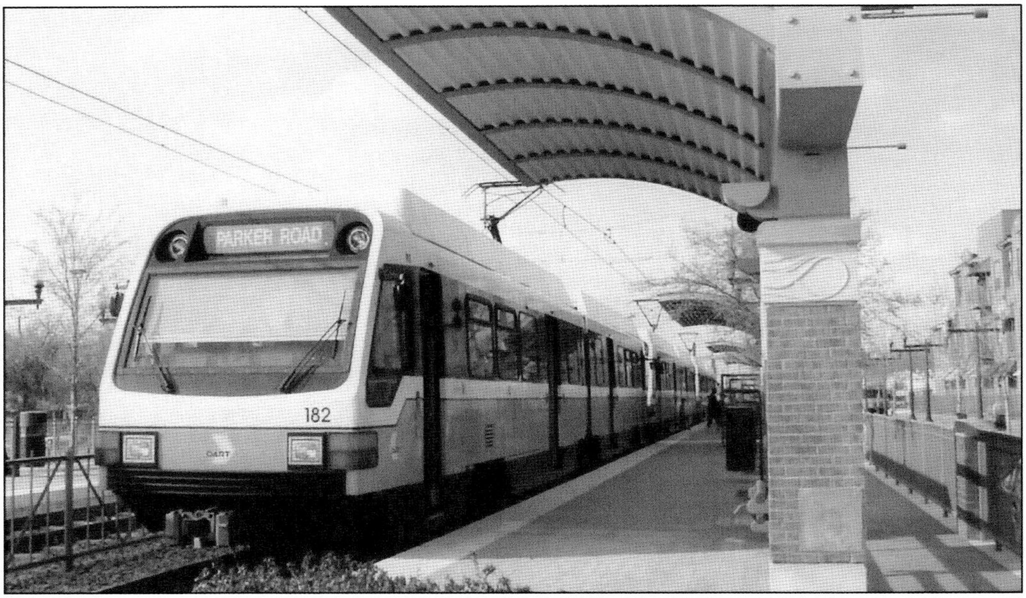

The historic business district has returned to its roots, "riding on the rails of success," according to Frank Turner, now deputy city manager, and former director of planning and economic development. Plano can be reached from Dallas via the DART light rail Red Line that stops right in the heart of uptown. For four Sacagawea golden dollar coins or the swipe of a credit card, riders can travel locally on a day pass, saving on gas as well as hours in major traffic delays. (Courtesy of the City of Plano.)

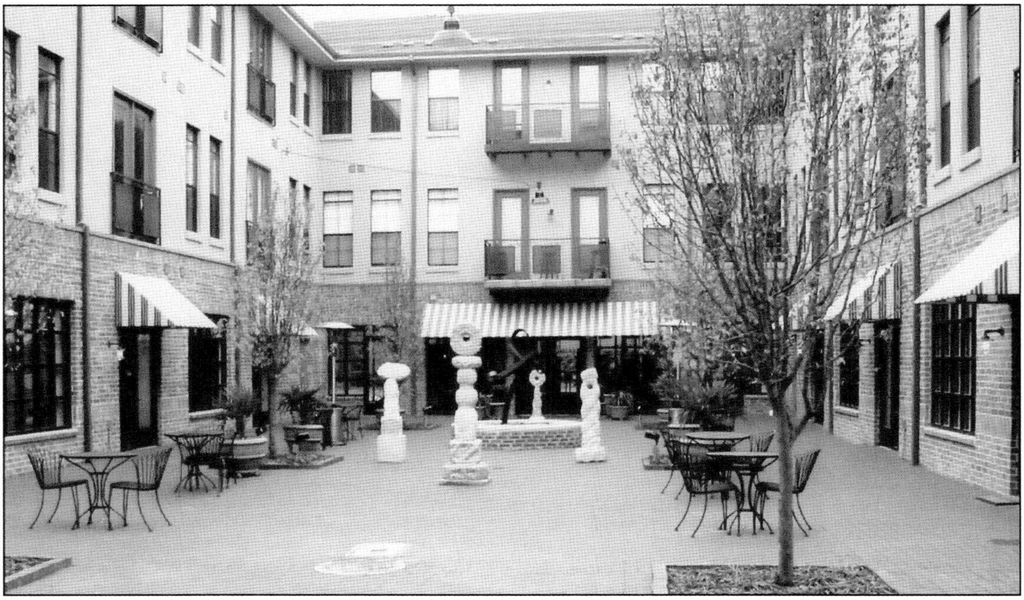
Eastside Village Apartments is part of the 90-acre downtown-business/government district where an infusion of new investment has motivated the owners of the original historic buildings to renovate and expand. Here is one of the courtyards at Eastside Village Apartments, offering flexible retail space on the ground level with living space above. Note the gathering area with seating, sculptures, and streetscape. Urban living coupled with the DART train has transformed Plano into an urban transit village. (Courtesy of the City of Plano.)

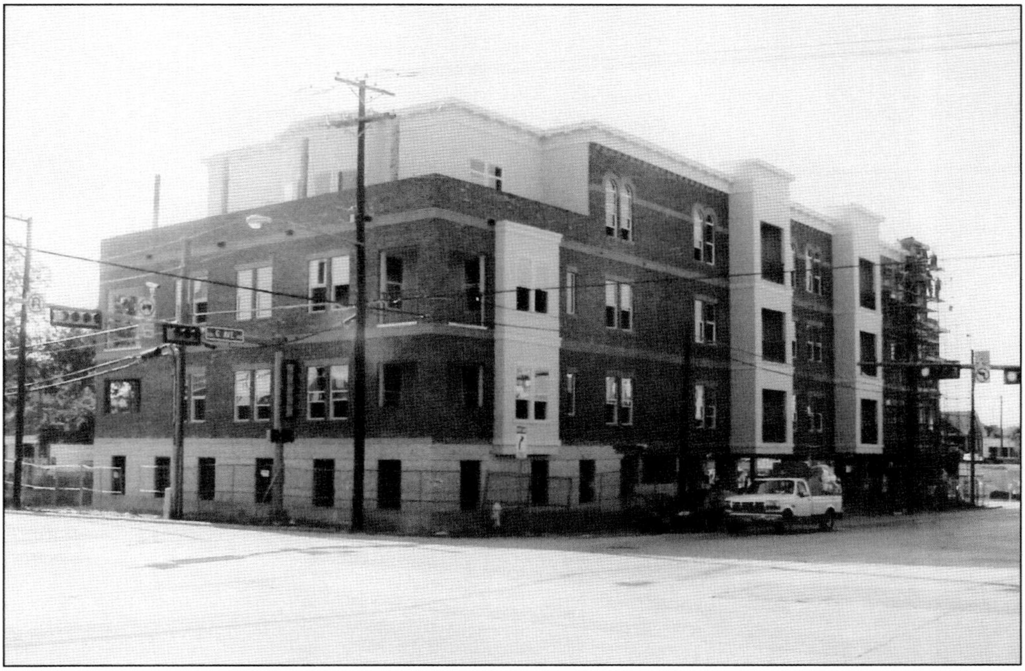

New shops and restaurants have sprung up with the demand from apartment dwellers giving historic Plano new life. Private development at Fifteenth Street and G Avenue has added over 120 townhomes and 34 condominiums. The Fifteenth Street Condominiums and Townhomes are the first signs of redevelopment when traffic exits US Highway 75 (Central Expressway) at Fifteenth Street and travels east to uptown Plano.

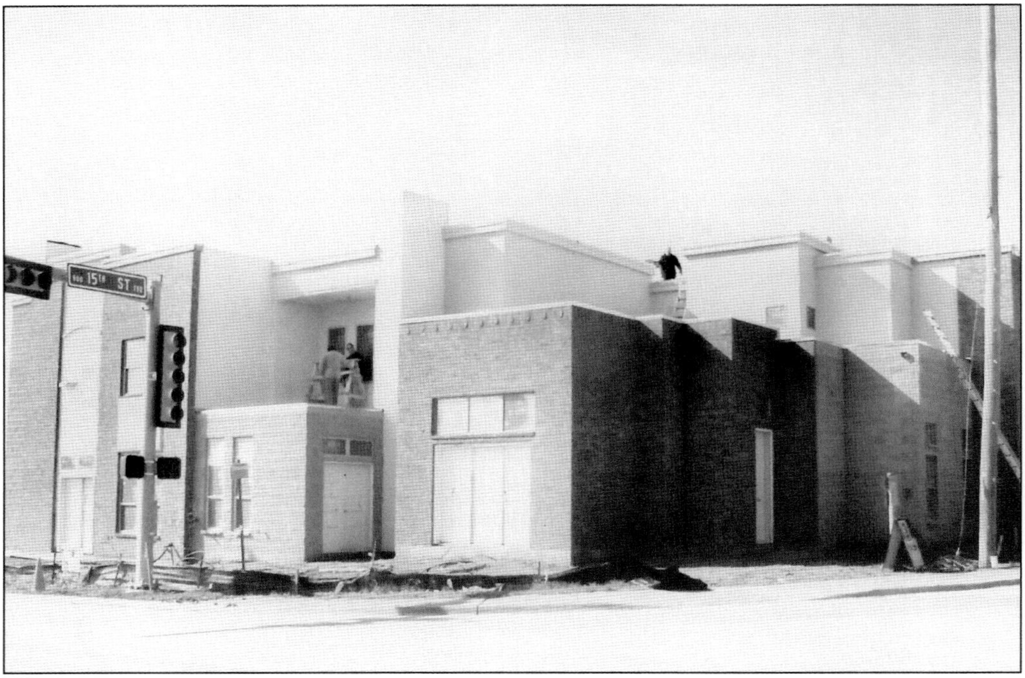

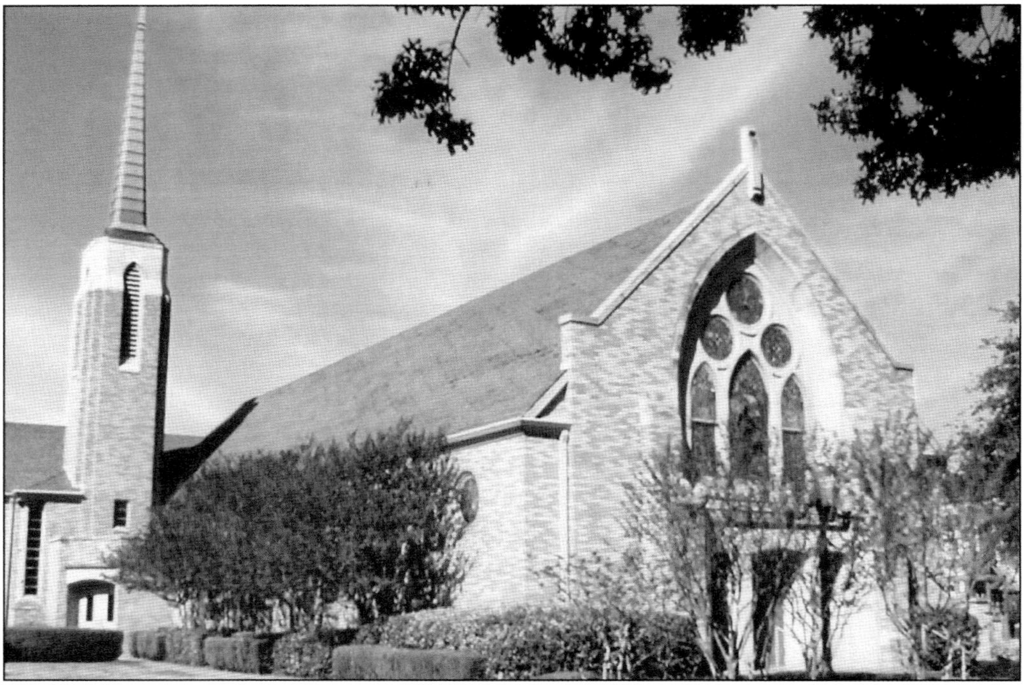

Approaching historic Plano from Route 75 along Fifteenth Street at the central Haggard Park, one begins to see what the Plano community was founded on—strong Christian faith with agricultural roots that have endured for over 150 years. In 2010, the church celebrated its 150th anniversary with historical displays of artifacts representing Plano through the years.

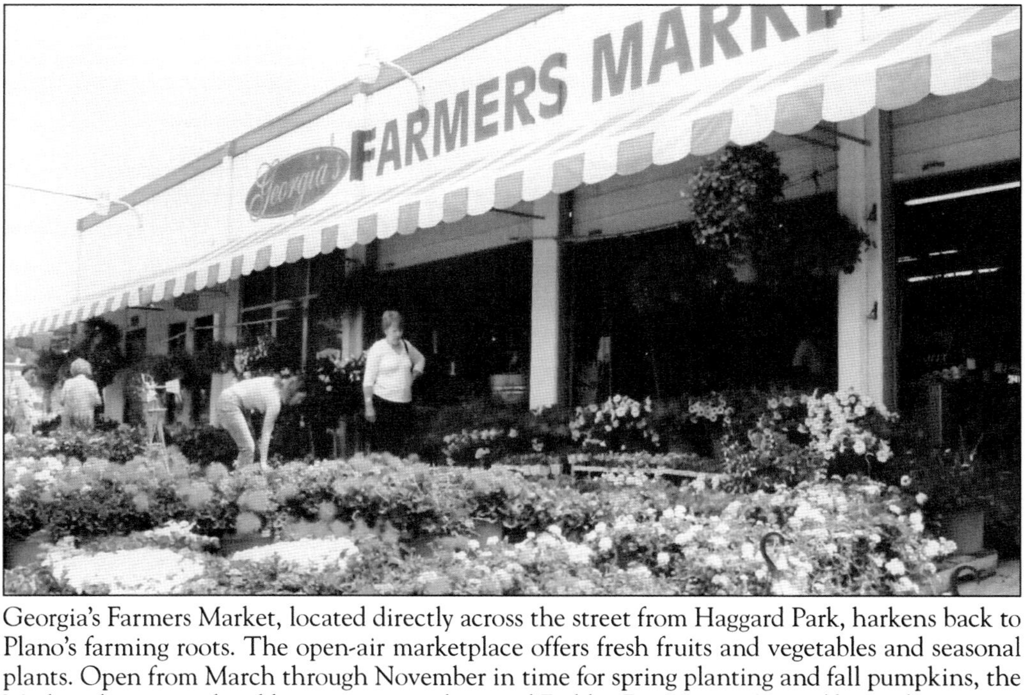

Georgia's Farmers Market, located directly across the street from Haggard Park, harkens back to Plano's farming roots. The open-air marketplace offers fresh fruits and vegetables and seasonal plants. Open from March through November in time for spring planting and fall pumpkins, the Market also carries local honey, spices, salsas, and Dublin Dr. Pepper. As a self-serve business, it is the next best thing to harvesting one's own garden.

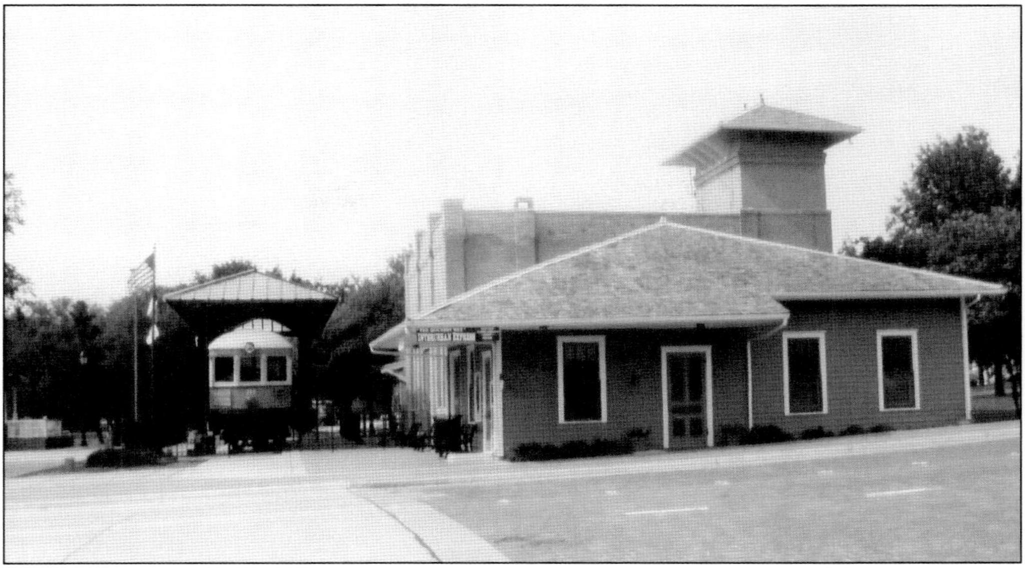

The Interurban Railway Museum is the last remaining restored station along the Texas Electric Railway. The 1908 depot museum features a model train, a hands-on science exhibit of the electric rail, and the recently restored ticket office. The building is one of only two National Trust Landmarks in Plano—the other one being the Heritage Farmstead Museum. A 2011 celebration commemorated the 100th birthday of restored Car 360, which is parked outside the museum in Haggard Park.

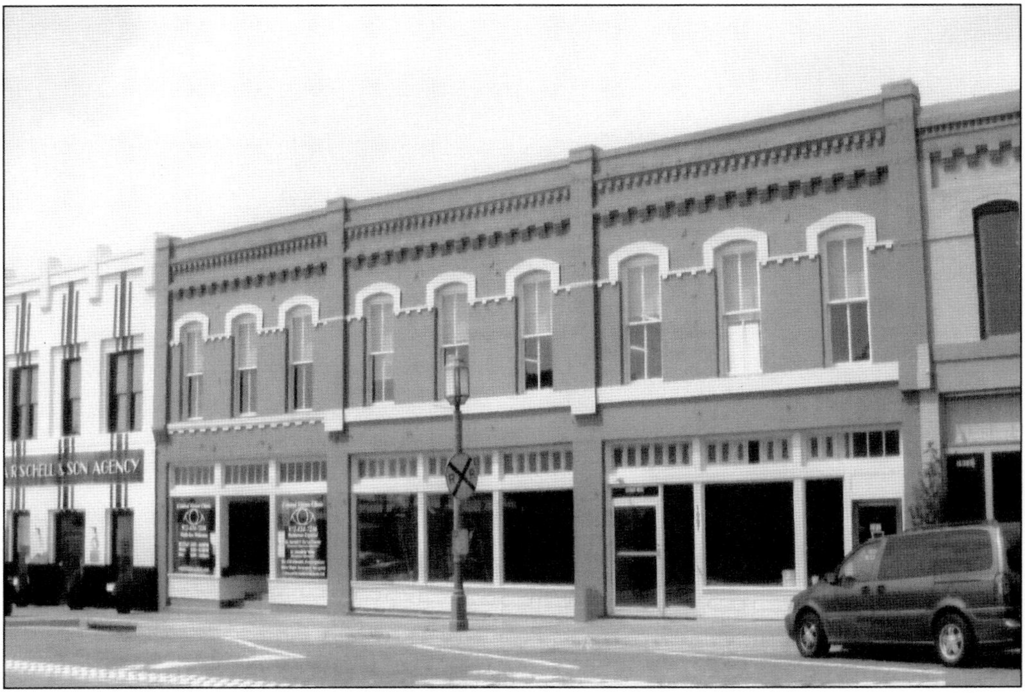

Crossing the railroad tracks into uptown Plano reveals a block of updated historic buildings, brought alive with the recent infusion of restaurants, bars, boutiques, art galleries, and cultural venues. Events are planned by the Historic Downtown Plano Association of merchants, interested citizens and residents, and some are sponsored by the city.

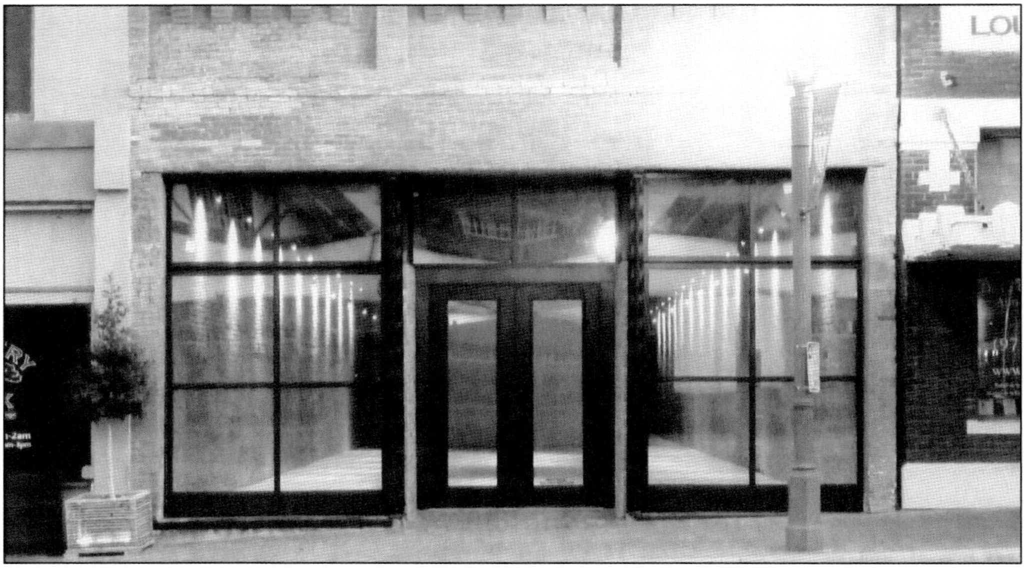

In 2010, the Plano Heritage Commission honored the Pierce family of California for its restoration of 1013 Fifteenth Street. The original ironwork was uncovered and the entry doors returned the building to its original splendor. Aged green stucco was removed and the brick exterior was exposed. The building has marked history as a liquor supplier, a hardware store, a general merchandise store, and a variety of department stores since being rebuilt after the fire of 1895.

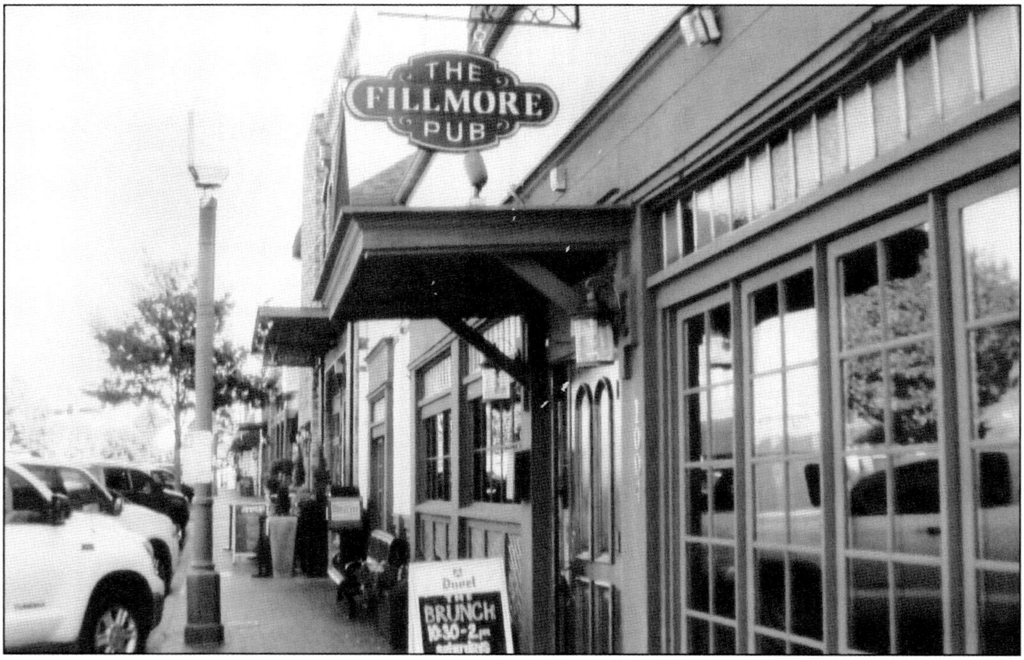

The Fillmore Pub brings an age-old use to this Tudor-style building, the only one of its kind uptown. Under the guidance of the Heritage Commission, the owner replaced the windows and doors with complementary materials in 2007 and received an award for its sensitivity to the building's design. Formerly the site of a grocery and Harrington Pharmacy, this building replaced the old structures, which burned in the 1970s. The Pub is now a popular gathering spot overlooking McCall Plaza and the DART train whizzing past.

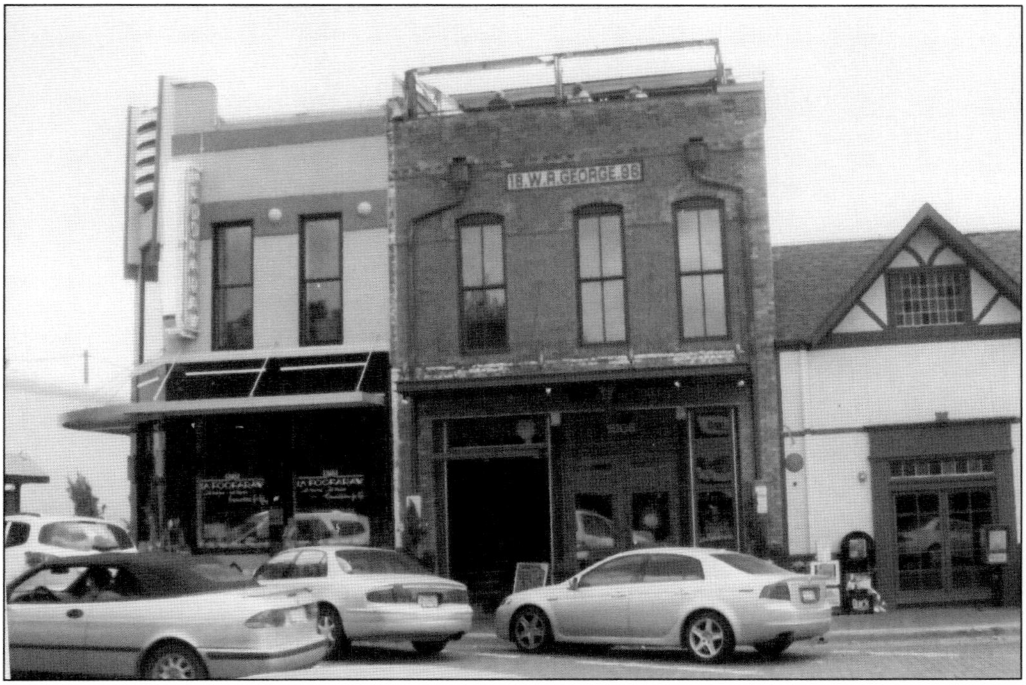

The W.R. George Building at 1006 Fifteenth Street (middle), was constructed in 1896 and completely restored in 2009 with a third-story rooftop patio addition. Restoration uncovered the second-story windows, which were covered for decades. The new Urban Crust restaurant pays homage to the former harness and saddle shop originally occupying the building, while adding a novel 30-foot-long frozen bar on the rooftop addition.

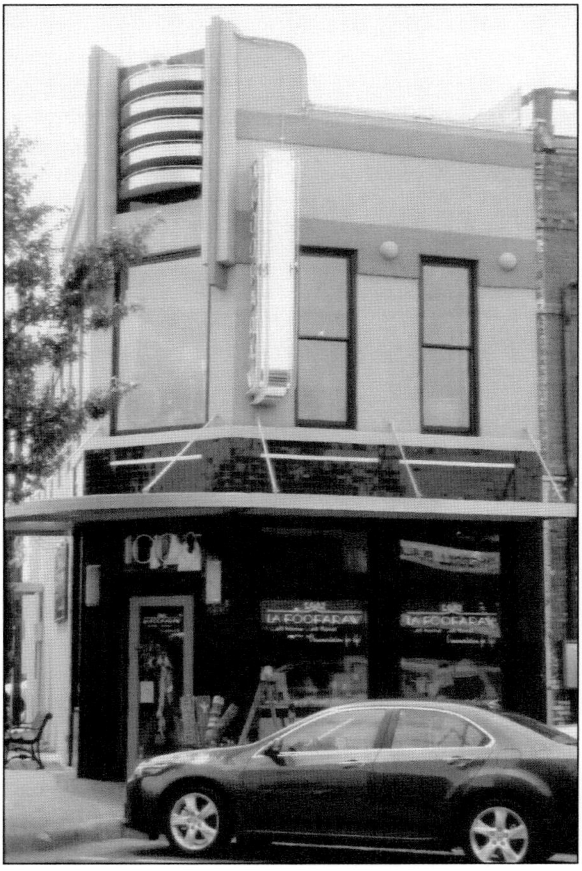

Next-door, at 1008 Fifteenth Street, the Love Photography building was painstakingly restored to its Art Deco design in 2010. Reminiscent of a 1930s cinema, the black marble tile is now accented with Art Deco sign and trim. The Crider family opened La Foofaraw to display the flashy, fun, and festive home ornamentation, mixing antiques with urban décor. The heritage commission commended both of these building restorations, and Plano is now distinguished as one of the only Texas towns to have two vintage Art Deco buildings.

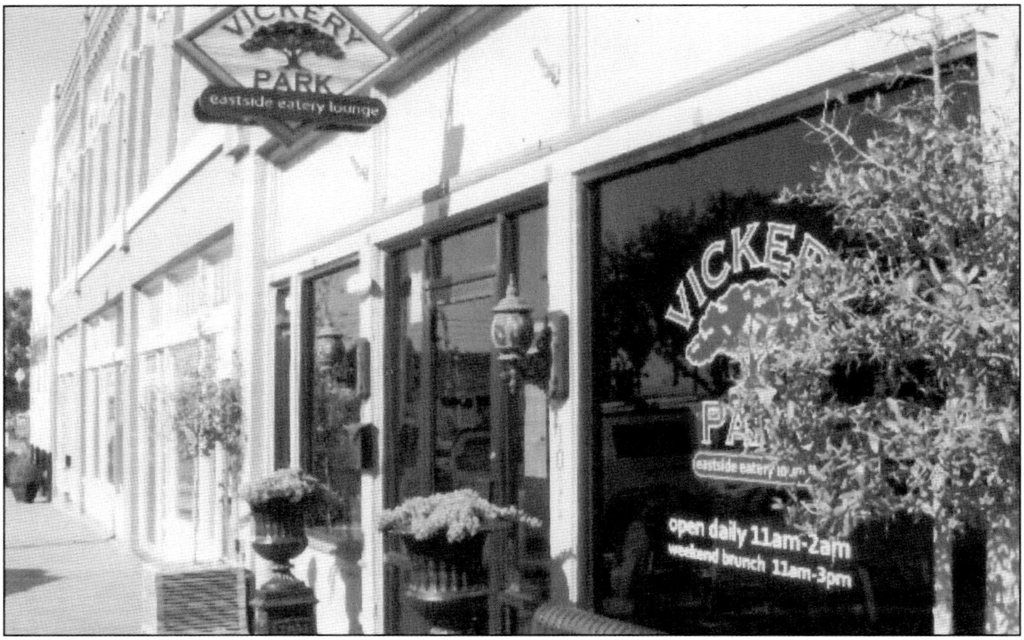

The owners of Dallas's Vickery Park discovered value in opening another eatery/bar uptown after years of success in Dallas. The McFarlin Building, longtime home to Allen Drug Store, is one example of the adaptability of old buildings. The nightlife has improved over the past few years as more restaurants and shops remain open after business hours and experience lively weekends. The merchants association schedules events including a pub crawl and Taste of Plano, renamed Feastival in 2011, to bring greater interest to uptown.

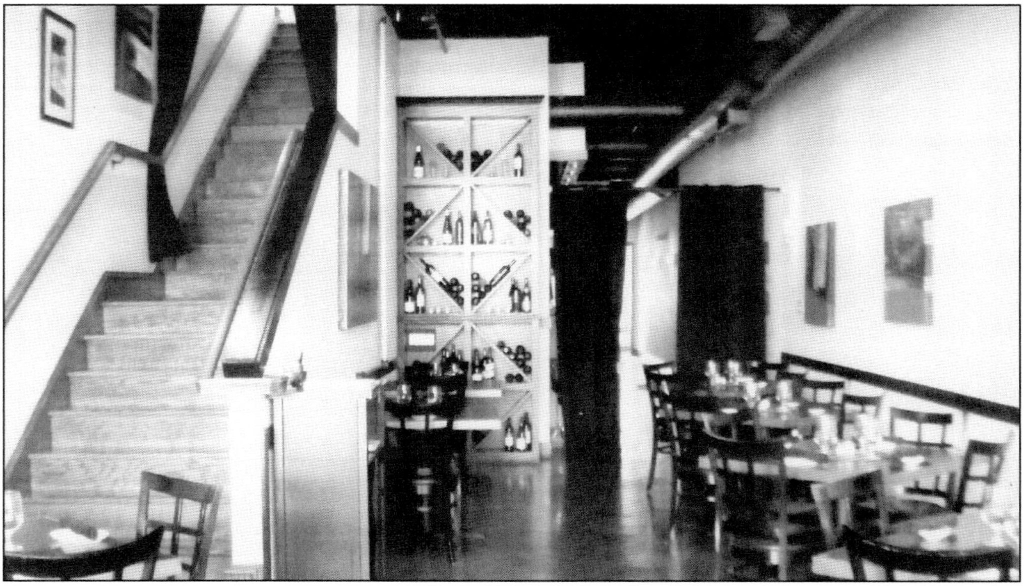
Increased private investment led the owner of this century-old building to complete a facelift, with new windows and a restored brick exterior. Zanata is now an upscale bistro with a rooftop patio, appealing to local residents and visitors alike. New dining choices continue to add to the allure of uptown. With the recent ban on smoking, bars and restaurants are enjoying popularity with improved air quality. Small business owners signify the restored confidence in uptown Plano.

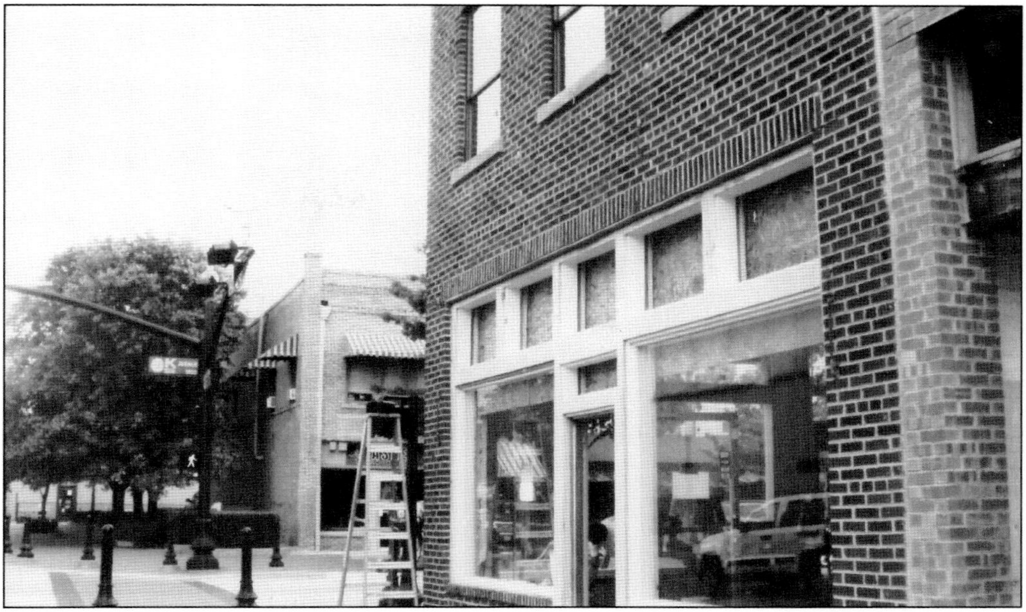

Private investment continues to improve the dining and shopping options in uptown Plano. The pedestrian-friendly neighborhood has transformed the original crossroads of Plano, but many remember this southwest corner of Fifteenth Street and K Avenue as the inimitable Queen of Hearts, which occupied the space for 20 years. The Chaddick Building will add to dining choices in the compact and walkable village uptown has become.

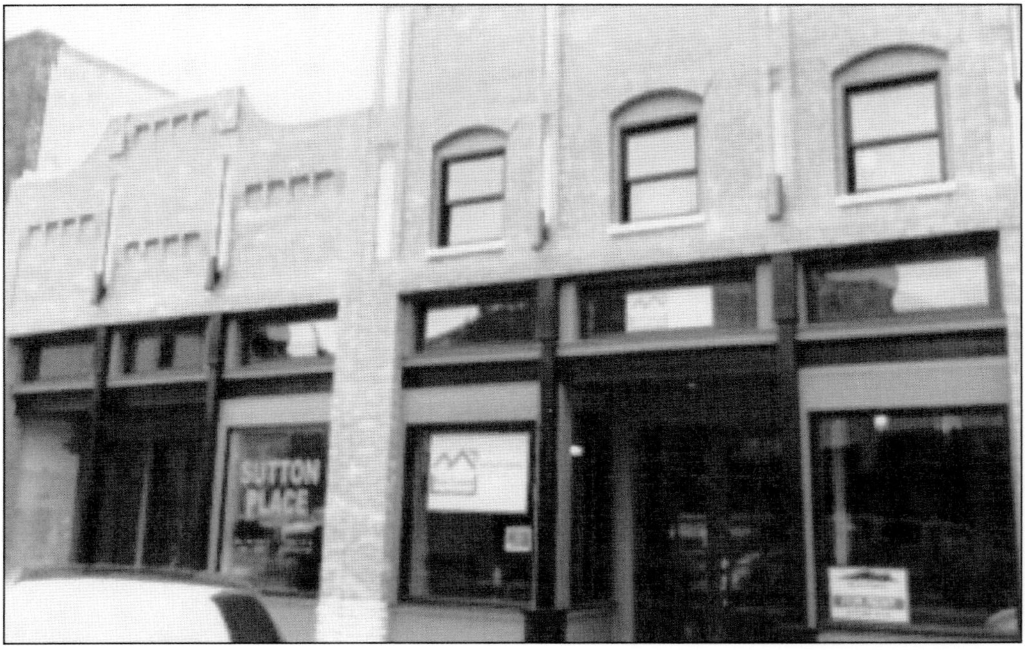

Restoring old buildings has its risks and its rewards, and Richard Sutton certainly has the experience to tackle this challenge. A longtime dealer in antiques and imported furnishings, Sutton uncovered the original second-story windows and reconstructed the brick façade on this Fifteenth Street anchor, rewarding uptown with another restoration adding to its newly claimed stature as an urban village.

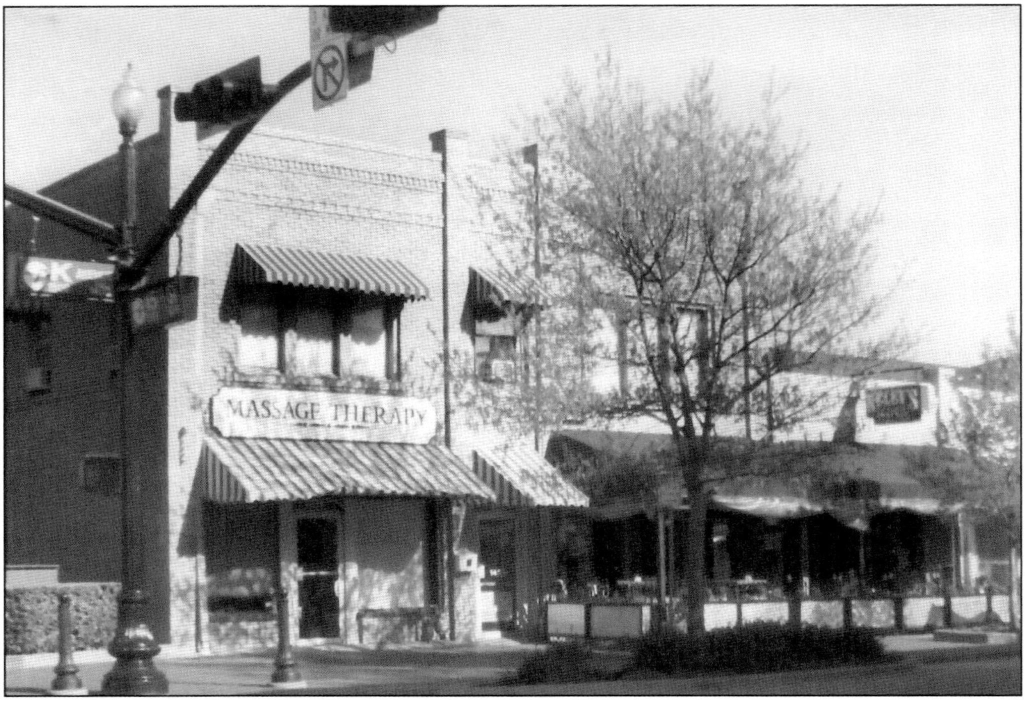

This view from the original crossroads looks southeast along K Avenue from Fifteenth Street. Kelly's Eastside, an established bar and grill, is a popular eatery featuring patio dining. Recently expanded into the adjacent building, the restaurant kept the original brick interior walls mostly intact. A horse sculpture on the sidewalk marks the site of Klepper's wagon yard and livery stable in the early days.

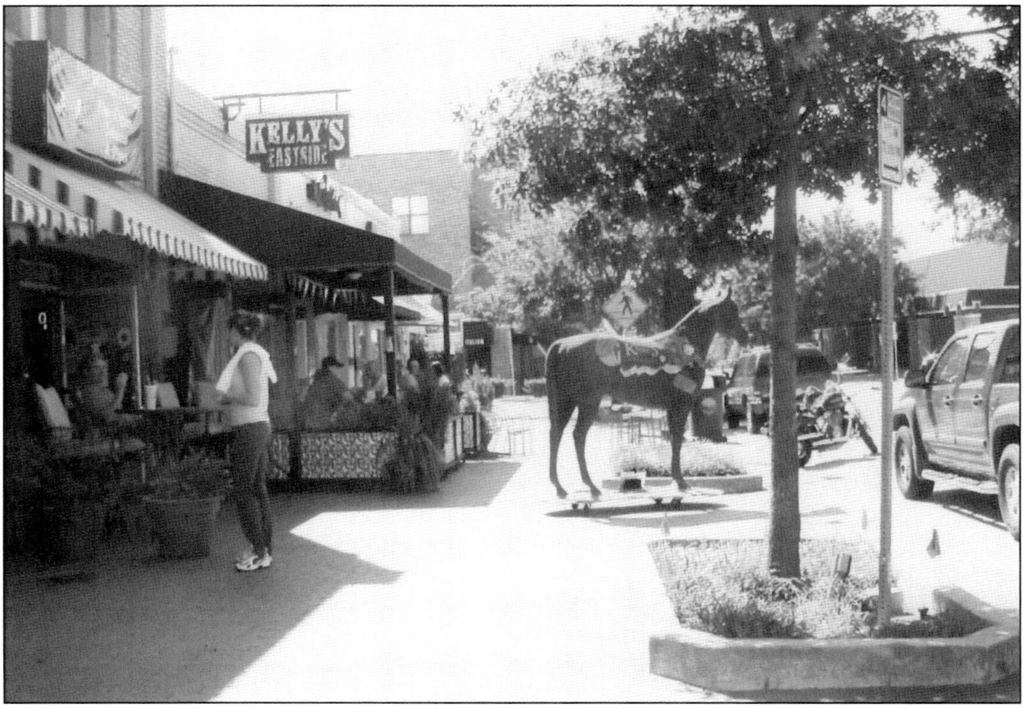

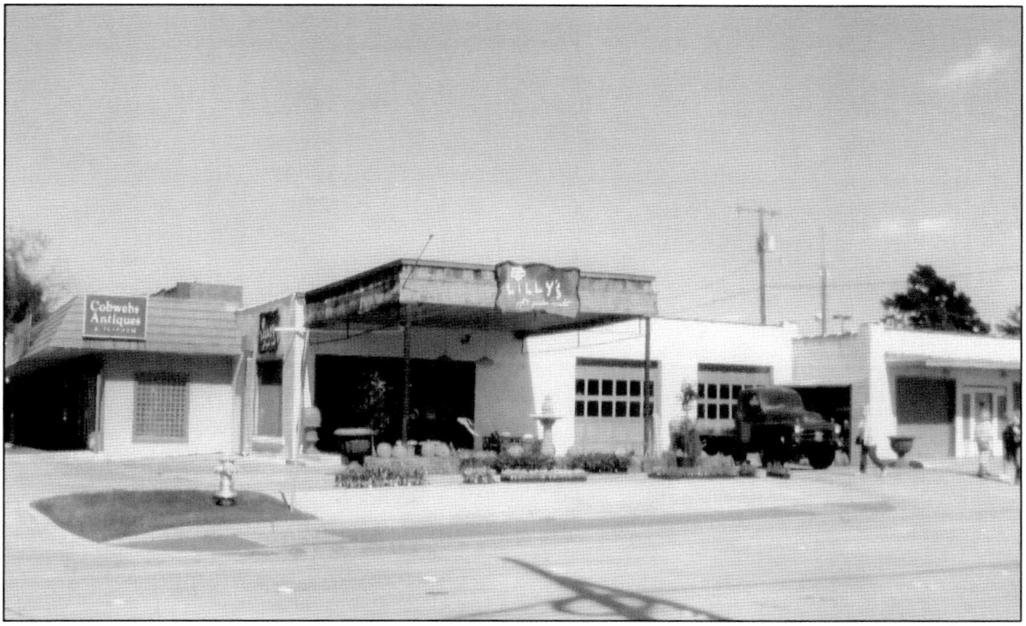

Adaptive reuse of this old service station as a garden center links the shops on Fifteenth Street southward along the Fourteenth Street corridor. Houses and businesses along Fourteenth Street have been redeveloped to expand the original business district. The former icehouse is across the street from this old filling station. The icehouse served other uses over the years, as Mac's Auto Repair and, most recently, a mail center. It was tastefully renovated for office use in the past few years. The owners are now redeveloping the adjacent parking lot into a multistory office building on the south side of Fourteenth Street, bringing more signs of an urban uptown where one can live, work, and play.

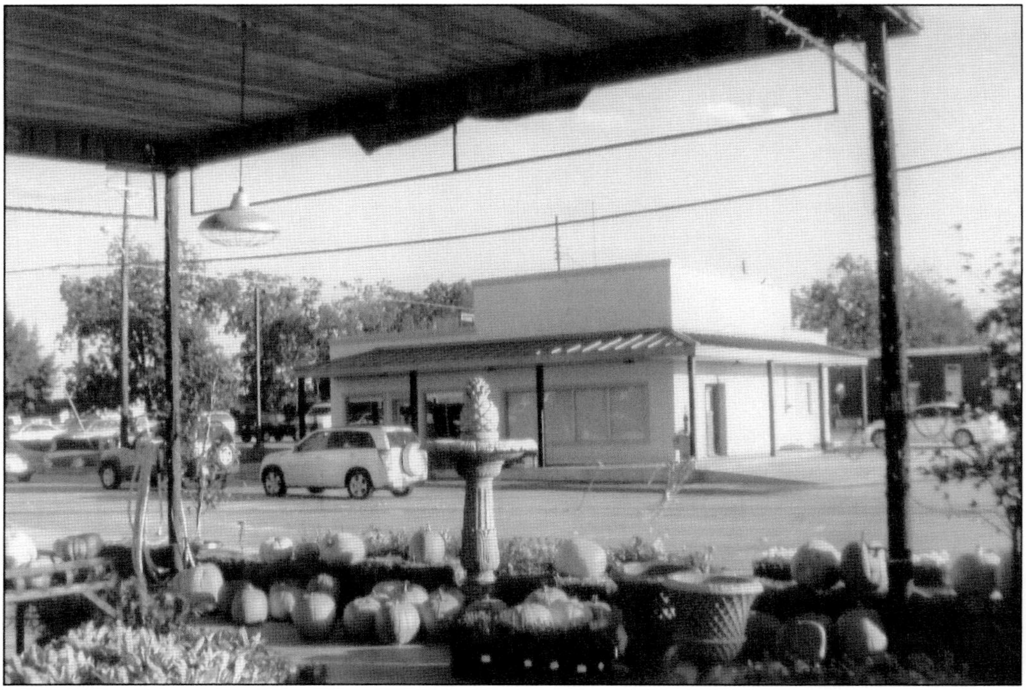

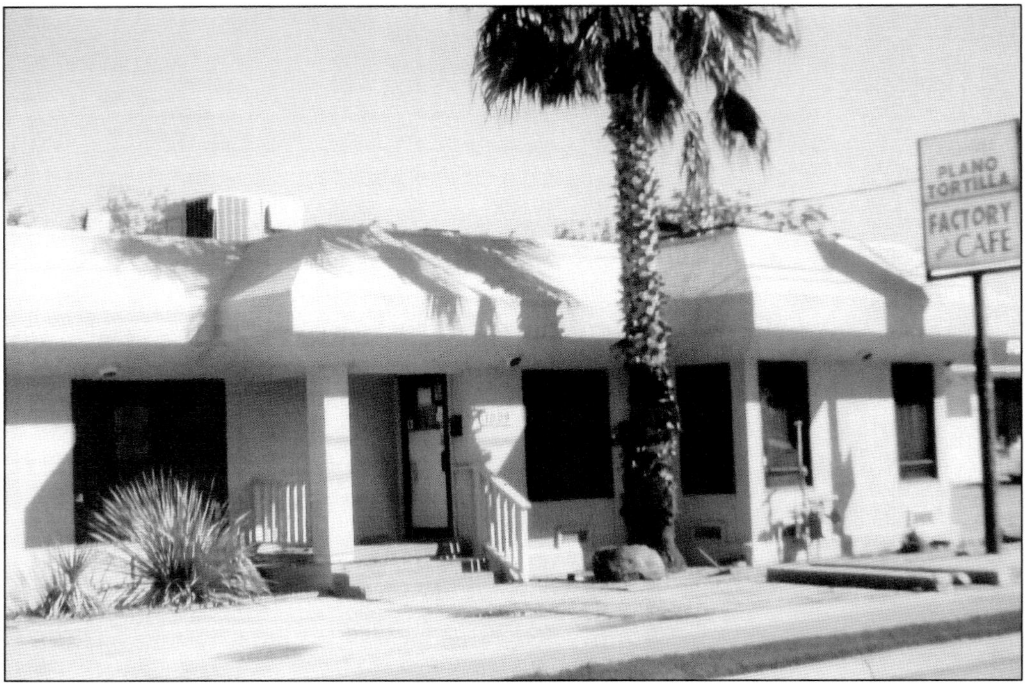

Retaining the small town, pedestrian-oriented nature in Plano has been key to its revitalization. As the only concentration of historic commercial buildings in the city, downtown and surrounding neighborhoods have been the major focus of the city's heritage preservation efforts. The Plano Tortilla Factory has been an icon on Eighteenth Street for many years. In 2005, the Aparicio family built a larger restaurant next to the DART line, retaining the old Tortilla Factory for its distinctiveness in this oldest part of the city.

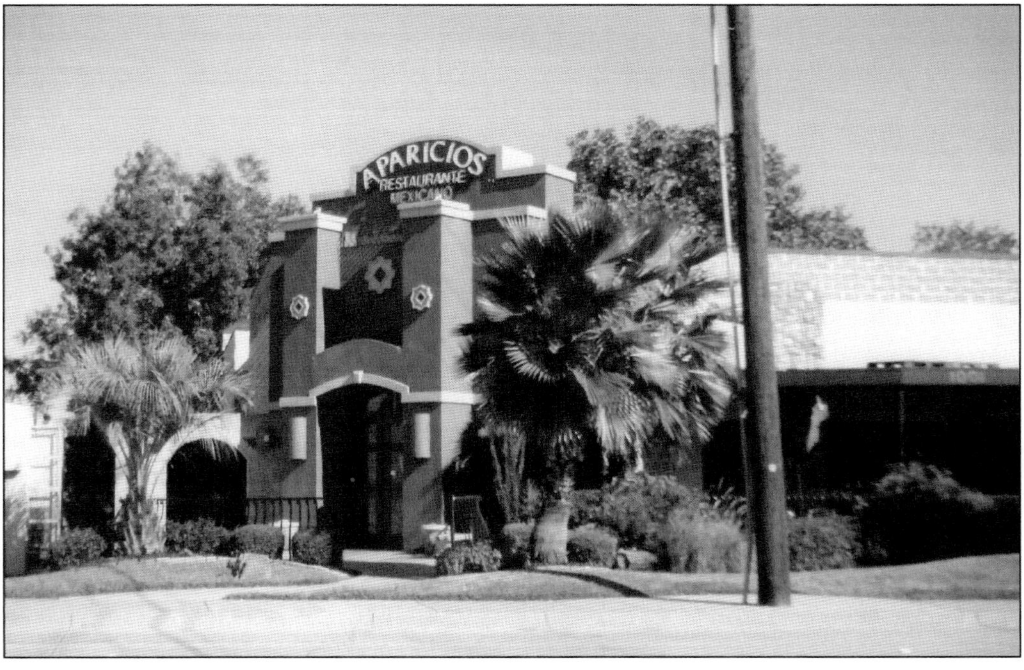

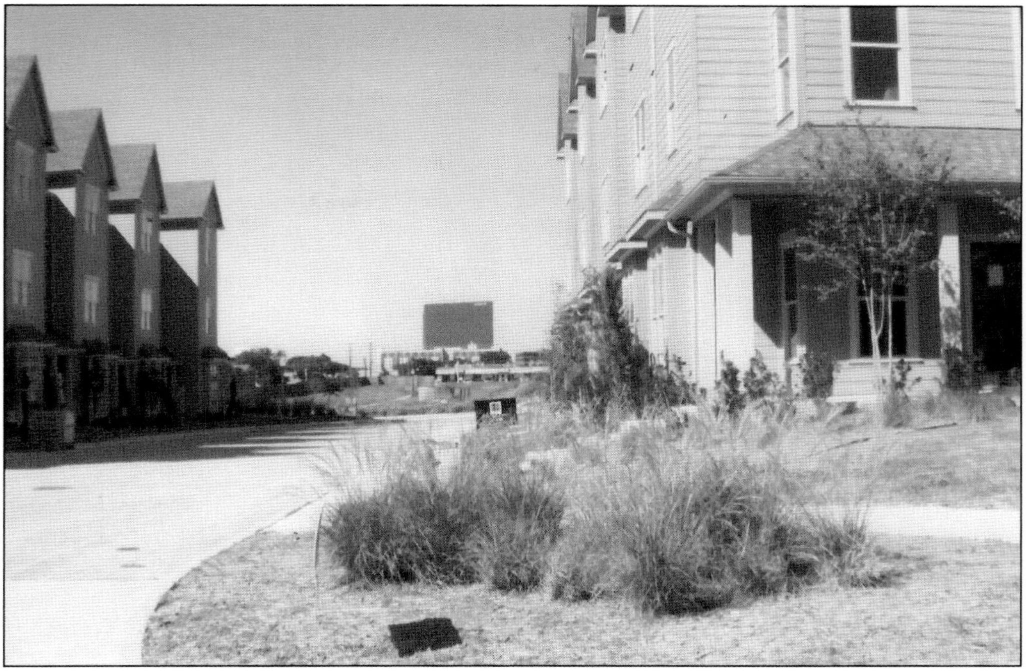

Public/private partnerships have been critical to the success of Plano's revitalization. Above, a former city-owned football field will offer almost 100 new townhomes within walking distance of uptown when redevelopment is completed. Partially located in the Haggard Park Heritage District on G Avenue between Sixteenth and Eighteenth Streets, the developer of Lexington Townhomes at Rice Field worked with the Plano Heritage Commission and local homeowners to plan the development. Below, the Ostranders built this mixed-use building to fit into the historic district. The building sits between the new Lexington project and the historic Mitchell House, across the street from the historic William Joel (W.J.) Carpenter House.

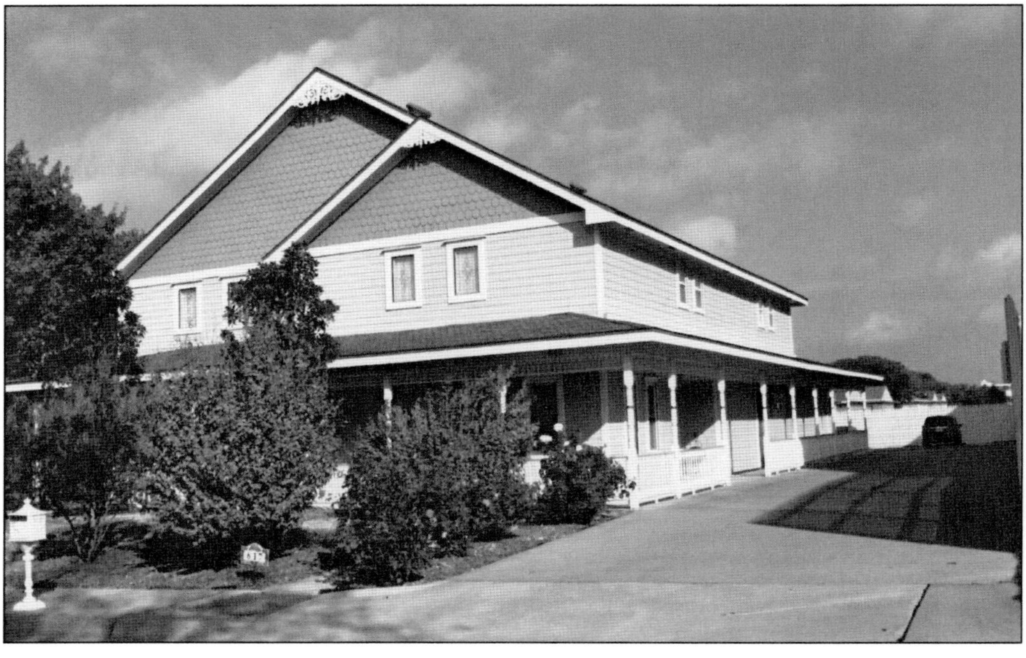

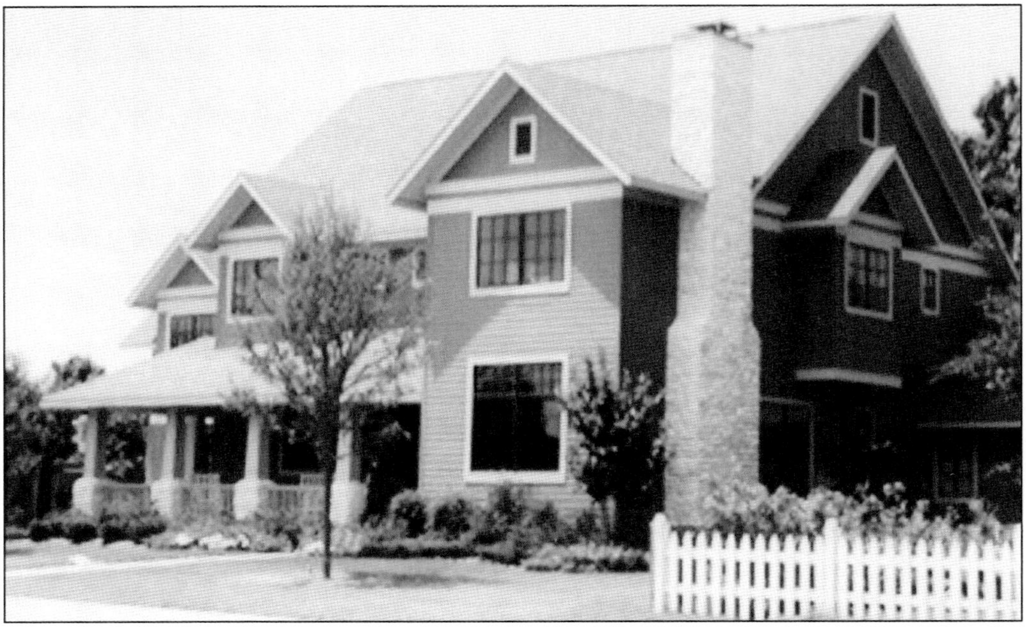

Newcomers and longtime residents take great pride in the old neighborhoods surrounding the original business district of Plano. In 1999, the Plano Heritage Commission adopted preservation guidelines following secretary of the interior standards for the Haggard Park Heritage Resource District. Built in 2001, the Campisi's house appropriately meshes with the Haggard Park neighborhood. The house was featured in *Southern Living* for early-1900s architecture.

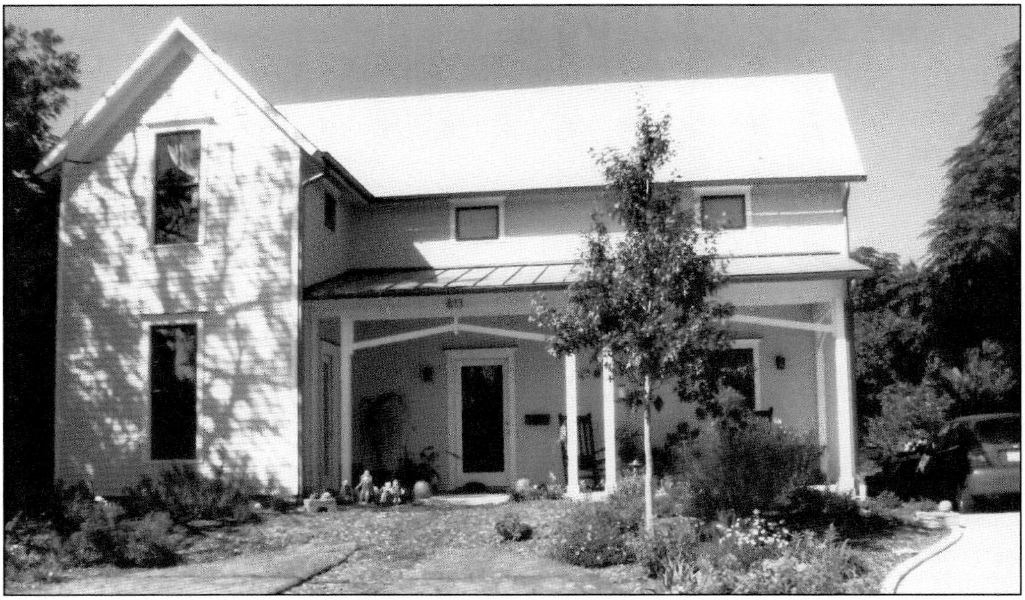

Also in the Haggard Park Heritage District, this new folk Victorian home won Plano Heritage Commission's Preservation Award in 2009 for creative new construction. Owner/architect John Brooks utilized new "green" technology in construction, and his wife, Kathleen, a master gardener, added low-care native landscaping. The Brookses designed their home in accordance with Plano Heritage Commission's preservation guidelines. The home contributes to the historic nature of the heritage district and enjoys partial tax abatement like others in the area.

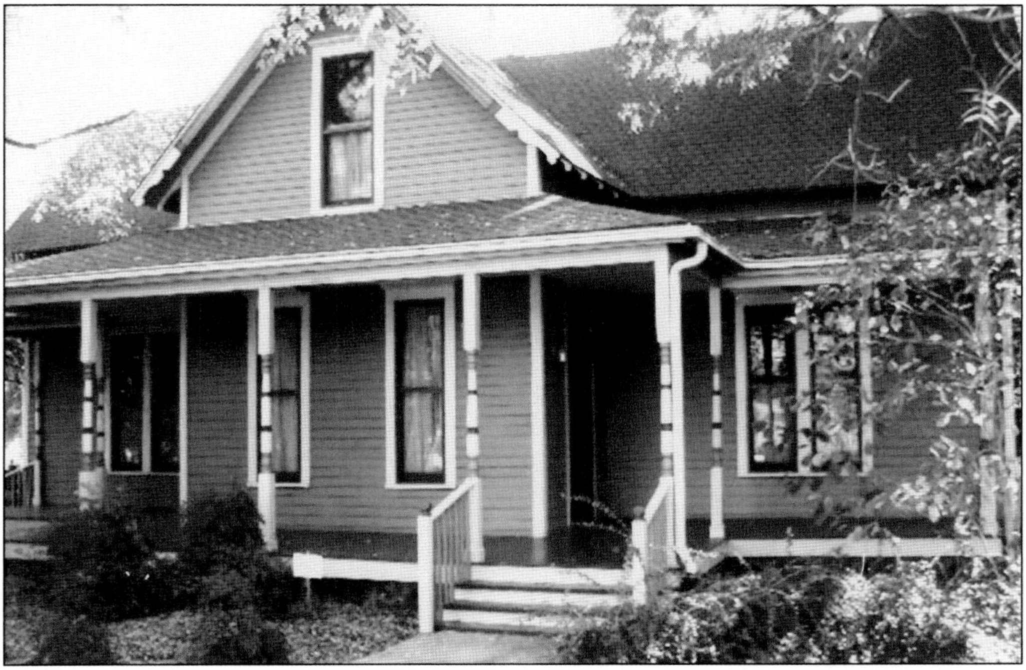

The Haggard Park Heritage District is the most intact residential neighborhood in old Plano. The Schimelpfenig-Dudley-O'Neal house was built around 1893. This 1.5-story vernacular Victorian had been condemned when Alvie and Melissa O'Neal bought and restored the original front part of the house. A modern addition utilized historically styled elements for a seamless transition.

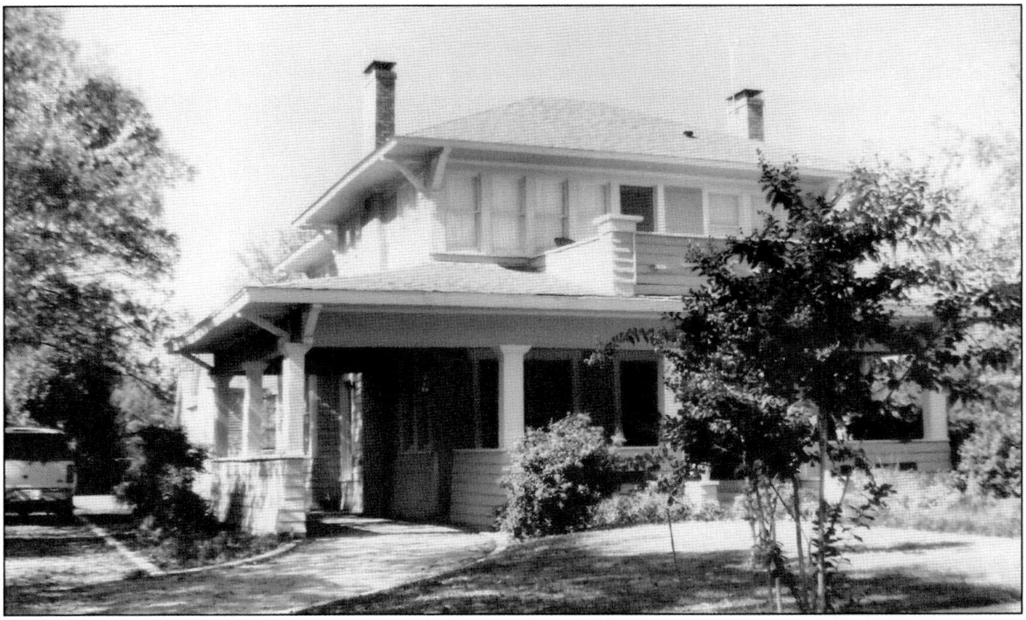

The Aldridge House is one of the few remaining examples of early-20th-century architecture left in Plano. Located on H Avenue and Seventeenth Street in the Haggard Park Heritage District, this foursquare-style home was purchased by Clint Haggard in 2006. A renovation was completed under the direction of award-winning Dallas architect Daron Tapscott in 2008. The Plano Heritage Commission commended the team with a preservation award.

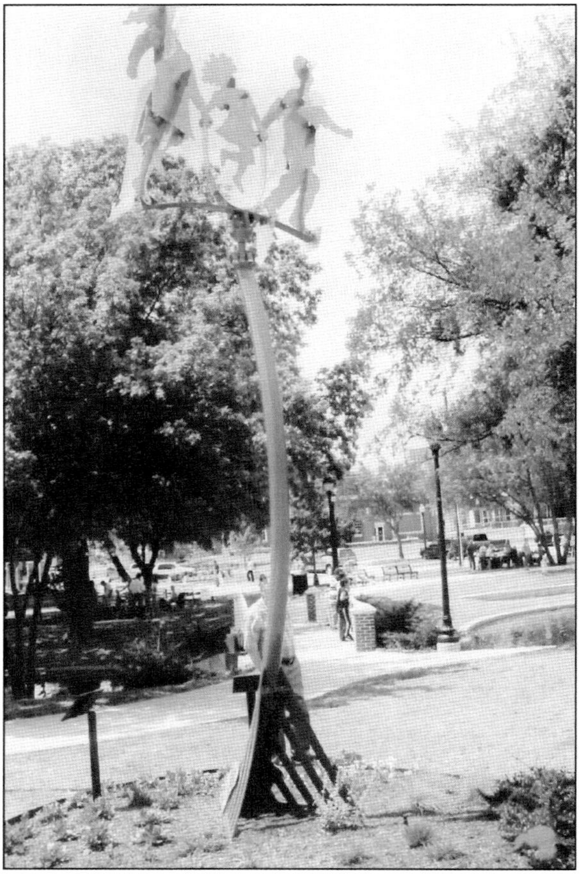

Uptown Plano is a cultural mosaic of art and ethnic diversity interwoven with both young and old who love the sense of community. New and old buildings are architecturally distinct and significant. The city has added sculptures to commemorate its historic past, like this one in Haggard Park designed to show the footpath of schoolchildren skipping uptown through the park for ice cream.

Tracks of Our Past and Future, a 76-foot-long mosaic wall, was commissioned by the Douglass Community Arts Advisory Council to represent the community and its history. Dedicated on "Juneteenth" 2006, mosaic artists Shug Jones and Lynne Chinn featured an image of Frederick Douglass, the original church, the old community oak tree, various members of the Douglass community, and the DART train. The hands of God on each side hold the Bible verse, "Love thy Neighbor as Thyself."

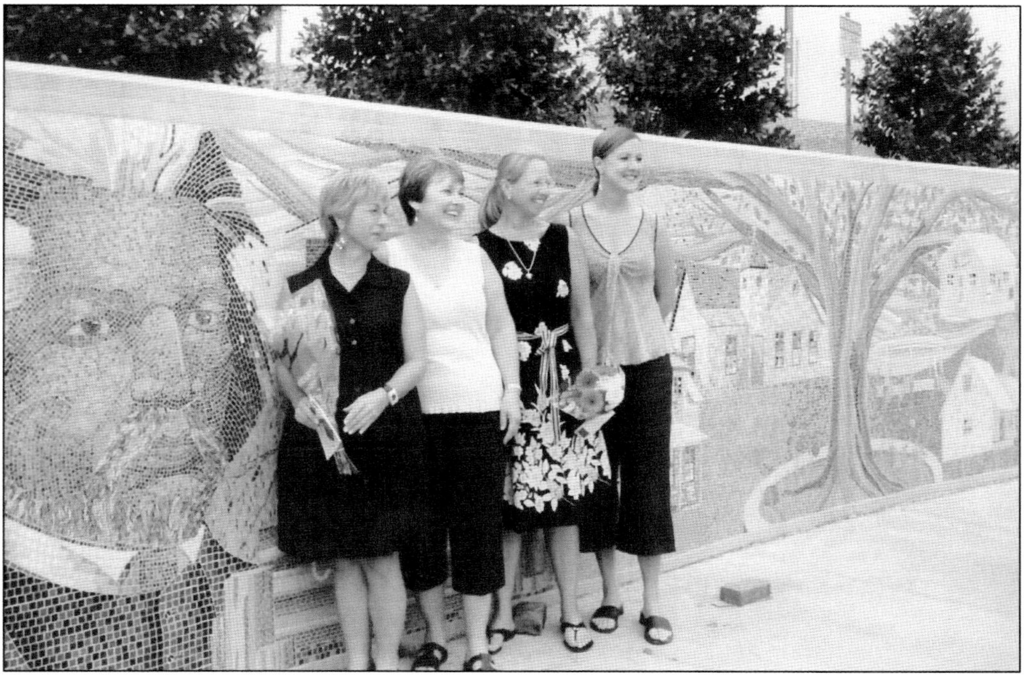

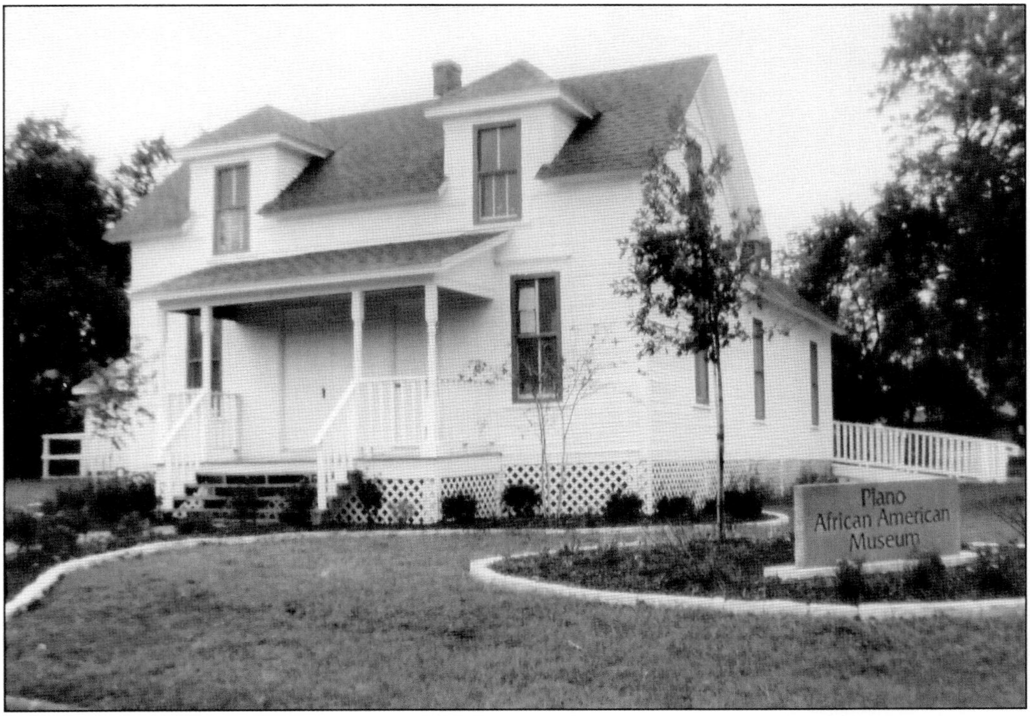

The Plano African American Museum (PAAM) is located in the historic Douglass Community at Thirteenth Street and H Avenue. PAAM educates visitors about the art, history, and cultural contributions of African Americans in the late 1800s and early 1900s. The centerpiece of the museum is the Thornton House, a prime example of the vernacular farmhouse construction commonly used in North Texas in the 19th century. The Community Church on the east end of the PAAM campus is thought to be over 130 years old. At one point, it was the church used by most denominations in the community.

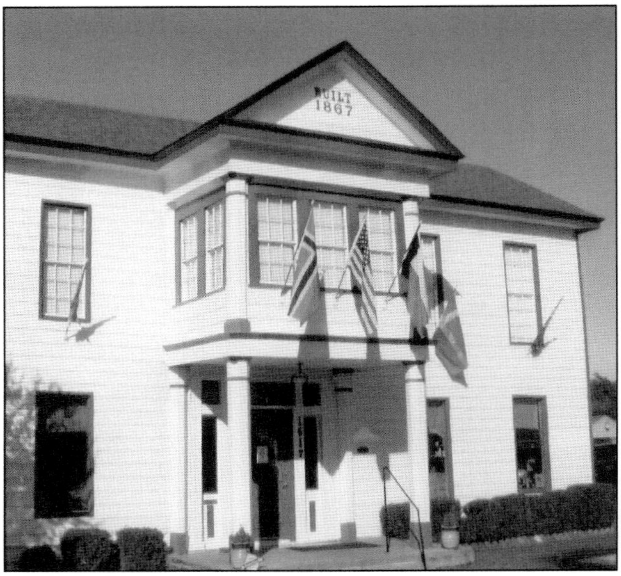

Built in 1867, the Forman House is the oldest house still standing in Plano, on K Avenue just north of the heart of uptown. Now a cultural center, the site of Plano's earliest post office and stagecoach stop has been lovingly preserved by the Workmen family with a Scandinavian flair. Other early-1900s homes have been converted to commercial use along Eighteenth Street. Along K Avenue in a municipal center courtyard, the city memorialized the former site of Biggerstaff Flowers, an icon in Plano for almost 50 years.

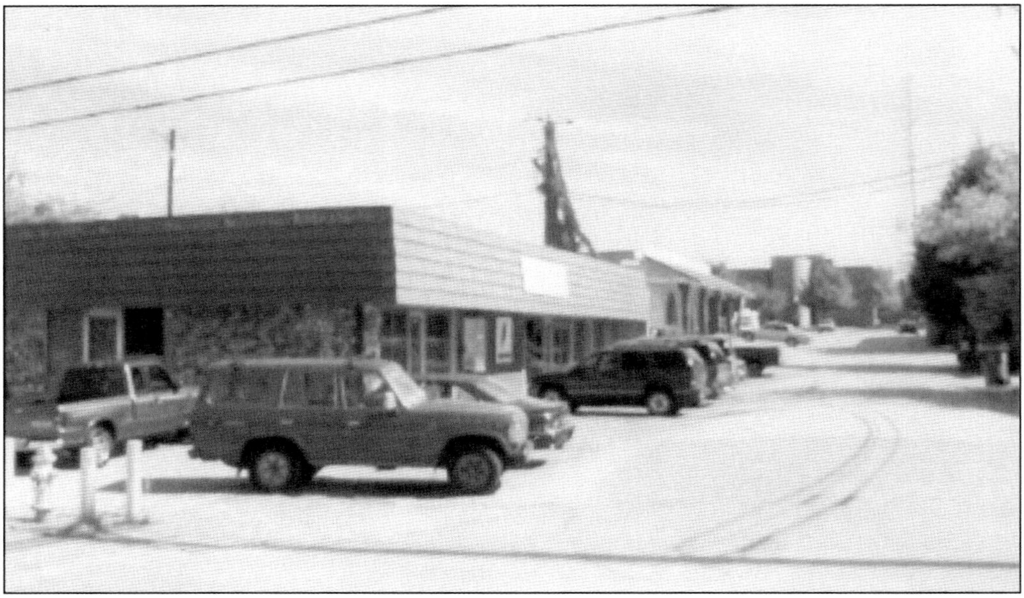

Plans are being made to develop more apartments along the west side of the DART lines across from Haggard Park in a public/private partnership. City planners are hopeful that by providing more residences, parking, retail, and entertainment venues, the development will connect Fifteenth Street along the DART line southward to Fourteenth Street. The so-called Douglass Walk would provide a pedestrian-friendly walkway similar to the north side of Fifteenth shown here in before-and-after photographs. While Vavra's and Willie Mae's bakeries are no longer there, Bake Rejoice and other service-oriented businesses are making history in the revitalized area surrounding the DART rail. (Courtesy of the City of Plano.)

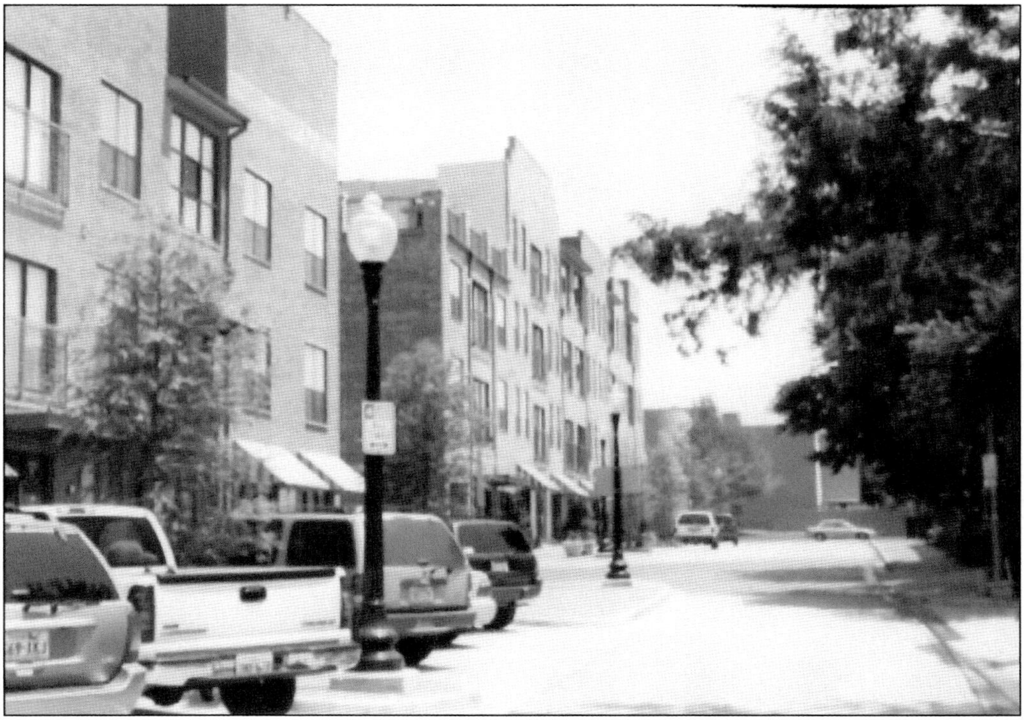

In recent years, Plano has been perceived as a city of new construction and corporate headquarters, but it is also a city of significant historical character, with two sites listed on the National Register of Historic Places, including the Heritage Farmstead Museum—a unique 4.5-acre farm interpreting life on the Blackland Prairie. In 2011, Spencer and Skylar Belloni spent a grand evening celebrating the freshly painted Ammie Wilson house, built in 1891—the centerpiece of the museum.

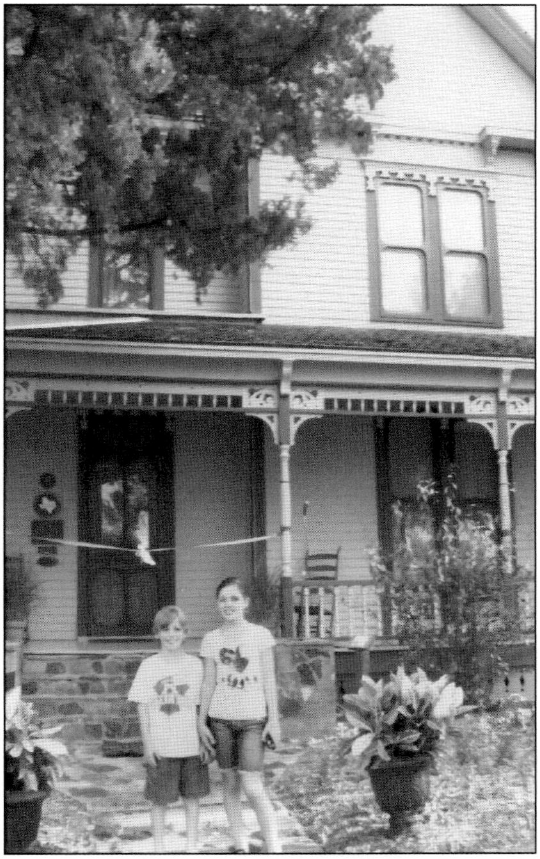

Plano's legacy is built on the sacrifices of the early settlers who toiled over the land and persevered to build a close-knit community. Now the world has come to Plano. We must enlighten and educate newcomers to nurture and preserve the roots of its success. Pictured below at Plano's First Christian Church in 2010 are some of those passionate historians who attended the Collin County Historical Commission's Preservation Celebration. From left to right, they are Maggie Sprague, Lolisa Laenger, Melissa O'Neal, Cheryl Smith, and Peggy Mitchell.

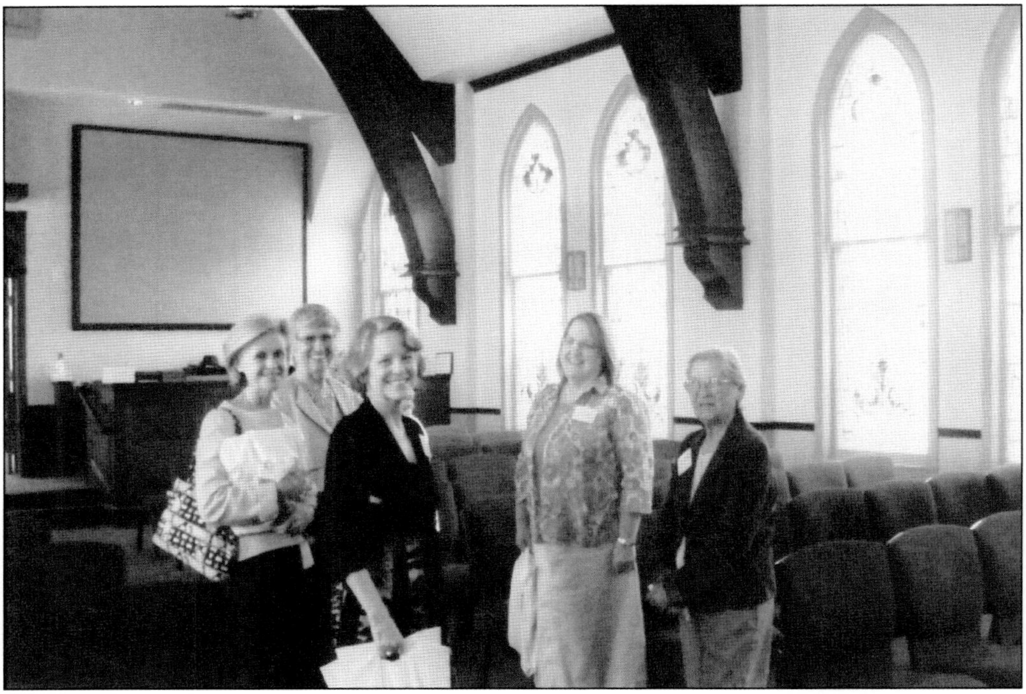

Discover Thousands of Local History Books Featuring Millions of Vintage Images

Arcadia Publishing, the leading local history publisher in the United States, is committed to making history accessible and meaningful through publishing books that celebrate and preserve the heritage of America's people and places.

Find more books like this at
www.arcadiapublishing.com

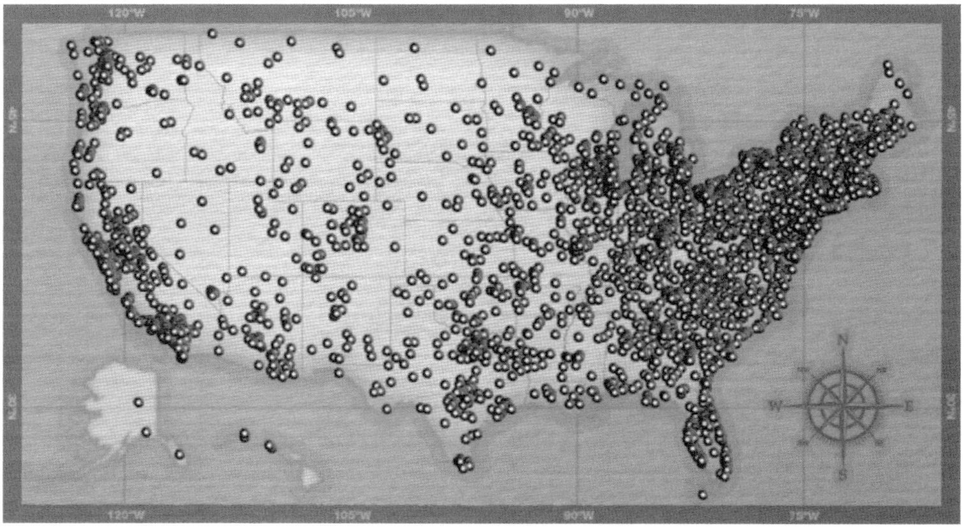

Search for your hometown history, your old stomping grounds, and even your favorite sports team.

Consistent with our mission to preserve history on a local level, this book was printed in South Carolina on American-made paper and manufactured entirely in the United States. Products carrying the accredited Forest Stewardship Council (FSC) label are printed on 100 percent FSC-certified paper.

MADE IN THE USA